GREAT GAA MOMENTS

2007 YEARBOOK

Finbarr McCarthy

MENTOR
BOOKS

First Published in 2007 by

MENTOR BOOKS
43 Furze Road,
Sandyford Industrial Estate,
Dublin 18,
Republic of Ireland.

Tel: + 353 1 295 2112 / 3   Fax: + 353 1 295 2114
e-mail: admin@mentorbooks.ie
www.mentorbooks.ie

ISBN: 978-1-84210-390-6

A catalogue record for this book is available from the British Library

Edited by: Treasa O'Mahony
Book and Cover Design by: Kathryn O'Sullivan
Photos supplied by: www.sportsfile.com
                                Ger McCarthy

Printed in Ireland by ColourBooks Ltd.

1 3 5 7 9 10 8 6 4 2

Contents

Acknowledgements

As with *Great GAA Moments 2006*, the writing of this book has been an enjoyable and fruitful experience, made easier by the support of so many people.

The staff of Mentor Books have been wonderful and by staff I mean everyone involved – they make me so welcome whenever I contact them.

Danny McCarthy, Managing Director of Mentor Books, was as supportive as ever. He even took it easy on me when his native Kerry beat Cork in the All-Ireland Football final. Thanks too to Treasa and Kathryn for all their help in editing and designing the book.

A special thanks to my wife Mary for her unstinting support especially in the last few months, and to all my family and friends, including St Nick's lads, for their help and encouragement.

Damian Lawlor is a true friend. I am honoured and privileged that such a renowned and well respected sports journalist would take the time to write the Foreword – something I greatly appreciate.

Once again I am indebted to my friends in the media, who on the many occasions when I sought their help were always ready to help. Special thanks to Peter Sweeney, Gordon Manning and Karl O'Kane of the *Irish Daily Star*, Michael Clifford of the *Irish Daily Mail*, Kieran Shannon of the *Sunday Tribune*, Eamonn Murphy of the *Evening Echo* in Cork and, of course, my colleagues in the news and sports department of 96/103 FM Radio who make working in 'sport' such a rewarding experience.

A word of thanks also to Sportsfile, whose fantastic colour photos make up such an important part of this book.

This book is about the people who generate the excitement on and off the field: hurlers, footballers, camogie players and ladies footballers, managers and officials. In their own way, they all contributed to some 'Great GAA Moments' in 2007. Thanks for making it yet another exciting season.

I hope those of you who read this book will enjoy it as much as I enjoyed writing about the stories that made the headlines.

Finbarr McCarthy

Dedication

This book is dedicated to my father-in-law John Newman,
whose spirit and determination since May have
been an inspiration to all who know and love him.
In the words of his grandson David,
'JJ's a legend'.
He certainly is.

Finbarr Mc Carthy.
October 2007.

Foreword

FINBARR MCCARTHY'S energy and enthusiasm for hurling and football is a constant source of wonder to me. A few years ago, just three days before Christmas, I rang his mobile to offer Yuletide greetings. I explained that my mission over the weeks ahead was simple; avoid turkey and generally keep as far away from a GAA field as possible. Which was precisely where Finbarr was at that moment and time; out in the howling wind and rain, at some minor 'C' relegation play-off or other. 'Sure what else would I be doing?' he replied rather indignantly after I questioned his sanity. That's Finny Mac for you, absolutely consumed by the GAA. Clearance for those bi-annual sunshine breaks of his only comes after a forensic examination of the official Croke Park fixtures calendar. And when this man holidays, it's a sure sign that the season either hasn't started or is long since over. In addition to all this, he seems to have served as club secretary for St Nick's forever, and is also part of the Glen Rovers administration, but of course it is as GAA Correspondent of 96 and 103FM that Finbarr is best known.

I first met him when I took myself Leeside to work with the *Evening Echo*. Not long after my arrival, Finbarr, poor soul, picked me to play in goal for the St Nick's junior team . . . to his credit he has never held it against me. Despite my goalmouth wobbles our friendship developed from there and over the next 10 years, he became a trusted lieutenant, a friend to bounce ideas off and an informed and balanced GAA man whose advice I have always taken. He has also played a huge part in helping the careers of many other young journalists looking for advice and contact numbers. For that we owe him a huge amount.

There's little or nothing that takes place in GAA circles that Finbarr didn't know about weeks before it happened. But he also has a great understanding and if he feels an issue is highly sensitive, no-one will ever hear of it. That aside, he will talk *sliothars* and *liathroids* all day long. Little wonder, then, that the pages of his second book, *Great GAA Moments 2007* radiate his knowledge, energy and informed opinion. From the first game on the calendar, Dublin and Tyrone under lights at Croke Park, to Kerry's demolition of his own county in the All-Ireland Football final, a stream of sagas and controversies rippled through the season. I know that the author has painstakingly researched each one of them, including the Semplegate and Clare hurling affairs, not to mention the feathers that Babs, Loughnane and company ruffled in the months afterwards. There were plenty of magic moments too; Sligo's much vaunted emergence from Connacht is just one that is dealt with. Finbarr's book is a delightful reportage of the season, an objective and informed view of its highs and lows. Only after reading the book will you realise that so much took place. It's a book to be consumed as the last cinders of 2007 are burned, a book that could only have been compiled by a GAA fanatic and fine writer. Finbarr McCarthy ticks those boxes.

Damian Lawlor

'Lights On' in Croke Park – a gala evening occasion with music, bands and the opening match of the Football League. Dublin and Tyrone teams parade before the start of the first game ever played under lights at Croke Park. 3 February 2007

1
Lights On in Croke Park

DUBLIN v TYRONE

On a clear February night, would the Dublin v Tyrone match provide sufficient drama for Croke Park's historic first nightime encounter?

1 Lights On in Croke Park

Dublin v Tyrone

Lights On

Almost a full house with 81,500 in Croke Park. Nothing unusual about that especially when Dublin are playing, but this was not an August or July afternoon, this was a cold February night.

Tyrone were the visitors in the opening game of the Allianz National Football League, a league match with a difference. It was to be the first ever to take place under the glare of the newly installed floodlights in Croke Park.

With rugby and soccer internationals due to be played at the venue in the following weeks, it was felt that the first game under lights would have to be one which the GAA had control over.

As well as the lights being turned on, the ultra modern under-soil heating was also being used for the first time.

What better way to mark the occasion than with the involvement of two of the biggest names in Gaelic football.

Who will ever forget the two titanic battles they had in the Championship of 2005, or indeed, but for all the wrong reasons, their clash in Omagh at the outset of the 2006 league?

It was a gala occasion and even the GAA entered into the spirit of the occasion by resisting the temptation to make a financial killing.

Normally a full house of 82,000 for an All-Ireland final would generate in the region of €4 million for the association, but this was more about promotion than profit.

A spokesman for the GAA said 'in promotional terms you just could not buy it. There is a real buzz around Dublin and normally you would not get that for a league game.'

Ticket prices were reduced, with entry to the stands just €15, the boys (and girls) on the Hill would only have to pay €13, while students, juveniles and concessions were admitted for €5 and there was also special rates for schools and clubs, all anxious to attend such a historic event.

It all meant a profit of less than €500,000 for the GAA, but then money was never the issue for this game.

From early on in the evening the crowds began filing into the stadium and pre-match entertainment was provided as the moment of reckoning inched ever nearer. Cumann na mBunscol Atha Cliath also contributed as young boys and girls carried the flags of many nations, paying testimony to the multi-cultural nature of Ireland and the participation of young people from different backgrounds in Gaelic games.

The Dublin Gospel Choir were first on stage and were followed by the hugely popular Saw Doctors who produced some wonderfully magical songs that went down a treat with young and old alike. Fans in the stadium quickly forgot the cold of the evening and warmly embraced the proceedings.

The atmosphere inside the stadium was, according to one seasoned journalist, 'electric, the best I have ever experienced at a game, summer or winter'.

Anticipation levels were high as GAA President Nickey Brennan and Director General Liam Mulvihill made their way to a specially constructed podium in the centre of the field, which was linked to the central electricity supply in the stadium.

As the two most powerful men in the

From a specially erected podium in the centre of the pitch, Director General of the GAA, Liam Mulvihill and President Nickey Brennan turn the power switch for the floodlights before the Dublin v Tyrone game. Croke Park, 3 February 2007

Conal Keaney, Dublin, gets his kick away despite the attention of Ryan McMenamin, Tyrone.
Dublin v Tyrone, National Football League, Croke Park. 3 February 2007

association made their way in relative darkness to the podium, they were greeted with sustained applause by the now almost full stadium – even the 'Dubs' decided to come early.

The stadium announcer then encouraged the crowd to begin the countdown as the President and DG, waited anxiously for the moment to arrive. It was almost time for 'lights on'.

It had been set up in such a way that when Nickey hit the button, the lights which were placed along the front of the three main stands with just one pylon behind the Dineen Hill 16 end of the ground, would come on individually.

This was to ensure maximum effect, but it would also take some time for the entire Dublin skyline to be lit up.

10, 9, 8, 7, 6, 5, 4, 3, 2, 1 go and

Nickey hit the button, a brief pause, was it going to work? It was, and then in an instant the first light flickered and to thunderous applause from the crowd, the full set soon came on and a new era in Croke Park was about to begin.

The delight on the faces of Nickey Brennan and Liam Mulvihill said it all – 'the stadium was now complete' and off they walked, proud of the achievement which is a tribute to all involved.

Afterwards, stadium manager Peter McKenna revealed that it was heart-stopping waiting for the 'lighting up ceremony'.

'When the lights flickered, it was a heart-stopper. You know something is going to work but you still have the moment of doubt.'

McKenna continued, 'normally they come straight on, but there was a few seconds when it felt like an eternity, but it all worked out well in the end.'

'Tonight is a special night for the association; this is a tribute to ourselves. This stands head and shoulders above what the association has done before, and it has catapulted Dublin's status as a world capital upwards.'

Now with the lights on, it was time for the match to begin.

A full moon shines over the Dublin fans on Hill 16, adding an eerie support to the new lighting system in Croke Park. Dublin v Tyrone. 3 February 2007

The Game Itself

The game itself could have been lost amongst all the razzmatazz that reigned at the venue on that February night, but to the credit of both teams they produced a match worthy of the occasion.

The crowd came to be part of a historic event but also to gauge early season form between two teams, with designs on big things in 2007, but also with some history and it soon surfaced.

It was a tough encounter, but to the credit of both sides it went nowhere near replicating the infamous battle of Omagh.

Yet 11 yellow cards were dispensed by experienced referee Pat McEnaney, while Tyrone's Ryan McMenamin received a straight red card late in the game.

It was a case of laying down a marker for the year ahead, no tackles were shirked, and there was plenty of heavy hitting, before the issue was finally resolved.

Dublin started well as Darren Magee and Declan O'Mahoney ruled the roost in midfield. The half-back line was also working hard, which was limiting Owen Mulligan's influence on proceedings.

Diarmuid Connolly and David Henry were among the scorers as Dublin opened up a 0-5 to 0-1 lead, but for all their dominance Dublin could only add 2 more points to their first-half tally. It meant that at 0-7 to 0-2 Tyrone were still in touch, and were capable of producing a much better second-half display.

Mickey Harte, sensing the difficulties,

reshaped his team for the second-half, introducing Colm McCullough to the attack and Kevin Hughes to a struggling midfield.

These changes worked and with Sean Cavanagh, one of the few to impress in the first-half, continuing to play well, Mulligan suddenly burst into life.

Mulligan and Raymond Mulgrew had early points, and when Mulligan had another from long range in the 47th minute it was 0-8 to 0-5 to Dublin, who were now getting caught in the glare of the oncoming Tyrone headlights or in this case floodlights.

With 55 minutes gone the gap was down to the bare minimum. Not long after, Mulligan, who was now running the show, landed the leveller before eventually firing Tyrone into the lead. The comeback was complete.

The crowd were enthralled by unfolding events as the game defied the cold February weather to produce a match played with Championship fervour – summer-like football in spring so to speak.

The atmosphere inside the splendidly-lit stadium was cranked up in the last quarter as both sides fought desperately for the two points on offer.

It was nail-biting stuff as the sides traded points, but Dublin's old failing

They say that a full moon and bright lights bring out all sorts of 'wildlife'. This streaker was caught in a fine rugby tackle by a nimble-footed steward. On his back the streaker had written 'Support Cystic Fibrosis'. One fan on the Hill suggested it should read 'Support Narcisstic Psychosis'.
Dublin v Tyrone, National Football League, Croke Park. 3 February 2007

(they only scored 2 points in 31 second-half minutes) came back to haunt them and despite their best efforts Tyrone (even though they finished with 14 men) held on to win by the narrowest of margins, 0-11 to 0-10.

| Tyrone | 0-11 |
| Dublin | 0-10 |

The respective managers Mickey Harte and Paul Caffrey expressed themselves pleased with the game, but both were absolutely delighted with the occasion which they hoped would be repeated in the future.

As the supporters left the stadium and made their way through the streets of the capital city they did so in the knowledge that they had just witnessed a

Alan Brogan, Dublin, has a shot on goal which is cleared by Tyrone goalkeeper and defenders.
Dublin v Tyrone, National Football League, Croke Park. 3 February 2007

unique event in Irish sport and more importantly in the history of the GAA.

Close on 82,000 people at a League game in February, a floodlit stadium that is the envy of most sporting organisations in Europe. And Europe and beyond would soon get to see the venue in all its wonderment as rugby and soccer came to Jones Road.

But on February 3rd 2007 the night belonged solely to the GAA, its supporters and its members and those who were among the capacity attendance felt it a privilege to have been present for yet another milestone for Cumann Luth-Chleas Gael.

Keith Higgins, Mayo, breaks through the tackle of Ciaran Bonner and attempted block by Brendan Devenney, Donegal. Mayo v Donegal, National Football League Final, Croke Park. 22 April, 2007

2

Donegal Take Title

NATIONAL FOOTBALL LEAGUE

With their places in 2008's competition determined by where they finished in 2007's competition, each team in the National Football League fought hard. One team, though, fought harder than all others.

2 Donegal Take Title

National Football League

New First-time League Champions

After the glamour and excitement of the opening night under the Croke Park floodlights (Chapter 1), the 2007 Allianz National Football League settled down and over the 7 rounds produced its usual share of shocks and surprises.

Of course in recent years the advent of floodlights in several grounds around the country has greatly enhanced the competition and helped attract many more supporters to the games. It appears evening games are the way forward.

The competition also had an extra and important dimension, and like the hurling league would impact on a number of counties before its conclusion.

A new format will be in operation for 2008, 4 divisions of 8 teams, and where a county finished at the conclusion of the 2007 competition would determine the groups for the 2008 league.

In effect it meant that the top 4 teams in Groups 1A and 1B would be in Division 1, the next 2 teams in the groups would be in Division 2 and the bottom 2 counties would head for Division 3. A lot

at stake then for several teams and their high profile managers.

Crucially the counties that would comprise Division 4 would not, unless they reach their Provincial Final, be eligible for the All-Ireland qualifiers but would instead have to contend themselves with the much-maligned Tommy Murphy Cup.

Division 1A

Tyrone, after their win over Dublin in the opening match in February, looked set to enjoy a good run but like so many teams, inconsistency would hinder their progress.

Mayo and Donegal were the early pacesetters, Mayo getting some measure of revenge for their hammering in the 2006 All-Ireland Final with a morale boosting win over Kerry – not the best of starts for Pat O'Shea in his first outing as Kingdom boss.

Donegal and Cork played out a bizarre game in Páirc Uí Rinn. Donegal won with a strong second-half display, but Referee Syl Doyle produced 16 yellow cards and 3 red cards, with James Masters and Nicholas Murphy of Cork being dismissed for innocuous offences.

It had ramifications also for Cork manager Billy Morgan who as a result of comments passed to the official was banned from the sideline for eight weeks.

Under the rules Billy was prohibited from any involvement with the team for the period of his suspension and selector Ted Owens was appointed temporary coach, not the ideal situation at a crucial stage in the competition.

A week later Kerry beat Cork in Tralee, Donegal and Mayo maintained their winning run and Limerick and Fermanagh were beginning to struggle, as Dublin picked up their first win.

It was a similar pattern as the group progressed. Cork hammered Tyrone and ultimately that derailed Mickey Harte's challenge for a semi-final place.

Dublin and Kerry found it hard to string two good results together and before the final round of games the semi-finalists were known.

Kerry's problems were complicated by the dual involvement of their manager Pat O'Shea who was combining both club and county jobs, as Dr Croke's were still chasing the All-Ireland club title.

Donegal and Mayo emerged as the two semi-finalists from Division 1A. In fact Donegal dropped only one point

Ciaran Bonner, Donegal, climbs high to field the ball ahead of Pat Harte, Mayo. Mayo v Donegal, National Football League Final, Croke Park. 22 April, 2007

and that was in a surprise draw to Limerick, which gave the Shannonsiders a slight chance of staying out of Division 3, but for that to happen they had to beat Cork in the last game.

Fermanagh's campaign lurched from one crisis to another and Division 3 beckoned for 2008 – a far cry from 2004 when they were All-Ireland semi-finalists.

The sequence of results also meant that there would be new champions as Kerry's failure to make the last four saw them relinquish their grip on the title.

There was little interest then on the last day, and Cork with a comfortable win over Limerick even minus a number of regulars guaranteed the Rebels a place in Division 2 and consigned Limerick to Division 3.

Division 1B

This group provided a bit more in terms of last day excitement. It was also a group many perceived to be weaker in content than 1A.

After all, 3 of the 4 provincial champions were bracketed together in 1A (Cork, Mayo and Dublin), while only the Ulster winners (Armagh) were in Division 1B.

Down, under new manager Ross Carr, were struggling from the very first game and never really recovered after being hammered by Galway. Indeed five successive defeats sent the once kingpins of Ulster football to Division 3 for 2008.

Down's demotion, though, was the only matter that was never in doubt as a combination of results kept the group competitive all the way through.

Galway lost a couple of games early on but battled back. Kildare and Laois under new boss Liam Kerins played out a thrilling draw before a 13,000 plus crowd in St Conleth's Park in Newbridge.

Derry, Westmeath and Armagh all picked up points and with the final round beckoning, all except Down had something to play for.

On the last day of the group series, the two semi-final spots were up for grabs with four teams in contention.

Kildare were on 9 points, Galway and Laois had 8 each with Derry on 7. In fact even though they had only 6 points, if results went their way Westmeath would have been propelled into the semi-finals – unlikely but possible. For that to happen they would need to beat Armagh convincingly, but they were not in control of their own destiny and there is little a team can do in such circumstances. It was a long shot, and it failed as they lost to Joe Kernan's men and only barely survived relegation. It was that tight.

The second relegation spot was filled by Louth who in losing to Derry, join Down in Division 3 in 2008.

At the top of the group a combination of results ultimately saw Galway and Kildare claim the semi-final places.

Kildare, by drawing with neighbours Laois, did enough to not only knock Liam Kerin's side out of contention but it set up a semi-final clash with unbeaten Donegal.

Galway by virtue of their win over Derry gave Peter Forde's team an early season date with Connacht rivals Mayo.

Both semi-finals were fixed for Croke Park and while there was some annoyance at dragging the Connacht teams all the way to Dublin, in general there was agreement that by playing the games in HQ they were raising the profile of the competition.

However, the poor attendance and lack of atmosphere at the games may force a rethink for next season.

Semi-finals

More accustomed to meeting in Connacht finals, the clash of Galway and Mayo was as competitive as any contest between these two age-old rivals.

In the end it was Mayo's ability to take scores and Galway's misuse of possession that swung the tie Mayo's way.

Galway actually made the better start – Nicky Joyce got the opening point, before his cousin Pádraig created a goal that was expertly finished to the net by Cormac Bane.

After the sides traded points Mayo struck for a goal of their own, when full-forward Ger Brady availed of a defensive blunder to blast the ball high into the net, and they were level when Alan Dillon had a neat point.

After both sides had scored four points apiece they left the field all square 1-5 each at the break, despite Joe Bergin dominating in midfield for Galway.

Eleven minutes into the second half, Galway, as a result of silly Mayo indiscretions, had scored 3 unanswered points, and Peter Forde's men were beginning to build a commanding lead.

Then as so often happens in games between these Connacht rivals, it took another turn and Mayo were thrown a lifeline.

In the 45th minute Conor Mortimer was upended in the square and referee Dave Coldrick immediately awarded a penalty.

Mortimer picked himself up, dusted himself down and the diminutive DCU student took the kick himself. However, Galway goalkeeper Paul Doherty made a good save but failed to hold on to the ball.

As the ball broke the quickest to react was Alan Dillon who drilled in the levelling goal, and it gave Mayo renewed vigour for the last quarter.

In that period both sides traded points but in the closing minutes Mayo grabbed the winner. It came from a driving run by half-back Enda Devenney in the 57th minute.

It sent Mayo to the final on a 2-10 to 1-12 scoreline, and Galway to contemplate their next meeting that would be in the Connacht Championship at Pearse Stadium.

Mayo	2-10
Galway	1-12

The meeting of Donegal and Kildare in the second semi-final was a unique affair, with the Ulster side chasing a first title. Having gone through the group stages unbeaten, Donegal were clear favourites to make the final.

Kildare, though, were coming along nicely under John Crofton and were keen to extend their interest in the league but a growing injury list was a cause of concern, and they were jinxed again during this game.

In fact one such injury, after just 6 minutes, to midfielder Killian Brennan clearly upset the Lily Whites who missed his industry in such a key area.

It produced an absorbing contest. Donegal were never behind once wing-back Paddy McConigley put them ahead in the first minute.

Indeed Kildare did not even gain parity despite the fact that Donegal finished with 14 men following Kevin Cassidy's dismissal for a second yellow card offence in the 64th minute.

It took Kildare 13 minutes to open their account, a John Doyle point, by which time Donegal had registered 3, and they continued to have the upper hand thanks to further scores (3) from Colm McFadden. It gave them an interval lead of 0-7 to 0-4.

Doyle, who was a constant threat to the Donegal defence, and Adrian Sweeney traded points, before the men from Tír Conaill scored a crucial goal.

On 44 minutes, McFadden's clever pass found Kevin McMenamin who drilled the ball powerfully to the net. Michael Hegarty quickly added a point and it looked 'game over'.

Donegal were now 1-9 to 0-5 ahead and just 15 minutes left to play.

Credit to Kildare, though, they

Alan Dillon, Mayo, right – buries the ball in the net to beat Galway goalkeeper Paul Doherty and score his side's second goal. Galway v Mayo, National Football League Semi-final, Croke Park. 15 April, 2007

battled their way back into the game. Pádraig O'Neill and Tadgh Fennin had points and they should have had a goal from Michael Conway but his only reward was a point.

It was now 1-10 to 0-8 in the 54th minute, when Kildare struck back. Fennin was hauled down in the square and Doyle duly dispatched the resultant penalty. He then had a point and now only the bare minimum separated the sides – 'game on'.

Cassidy eased the pressure with a Donegal point, before his second yellow card saw him depart proceedings early.

Doyle had another Kildare point, but in true Donegal fashion they played keep ball in the closing minutes and further points from McFadden and Hegarty put them 3 ahead with time almost up.

Kildare came in search of the levelling goal, but O'Neill's late effort sailed over for a point, the final score in a game that had many twists, but in the end Donegal emerged winners by 1-13 to 1-11.

Kildare boss John Crofton was not too downbeat – 'we are disappointed but we had a good campaign and we secured Division 1 status for next year which is important.'

Donegal boss Brian McIver was looking forward to the final as he paid tribute to Kildare – 'it was a tough game and Kildare are a good side. We won and now we will be going all out to win the final, no point in saying otherwise. Finals are there to be won and even with a few injury worries, that is what we will be trying to do.'

Donegal	1-13
Kildare	1-11

Donegal deliver first title

It was an important and crucial game for both counties – Mayo determined to erase the memory of the trashing in the 2006 All-Ireland Final and to win something at last in Croke Park. As for Donegal it was only their fourth final appearance and Brian McIver, their manager, stressed the importance of continuing their winning run.

There was contrasting team news before the start – Mayo would be without Kevin O'Neill although he would make a late appearance, while Donegal were boosted by the return from injury of key forward Brendan Devenney. But his comeback only last 30 minutes before being replaced due to a re-occurrence of the injury that forced him out initially.

However, his value to the team was clear as in that period he made an important contribution.

In fact it was Donegal who made all the early running, scoring 4 points without reply in the opening 13 minutes, helped by good combination play from Brian Roper and Colm McFadden. Worryingly, they created 3 goal-scoring chances in 30 minutes but failed to take them. Interestingly, Devenney was involved in 2 of these before departing.

Mayo's recovery began when their half-back line improved and, given further impetus by good play from attackers Alan Dillon and Conor Mortimer, the gap was quickly down to a single point.

However, Donegal still led by 2 points, 0-7 to 0-5 at half-time. This was increased to 3 early in the second-half but once again persistent and good play from Mayo had it down to 1 point.

Mayo continued to improve and with just 16 minutes left they were level. With momentum now on their side, the odds favoured the Connacht champions.

A pivotal moment arrived just after Donegal had regained the lead with a

Colm McFadden, Donegal, looks up to find a good pass as David Lyons, Kildare, closes in.
Kildare v Donegal, National Football League Semi-final, Croke Park. 15 April, 2007

Kevin McMenamin point in the 57th minute – Mayo missed another goal chance.

Donegal defender Andy Devenney under pressure spilled a harmless looking lobbing ball. It fell to Andy Moran who blazed the leather over the bar when he really should have drilled it into the net, a let-off for Donegal.

One more time the sides were level at 0-10 each as the match entered the first of the 8 minutes of added time that efficient referee John Bannon had signalled.

In the first of these Donegal took the lead, after both sides had missed chances. This time Rory Kavanagh got the score (a marvellous point), and with more energy and more importantly confidence, the Ulster side set about clinching the title.

Further points from Neil McGee and the wily Adrian Sweeney sealed victory, 0-13 to 0-10, for a proud football county as their supporters in an attendance of 29,433 celebrated a famous win.

Captain Neil Gallagher, who through injury was replaced with 20 minutes remaining, thus became the first Donegal man to take possession of the Allianz National Football League trophy from GAA President Nickey Brennan who praised both teams for their wonderful commitment in a game that lasted almost 80 minutes.

Afterwards a jubilant Donegal manager Brian McIver said 'I am delighted for the panel who worked very hard to bring the title to the county. We can now enjoy tonight and then we start to concentrate on the upcoming Championship.'

Across the corridor, Mayo boss John O'Mahoney was naturally very disappointed at a second defeat in Croke Park for his side inside 7 months – 'of course it's disappointing. It is after all a national final. It does not put us under any extra pressure going into the Championship but we have a few knocks and we will try and get them right for Galway on May 20.'

So as one campaign ends another begins or in O'Mahoney's case two begin, as the Mayo manager enters the race not only for Sam Maguire but also for Dáil Éireann as a Fine Gael candidate in the constituency of Mayo. It will be interesting to see how they both evolve in the weeks ahead.

No such worries for Donegal – worthy and deserving National League Champions for 2007.

Donegal	0-13
Mayo	0-10

For the record

Meath under new boss Colm Coyle bounced back from relegation in 2006 to claim the Division 2 title with a comprehensive 2-12 to 0-10 win over John Maughan's Roscommon.

Finally with the competition at an end the groups for 2008 are as follows.

Division 1
Donegal, Mayo, Kerry, Tyrone, Galway, Kildare, Derry and Laois.

Division 2
Dublin, Cork, Westmeath, Armagh, Monaghan, Roscommon, Cavan and Meath.

Division 3
Limerick, Fermanagh, Louth, Down, Longford, Leitrim, Wexford and Sligo.

Division 4
Offaly, Clare, Waterford, Carlow, London, Wicklow, Antrim and Tipperary.

It means yet another intriguing league to look forward to in 2008 and some big names in unfamiliar places.

Offaly, Leinster finalists in 2006, are now in Division 4 and were it not for an administrative error they could have avoided the drop.

In a group game they drew with Leinster rivals Longford but unknowingly played a player who had been sent off in an Under 21 Championship match.

Longford queried this and the Central Competitions Control Committee ruled in their favour and awarded them (Longford), the two points, and that point loss effectively sent Offaly to Division 4. How cruel can sport be?

Below in Division 4, will Mick O'Dwyer be at the helm for Wicklow and what of Division 2 – three big guns battling for two promotion spots – Dublin, Cork and Armagh?

And who said the League is boring?

Dan Shanahan, Waterford, scores a great point watched by Tommy Walsh, Kilkenny. Waterford v Kilkenny, National Hurling League Final, Semple Stadium, Thurles. 29 April, 2007

Waterford Win League

NATIONAL HURLING LEAGUE

In a hurling season that threw up more than its fair share of surprises, Waterford's steely determination to recapture the league title after 44 years provided some fantastic hurling.

3 Waterford Win League

National Hurling League

National Hurling League

On a cold February morning iconic hurling figures assembled in Dublin along with GAA President Nickey Brennan to officially launch the 2007 Allianz National Hurling League.

The 2007 season's competition promised much. It had another new format and several marquee names in the game would command centre stage.

At the end of 2006 a number of counties had appointed new managers. This helped generate renewed vigour and enthusiasm for a competition that had lost its sparkle in recent years.

Gerald McCarthy had taken over as Cork boss and made no secret of his desire to win the league – a feat last achieved by the Rebels in 1998.

John Meyler, an All-Ireland winner with Cork, had assumed control in his native Wexford; Tony Considine replaced Anthony Daly in Clare, but it was a Clareman who would attract the full glare of the media.

Ger Loughnane, the school principal from Feakle and the man who led the Banner County to the promised land in 1995 and again in 1997, was given the task of awakening Galway hurling from its slumbers.

Elsewhere, Babs was still in charge of Tipperary, Ritchie Bennis was beginning his first full season at the helm in Limerick, another Corkman, Justin McCarthy, was guiding the fortunes of Waterford, but the team they all had to beat were reigning champions Kilkenny and their genial coach Brian Cody.

As for the format there was a slight but important change, with the re-introduction of quarter-finals.

It all began on February 18th, with the following groups:

Division 1A
Cork, Offaly, Waterford, Wexford, Down and Clare.

Division 1B
Kilkenny, Dublin, Galway, Limerick, Tipperary and Antrim.

There was a mild shock on the opening day when Dublin drew with Kilkenny, but Brian Cody had no complaints – 'it was well deserved and hopefully Dublin can build on this, but we (Kilkenny) have little done after the winter but we will pick it up as the league evolves'.

In the same group Limerick had a win over Tipperary, while Loughnane got his tenure in the West off to a winning start.

In the second series of games, a defeat for Kilkenny at the hands of Tipperary, the champions with just one point from four, a slight sign of slippage perhaps.

Dublin's game with Antrim was postponed. On the same day the Cork v Waterford game was also a victim of the weather, and its re-fixture would spell trouble for the Dubs.

No real shocks in the other section. Cork opened with a win over Offaly, under pressure Clare boss Tony Considine got a win over Down, and Waterford hammered Wexford, a bad

Jackie Tyrell, Kilkenny, ball in hand, tries to get past Eoin Kelly, Waterford.
Waterford v Kilkenny, National Hurling League Final, Semple Stadium, Thurles. 29 April, 2007

start for Meyler, but it would improve.

Dublin's revival gathered momentum when on a dreadful day in Parnell Park, snow and sleet envelope the ground, they defeated Galway and followed that a week later with a win over a poor Limerick side in the Gaelic Grounds.

Five points from three games guaranteed them Division 1 status next year, but more importantly a win over Antrim in the re-fixture would send them to the play-offs.

Elsewhere Kilkenny, even without the Ballyhale-Shamrock's contingent, with successive wins over Limerick and Antrim were back in the equation, while the latter two were destined for the relegation battle.

Regrettably for Dublin, the wheels came off the wagon when they lost to Antrim in the re-fixture, but the timing of this game was a source of debate.

It was played on a Wednesday evening under lights in Casement Park, Belfast and Antrim won by 4 points.

The question being asked is why was it fixed for a Wednesday evening, unlike the Cork v Waterford game which was played on a Saturday afternoon, a game Waterford won?

Would the Dublin footballers have agreed to a similar scenario? Or did Tommy Naughton, the Dublin manager,

underestimate Antrim? Whatever – that defeat coupled with a heavy loss to Tipperary ended their play-off ambitions, but they had the consolation of Division 1 hurling to look forward to in 2008 – and that for Dublin is progress.

It all meant that the final series of games in Division 1B were of little consequence as the play-off places were decided. Kilkenny – did someone mention slippage? – were in the semi-final, with Galway and Tipperary in the quarter-finals.

It was a bit more competitive in Division 1A. Wexford despite a second loss, this time to Cork, regrouped and went to Ennis and beat Clare. Waterford also came a cropper in Ennis; Cork struggled to win in Down, but at least it ensured the last series of matches had a sense of purpose about them.

Four of the six teams, Cork, Clare, Waterford and Wexford were in contention for three places. Offaly and Down were out of the equation, the latter consigned to Division 2 after a pointless campaign.

Wexford hammered Down to secure a quarter-final berth. Offaly sprung a surprise by winning in Walsh Park and in the process denied Waterford a semi-final place.

The focus was now on Cusack Park in

Ennis, where the respective managers Gerald McCarthy and Tony Considine were under a little bit of pressure.

Considine's battle with Davy Fitzgerald (see Chapter 21) had shown no signs of abating and the goalkeeper was still absent.

Meanwhile in Cork, McCarthy had seen three players leave the panel, the most notable being former All-Star Wayne Sherlock, fuelling speculation that all was not well on Leeside.

As it was, Cork won a strange game, thanks mainly to a strong second-half showing, and coupled with Waterford's unexpected loss to Offaly, the Rebels were now in the semi-final. Clare were out and McCarthy's Waterford joined Wexford in the quarter-finals.

After the game in Ennis, Cork boss Gerald McCarthy faced the media and dismissed claims of unrest in the camp and felt 'that the performance today especially in the second-half was proof of that.'

Quarter-finals

Nowlan Park, Kilkenny, was the venue for the pairings and on a gloriously sunny afternoon a fine crowd witnessed two entertaining games.

Galway v Wexford was first up,

followed by the all-Munster clash of Tipperary and Waterford.

John Meyler had worked wonders with Wexford in a few short months and the improvement was maintained in this game.

Galway under Loughnane had stuttered into the quarter-finals and this would be a big test. It was one they would fail, despite a good start.

Early points put the Tribesmen in front, but Wexford battled back to draw level. In fact they were level five times in the opening half. No surprise then that it was all square, 0-9 each, at the break. Although Wexford were grateful to veteran goalkeeper Damien Fitzhenry who made several important saves, as the pendulum swung Wexford's way.

Loughnane reshaped his team for the second-half and once again Fitzhenry made a vital stop in the 45th minute. It was the signal for Wexford to assume control.

Sparked by the introduction of Mitch Jordan, Wexford proceeded to dominate the closing quarter. They had edged 3 points ahead when the decisive score came. A long delivery from Rory Jacob was doubled on superbly by Eoin Quigley for a brilliant goal.

Galway were visibly tiring. Wexford tacked on a few points and at the end were worthy winners by 1-16 to 0-14. A semi-final with neighbours and champions Kilkenny was their reward.

The second game between Tipperary and Waterford produced reasonable entertainment, even if Tipperary were hampered by the loss of four players through injury. John Carroll also failed to finish the game, but in different circumstances. He was sent off with a straight red card in the 40th minute.

It was 1-11 to 0-7 at half-time, the Waterford goal coming from Eoin Kelly.

In fact his namesake in the Tipperary jersey was one of those who left the field injured, as did his brother Paul. Their presence was missed in the closing stages.

Waterford were hurling well even if they were a bit reliant on Kelly for scores. He finished with 1-9, but they were put under pressure as Tipperary began the fightback.

It was 1-11 to 0-9 when Carroll was sent off. Following his dismissal, Lar Corbett fired over a couple of points and then Paul Kelly, drilled in a great goal – 'game on'.

A couple of more points, especially from Corbett, and with the game now in injury time, it was level at 1-19 each and extra-time looked certain. But Waterford had other ideas.

Up popped substitute Shane Walsh with what proved to be the match winning point. Despite a late effort from Tipperary, it was Waterford who would face Cork in the semi-final a week later, narrow winners 1-20 to 1-19.

After the game Babs was annoyed with the sending-off. He felt a yellow card would have been sufficient, but he was more concerned about the injuries, as the dressing room resembled an A&E ward, but time would heal the wounds.

Wexford	1-16
Galway	0-14
Waterford	1-20
Tipperary	1-19

Semi-finals

A week later a renovated Semple Stadium in Thurles would welcome two Leinster and two Munster teams as the last four in the Allianz National Hurling League.

The all-Leinster clash of Kilkenny v Wexford opened proceedings with Cork and Waterford to follow.

Wexford were dealt a harsh lesson by the champions who quickly established control and maintained it for the 70 minutes.

Sloppy Wexford defending allowed

Tommy Walsh, Kilkenny, ball in hand, tries to shake off Eoin Quigley, Wexford.
Kilkenny v Wexford, National Hurling League Final, Semple Stadium, Thurles. 15 April, 2007

Aidan Fogarty in for a goal in the first minute. Darren Stamp did get one goal for Wexford in the fourth minute but Kilkenny were relentless in their pursuit of victory.

Fogarty had a second goal in the 14th minute and a succession of points gave the 'Cats' an interval lead of 2-10 to 1-3, and Wexford were staring defeat in the face.

The second-half was a formality for Kilkenny who used their full complement of substitutes, as they tacked on 11 more points. Stamp got a second goal in injury-time, but it barely raised a ripple from the large Wexford following who were once again taught a harsh lesson, and a clear indication that a huge gap in standards still exists between Kilkenny and the rest of Leinster.

The full time scoreline tells its own tale – Kilkenny 2-22 Wexford 2-7.

At least Cork and Waterford produced a much better contest in the second semi-final with the result in doubt right to the end.

Cork welcomed back Ben O'Connor for his first game in the campaign, but Joe Deane was absent with a leg injury. After 5 minutes Niall Ronan was also forced off, and the attack suffered as a consequence.

They seemed untroubled by these events as the game began. Ben announced his return in spectacular style, a point from a sideline cut in the third minute was followed by a great goal in the 13th minute. Cork were flying, Waterford were struggling with 23 minutes played, the Rebels were ahead 1-7 to 0-4.

A minute later came the score that altered the direction of the contest – a Waterford goal with a hint of good fortune about it.

Cork goalkeeper Donal Óg Cusack made a brilliant save from Dan Shanahan but the ball struck full-back Diarmuid O'Sullivan's hurley and rebounded into the net.

It re-ignited the Waterford challenge and with Eoin Kelly and Seamus Prendergast prominent they took over and led at half-time by 1-10 to 1-8, and set the scene for a stirring second-half.

On the resumption Cork posted their intent with 5 points as against 2 for Waterford to regain the lead 1-13 to 1-12.

Waterford, though, were in no mood to surrender and Kelly and John Mullane between them scored 4 points, putting the Decies back in front 1-16 to 1-13. It was now developing into a cracker, in keeping with so many of their recent clashes.

John Gardiner nailed two long range frees for Cork. With 68 of the 70 minutes played, just 1 point divided the sides, Waterford in front 1-17 to 1-16.

Cork came in search of the levelling score that would have forced extra-time, but Waterford had no desire to let this game slip from their grasp and late points from Prendergast and Dan Shanahan, his first of the game, sent Justin McCarthy's men into the final 1-19 to 1-16 and on balance well deserved.

So the stage was set for a unique decider between keen rivals from the south-east of the country – Kilkenny v Waterford and once again Tom Semple's field in Thurles would be the venue.

Kilkenny	2-22
Wexford	2-7
Waterford	1-19
Cork	1-16

The Final

Despite their intense rivalry it was the first ever meeting of Kilkenny and Waterford in a league final. It was the champion's third successive decider, while the last appearance of the men in 'blue and white' in a final was their defeat to Galway in 2004.

Kilkenny were bidding for their 14th

Seamus Prendergast, Waterford, heads towards goal, trying to pass Diarmuid O'Sullivan, Cork. Cork v Waterford, National Hurling League Semi-final, Semple Stadium, Thurles. 15 April, 2007

title which would bring them level with Cork. Tipperary lead the roll of honour with 18. For Waterford their sole success in the league came in 1963. Could they end the long wait for a national title?

The setting was perfect as a crowd of close on 26,000 attended the eagerly awaited contest with Tipperary's Seamus Roche the man in the middle.

Flags in the stadium flew at half mast and prior to the commencement of the game a minute's silence was observed in memory of former GAA President Con Murphy, who passed away that morning after a brief illness.

Kilkenny lost centre-back John Tennyson with illness before the game and he was replaced by PJ Delaney, an experienced defender in his own right.

As expected there was a lively start. Waterford's Jack Kennedy got the game's first point, but the teams were level 5 times in the opening 26 minutes. Worryingly though, Waterford hit 8 wides to Kilkenny's 3. However, a strong finish which yielded 5 points gave them a deserved interval lead of 0-11 to 0-9.

It was a strange half and several of the Kilkenny players were playing well below par, notably James 'Cha' Fitzpatrick in midfield, while in attack Henry Shefflin was making little progress.

However, they upped the ante on the resumption and the crowd got a glimpse of the real Kilkenny.

In 10 minutes they fired over 5 points, 4 from Shefflin frees and they now led 0-15 to 0-12, after Kelly had a Waterford point.

But Waterford were determined to land a national title and responded in style. Urged on by their loyal supporters, they quickly drew level, when Dan Shanahan and substitute Paul Flynn had points. Now it was Kilkenny who were struggling, but their innate sense of survival kept them in touch.

It was gripping stuff entering the last quarter as the sides shared 6 points, a Shefflin free on 70 minutes levelling the contest for the tenth and what would prove to be the final time.

At 0-18 apiece, 3 minutes of added time was signalled by the fourth official. Would there be a winner or a replay a week later?

Waterford's insatiable hunger surfaced in those crucial minutes. Kelly hit a fabulous point, followed immediately by a beauty from Seamus Prendergast. The 'Decies' are now 2 points ahead – a dangerous lead as Kilkenny went in search of the winning goal.

It never came and when referee Roche sounded the full-time whistle a long famine in hurling was over. The men of 1963 could relax, the baton would pass to a new generation of hurlers as Waterford are the National League champions for 2007.

| Waterford | 0-20 |
| Kilkenny | 0-18 |

Their supporters gave full vent to their feelings and invaded the sacred sod of Thurles. Amidst huge celebrations, GAA President Nickey Brennan, proclaimed 'this is a great day for hurling'. Few would argue with these sentiments as a proud hurling county basks in the glory once again.

The curtain comes down then on an exciting campaign, new champions and a new format to look forward to in 2008 – but now as they head to Portugal for a week of warm weather training, the thoughts of Justin McCarthy and the Waterford hurlers turn to the Championship.

So on the day Taoiseach Bertie Ahern signalled the start of the general election campaign, the race to Croke Park on the 1st Sunday in September was also well underway.

Note

On the same day Laois easily defeated Wicklow to take the Division 2 title, while after a series of relegation play-offs, Limerick, by beating Offaly and Laois, preserved their Division 1 status for 2008. However, a Special Congress on September 29 decided that there would be no change to the format of the league for 2008. So Offaly were allowed retain their Division 1 status.

2008 Division 1

Group 1

Cork, Wexford, Waterford, Kilkenny, Dublin, Antrim

Group 2

Tipperary, Clare, Limerick, Galway, Offaly, Laois

Colm 'the Gooch' Cooper, Dr Crokes, tries to head towards goal, but runs into John Donaldson and Aaron Kernan, No 5, Crossmaglen Rangers. Crossmaglen Rangers v Dr Crokes. All-Ireland Football Club Final, Croke Park. 17 March, 2007

4

Ballyhale and Crossmaglen

As Ballyhale Shamrocks did battle with Loughrea in a somewhat one-sided encounter, the football final was mired in controversy. Crossmaglen and Dr Crokes played not one, but two feisty finals.

4 Ballyhale & Crossmaglen

All-Ireland Club Finals

Clubs battle for top honours

Croke Park on St Patrick's Day is the aim, the ambition and the drive of every club player in the country. It's AIB Club Finals day in hurling and football and there is no better place to be.

Of course getting there is the hard part. Some clubs arrive on the big stage once and then disappear. Others like the Rangers of Nemo and Crossmaglen in football and Birr in hurling seem to be regulars on Lá Le Pádraig.

The first objective is to win the local County Championship, advance to the Provincial campaign and then tackle the All-Ireland series. It can often mean 12 months of sheer hard work, sometimes in the most difficult of conditions imaginable.

The inter-county Championships, which run from May to September, capture the headlines and generally the good weather, while the club competitions that take place in the autumn and winter months can be blighted by wind and rain with the odd snow shower thrown in. It is a real test of endurance for players and officials alike. Is it any wonder that retaining the All-Ireland club title is a rare feat?

This year finalists in both codes went through every gambit of emotion in their efforts to reach Croke Park. Now would they reap the ultimate reward and be crowned All-Ireland Club champions for 2007?

Sixty plus more minutes would determine their fate. Would they savour the joy of victory or would the bitter pill of defeat be theirs to swallow? Let's find out.

Shamrocks bid for renewed glory

Not since the days when the renowned Fennelly brothers backboned their teams had Ballyhale Shamrocks from Kilkenny enjoyed glory on All-Ireland day. Now the present crop of hurlers from the famed club were on the cusp of something special.

Having annexed the Kilkenny Championship and followed that with a comfortable march through Leinster, their mettle was severely tested on a cold February afternoon in Portlaoise.

Tipperary and Munster champions Toomevara were in the other corner and early in the second-half opened up a

Kenneth Colleran, Loughrea, tries to get away from Paul Shefflin, Ballyhale Shamrocks.
Ballyhale Shamrocks v Loughrea. All-Ireland Hurling Club Final, Croke Park. 17 March, 2007

commanding lead.

It looked certain that Shamrocks would have to wait a while yet to emulate their predecessors but the character of the team surfaced and with hurler of the year, Henry Shefflin, leading the charge they fashioned a fabulous win and were immediately installed as favourites for the final.

Loughrea, the Galway and Connacht champions, were their opposition on March 17th, and while the Provincial campaign had been easy (little opposition in the West it must be said),

the Galway Championship had been a fractious and controversial competition with some games grabbing the headlines for all the wrong reasons.

In fact Portumna were so annoyed with the Galway County Board, it is felt that the talented Joe Canning's decision to opt out of the county senior hurling panel was directly linked to his club's treatment after an investigation into events in the county final, which Loughrea won.

The stage was then set for the biggest club game in the hurling season and it was Loughrea who made the more positive start as Ballyhale hit 4 wides in the opening minutes, and the Galway champions took a 0-4 to 0-2 lead.

Ballyhale soon settled and Henry Shefflin began to move. He laid on a couple of scores and then rifled over 3 frees to help his side into a 3 point lead, and now the favourites were moving up a gear. Loughrea were coming under increasing pressure and to compound their difficulties they conceded a goal. TJ Reid was the scorer for Ballyhale with a neat drop shot that was finely executed thus avoiding the attempted hook by Loughrea defender Ray Regan.

Loughrea themselves nearly got in for a goal as the game entered the final minutes of the first-half but Brendan Dooley's effort flew over the bar. It left the Kilkenny side 1-9 to 0-7 ahead at half-time, and Loughrea in trouble. For the Connacht side to make an impact they needed a good start to the second-half, but they got the worst possible one when they were hit for a second goal.

With just 3 minutes gone in the half, Shefflin's 65 was picked up by Patrick Reid and despite the presence of several Loughrea defenders, Reid drilled the ball into the net and for his troubles picked up a knock on his hand, but the goal eased the pain.

This goal, coming when it did, effectively finished the game as a contest and yet there was still 26 minutes to play. In fact Loughrea failed to add to their tally until the 46th minute. It made for a very poor contest as Loughrea were unable to penetrate a strong Ballyhale defence who were in mean mood, that is until the game was done and dusted. Well-known inter-county referee Michael Haverty was introduced by Loughrea in an effort to boost their flagging chances but it made little difference. Late on in the game Loughrea did pinch 2 goals by the Mahers, Johnny and Vinnie, but in between TJ Reid had raised a third green flag for the Leinster champions.

Long before the finish the outcome was decided and in the end the winning margin of 3-12 to 2-8 tells its own tale of a one-sided encounter.

Ballyhale manager Maurice Aylward, believes there is a lot more in his side. 'We have a young team and we are quite capable of coming here (Croke Park) and winning again, I have no doubt in the world about that.'

On a day when they joined Birr on top of the roll of honour (they both have four titles), Aylward's ambition now is for Ballyhale to overtake the Offaly side. 'We would love to go ahead of them at some stage, but we are very proud to be here on our National Holiday and be crowned champions. We will think about the future after we enjoy the celebrations.'

Loughrea had no complaints. Team boss Pat O'Connor said. 'It's disappointing; it's a long hard road to get here and we did not perform to our best, but hats off to Ballyhale. We gave them a chance and as Kilkenny teams will do you get punished and we were chasing the game after that.'

So the blinds are drawn on yet another club hurling Championship and in a season when the Kilkenny senior team won all before them it's no real surprise that the best club side in the country did also emerge from the Marble County.

Ballyhale-Shamrocks	3-12
Loughrea	2-8

Controversy in Football Final

Crossmaglen Rangers and St Patrick's Day go hand in hand as the boys from the County Armagh, along with Cork's Nemo Rangers are the most successful clubs in the competition.

Having won their 11th successive Armagh County Championship, 'Cross' as they are popularly known, survived a scare or two before collecting yet another Ulster title. In the All-Ireland semi-final they defeated St Brigid's from

Roscommon to book their place in the final as they went in search of their fourth club title.

Dr Crokes were beaten in the Kerry County Final by South Kerry but as divisional sides are not allowed participate in the club Championship the Killarney-based side were nominated to represent Kerry in the Championship. To their credit they came to Cork and

Liam O'Connor, renowned 'box' player, with his son Oisín on bodhrán, entertain the match crowd at the interval on St Patrick's Day. All-Ireland Club Finals, Croke Park. 17 March, 2007

beat Nemo Rangers in the semi-final, only the second time the Championship specialists had lost a game in the province.

Crokes then beat The Nire from Waterford in the final before accounting for Kildare's Moorefield after a replay in the semi-final.

The final would also see two of the games best forwards in action – Oisín McConville for Crossmaglen and Colm 'Gooch' Cooper seeking his first All-Ireland club medal with Dr Crokes who won their only title in 1992. It was a difficult day in HQ with a cross-field wind hampering the efforts of both sides to play constructive football. Indeed the first-half was a dogged affair that produced little in terms of quality.

Cooper got the game's opening score from a free, which was extended by Brian Looney's wonderful point. After Michael McNamee scored Cross's first point, Crokes lost their influential centre-back Brian McMahon with an injury that upset the balance of the team.

The yellow card count was mounting before the Ulster champions got their noses in front with a McNamee point. Aaron Kernan doubled their advantage with a pointed free, but a late point by Ambrose O'Donovan closed the first-half scoring and it was 0-4 to 0-3 for Crossmaglen at the interval.

Both sides were guilty of early misses on the resumption and there was little sign of an improvement, before the game suddenly sprung to life, courtesy of 2 goals inside a minute.

The first arrived in the 34th minute when a powerful solo run by Oisín McConville unlocked the Croke's defence. He then sold goalkeeper Kieran Cremin an outrageous dummy before planting the ball in an empty net. However, the Cross fans had barely time to digest this lovely goal when they were rocked back on their heels by an instant reply from Crokes. Cooper was the provider and Shane Doolin drilled the ball past Paul Hearty, game on, at last.

The tempo of the contest now improved. David McKenna and Croke's captain James Fleming traded points before Looney squared the game at 1-5 each after 37 minutes. It was still level on 48 minutes, before Crokes moved 2 clear with points from Cooper and Kieran O'Leary – a lead they stretched to 3, 1-9 to 1-6, with 8 minutes remaining.

Crossmaglen, who had the unique record of never having lost a club final, were eyeballing defeat in the face, but in keeping with their character they battled back. Crokes didn't help their cause by retreating into a defensive mode,

Oisín McConville, Crossmaglen Rangers, evades Vince Cooper, Dr Crokes, to go on and score a last-second point for Crossmaglen Rangers to draw the game. Crossmaglen Rangers v Dr Crokes. All-Ireland Football Club Final, Croke Park. 17 March, 2007

deciding to circle the wagons and protect what they had. It was an invitation for Cross to pile on the pressure and in the end Crokes cracked, if somewhat controversially.

John McEntee hit a long range point as they painfully reeled in the Killarney side and reduced the deficit to the bare minimum, thanks to a McConville free with time running out.

Then came the controversy and it left Crokes regretting their inability to close out the game when Cross were on the ropes. Three minutes into injury time

McConville snaffled a breaking ball 35 metres from Croke's goal. His shot appeared to drift wide but to the consternation of the entire Kerry contingent in the stadium the umpire waved the white flag to signal a point, level at 1-9 apiece.

| Dr Crokes | 1-9 |
| Crossmaglen Rangers | 1-9 |

To add salt into the gaping wounds of Crokes, McConville over-carried the ball, taking 7 steps, 3 over the permitted 4.

Television pictures confirmed that the ball had gone wide but all the protests were in vain. It was level and a replay was scheduled in O'Moore Park, Portlaoise on April 1st.

More talking points in replay

Replays seldom match the excitement of the drawn game and this final followed a similar pattern, but the match and subsequent events on and off the field, gave rise to much debate. Both sides finished with 14 players and Crossmaglen's John McEntee was at the centre of controversy, when he appeared to receive a second yellow card in the game but referee Eugene Murtagh did not send him off.

The match itself was a tough uncompromising affair, especially in the first-half. Crossmaglen made the perfect start and had the game's opening 3 points, but with Colm Copper scoring a nice brace for Crokes the sides were level at the end of the first quarter. Cooper, one of the game's marquee forwards, was coming in for some disgraceful treatment as he made his way out to take a 30 metre free. It was ignored by the match officials, but the 'Gooch' answered in the best possible fashion by landing a massive point. Minutes later he

was almost in for a goal but his blistering drive went over instead of under the bar, a bad miss and a let-off for Crossmaglen who had now seen McEntee receive the first of his 'yellow cards'.

The Kernan brothers, Aaron and Stephen, then upped the ante for the Ulster champions with points, ending a 15-minute spell without a score. Oisín McConville added 2 more and at the end of a tempestuous 30 minutes Crossmaglen were 0-7 to 0-5 in front.

Aaron Kernan's second point in the 6th minute of the second-half extended the lead, before Cooper showed his class. He chased and won a poor delivery from midfield, skipped past a couple of defenders before crossing for the in-rushing David Moloney to fire the ball to the net – the sides level, Crokes 1-5 Crossmaglen 0-8.

The tackles and the cards continued to mount, 10 yellow and 2 red in total, as Crokes missed a glorious opportunity in the 37th minute. A lovely flowing move ripped the Cross defence apart and Shane Dollin was hauled to the ground and the referee awarded Crokes a penalty. However, goalkeeper Paul Hearty saved Cooper's effort, and crucially the Killarney side did not score again as the game ebbed away from them.

Sensing they had been let off the

hook, Crossmaglen responded in style. McConville inched them in front with a lovely point, followed soon after by John Donaldson's departure with a second yellow card. However, they kept their composure and extended their lead with another Stephen Kernan point. Crokes were now in difficulty, compounded when Ambrose O'Donovan suffered a similar fate to Donaldson with his second yellow card. Crossmaglen then withdrew McEntee after he picked up a yellow card, his second, and it should have been red.

The men from Armagh were now rampant and further scores from Aaron Kernan and McConville finally closed the door on Crokes' challenge and at 0-13 to 1-5, the Andy Merrigan Cup was Crossmaglen-bound for the fourth time.

Crossmaglen Rangers	0-13
Dr Crokes	1-5

Regrettably there were many talking points. Crokes were incensed at the failure to send off McEntee and were also angry with the behaviour of some Crossmaglen supporters and officials. In relation to McEntee, referee Murtagh commented afterwards that he did not intend giving him his first yellow card and it should have been a ticking off and

that is why he did not send him off.

To their credit Crokes made light of the referee's mistake and coach Pat O'Shea said afterwards, 'we had our chances and did not take them and paid the price.'

The Dr Crokes club did write to the GAA expressing their annoyance at a 'number of unsavory incidents which took place during the game'. However they also made a point of congratulating Crossmaglen Rangers on their win and wished them well in the future. And that future is another assault on the Armagh county Championship as they seek a 12th successive title and then a tilt at retaining their All-Ireland title as they chase Nemo Rangers who lead the way with 7 titles. (Note: Crossmaglen succeeded in their bid to become Armagh county champions for the 12th time.)

One sad note in relation to the game – a few short hours after acting as an umpire for Eugene Murtagh in the club final in Portlaoise, well-known Longford GAA official, TP Petit, was killed in a tragic accident.

Mr Petit was highly respected in his native county and his death cast a shadow over Longford GAA, as the tragedy touched all who knew TP. He was also a referee of high standing in the GAA.

Ar dheis Dé ar a anam dhílis.

Paul Casey, Dublin, gets his pass away despite
the attention of Graham Geraghty, Meath.
Dublin v Meath. Leinster Football Championship
Quarter-Final Replay. Croke Park 17 June 2007

5

Dublin's 3-in-a-Row

The build-up to the final of the Leinster Football Championship had internal divisions (Meath), replays of ancient rivals (Dublin v Meath) and reports of rows in dressing rooms (Louth). But none of this was enough to put the Dubs off their stride.

5 Dublin's 3-in-a-Row

Leinster Football Championship

Old rivals ignite Leinster Football Championship

The sight of a packed Croke Park with the 'Dubs' in action is one of the most enduring in Irish sport, but when the opposition is provided by Meath, then the atmosphere is electric. It was exactly that when Leinster's big two met on the June Bank holiday weekend, and true to form they did not disappoint.

Before that clash the Championship had got off to an exciting start, helped by the sight of the legendary Mick O'Dwyer guiding the fortunes of Wicklow. Having bowed out after Laois exited the Championship of 2006, the Waterville maestro now in his 70th year succumbed to temptation and assumed responsibility for the Garden County and it had an immediate effect.

Louth were their first round opponents and the expectation was that Eamonn McEnaney's side would win with a bit to spare, but they were in for a rude awakening. Micko had his team fit and ready for action and in the end they forced a draw to set up a replay in Parnell Park a week later.

Louth retained the favourite's tag, but once again Wicklow backed by a huge and vociferous support battled away and at the end of yet another gripping contest not even extra-time could separate the sides. The game was played just 24 hours after the Wee County had bade farewell to the legendary musician Dermot O'Brien who passed away after a long illness. O'Brien had been captain when Louth shocked every GAA football fan in Ireland and around the world by defeating Cork in the 1957 All-Ireland football final.

So a second draw meant another replay, this time back in Croke Park as a curtain raiser to the Dublin v Meath game.

Elsewhere in front of a packed crowd in Pearse Park Longford staged a fabulous second-half comeback to defeat Westmeath and sent Tomás Ó'Flaharta's side to the qualifiers. The same fate awaited injury-hit Kildare as they were hammered by Meath, who now had Dublin firmly in their sights.

In advance of their clash with Laois, Longford manager Luke Dempsey feared for his team as he felt 'Liam Kearns the Laois boss had gone for a more physical type of player'. As it happened Longford

Ciaran Whelan, Dublin, is determined to shrug off the tackle of Mark Ward, Meath. Dublin v Meath. Leinster Football Championship Quarter-Final Replay. Croke Park 17 June 2007

were undone by a poor refereeing decision. It came in the 57th minute when they had what appeared to be a perfectly good goal disallowed. From the resultant free Laois got a point to signal the end of Longford's challenge as the men from the O'Moore County went on to win by 0-14 to 0-9.

Micko's challenge for Leinster honours finally came to an end in the third clash with Louth who won convincingly on a 2-18 to 0-11 scoreline, sending Wicklow to the Tommy Murphy Cup, but reassured that O'Dwyer would remain in charge.

The stage was now set for the first instalment of Dublin and Meath and 82,000 supporters crammed into HQ on a day when the rain cascaded down from the grey leaden-filled skies. This only added to the drama, of which there was plenty.

Dublin, with manager Paul Caffrey confined to the stands (as was Meath boss Colm Coyle) made a blistering start and with 20 minutes played were 0-5 to 0-0 in front.

Gradually the fighting qualities always associated with the Royal County surfaced and when Joe Sheridan notched their first point, the comeback began.

Meath also had a goal disallowed when excellent referee Jim McKee adjudged that defeated Fine Gael general election candidate Graham Geraghty had fouled his man when winning possession of the ball. It prompted one wag on the hill to comment 'the ref must be a Fianna Fáil man.'

Dublin themselves got a goal from Alan Brogan, which looked dubious to say the least. It helped them to an interval lead of 1-6 to 0-6.

By the 47th minute the lead was extended to 1-9 to 0-7 and the Dubs looked set for victory. However, not for the first time their inability to close down a game surfaced as Meath battled back. In fact in the closing 23 minutes Dublin only managed to score 0-2, not Championship winning form.

Cian Ward was the hero for Meath. Introduced as a 47th minute substitute he proceeded to score 0-5, including a difficult sideline kick deep in injury time to force the draw that their efforts deserved.

It was a fabulous match and with the replay set for two weeks later on June 17th, it meant a financial bonanza for the Leinster Council as yet another chapter in an age-old rivalry was about to unfold. Shades of 1991, perhaps, when it took

three games to eventually separate these two sides.

Dublin	1-11
Meath	0-14

The Replay

Once again the house-full signs were up as 82,000 enthralled spectators packed into Croke Park for the second meeting of Dublin and Meath and it was every bit as good as the drawn encounter.

Dublin were the dominant team for the most part but their old failing, an inability to kill off the opposition, left them vulnerable as the Royals mounted a comeback.

However, on this occasion the 'Dubs' answered their critics by scoring the last 3 points. Conal Keaney and Alan Brogan did the business to finally consign Meath to the qualifiers.

However, it was a player who was not named on the original starting fifteen, Mark Vaughan, who emerged as the scoring hero by bagging 0-8 – exactly half of the winner's total.

Meath started better as Cian Ward opened the scoring with a pointed free. But they were lucky in the sixth minute when a mix-up between goalkeeper Brendan Murphy and Anthony Moyles left Collie Moran clear on goal but somehow even from 8 yards out, Moran missed a glorious chance.

Dublin were improving but still found themselves behind by 0-5 to 0-3 on 14 minutes. Gradually Shane Ryan and Ciaran Whelan got on top in midfield and their dominance allowed the Dubs hit a purple patch that yielded 5 unanswered points.

However, when Stephen Bray kicked his third point of the game not only did it end a long scoreless period for Meath, it also meant they only trailed by a single point 0-8 to 0-7 at the break.

Dublin were playing into the Hill for the second half and it seemed to inspire them. Vaughan quickly landed 2 frees, and suddenly Meath were 4 points in arrears. They deployed centre-forward Kevin Reilly as an extra defender in an effort to stem the Dublin tide.

In keeping with their battling qualities, Colm Coyle's men were in no mood to surrender without a fight and were desperately unlucky not to get a goal in the 43rd minute.

Graham Geraghty's effort came back off the post after a great pass from Brian Farrell, but Geraghty did open Meath's second-half account with a point almost immediately.

Dublin though were still maintaining their 4-point advantage. Caffrey introduced Jason Sherlock to the attack, just as the Meath fightback began by displaying their typical 'never say die' spirit.

Farrell had a point followed by two from Stephen Bray after he had earlier missed an easy free. With just 7 of the 70 minutes remaining the bare minimum divided the sides – Dublin 0-13 Meath 0-12.

Extra-time now looked a distinct possibility. As Keaney and then Brogan missed good chances, Dublin fans must have feared another late collapse. Not this time though and when the hard questions were asked the 'boys in blue' came up with the right answers much to the delight of the hordes on the Hill. Keaney pointed twice in quick succession and despite having hit 5 wides, Alan Brogan finally found the range in the 72nd minute after a pass from Sherlock.

It put 4 points between the sides. There was no way back for Meath and at the end of yet another titanic battle for supremacy, Dublin moved on to the semi-final with a 0-16 to 0-12 win and a meeting with Offaly.

| Dublin | 0-16 |
| Meath | 0-12 |

As for Meath they encountered choppy waters after this game. First of all Joe Sheridan withdrew from the panel.

Having played with his club on the weekend he attended training on the following Tuesday night before informing Colm Coyle of his intentions. Sheridan had been substituted before half-time in the defeat to Dublin and said he had lost interest in the game and needed a rest.

To compound Coyle's problems as they prepared to face Down in the qualifiers, Graham Geraghty was involved in a training ground bust-up that led to him being removed from the panel by the manager.

According to reports, Geraghty reacted angrily to a challenge from a 19-year-old squad member and allegedly lashed out repeatedly as the session neared its end.

Team-mates and onlookers were shocked at the serious nature of the incident. The session was ended almost immediately as Coyle attempted to calm things down. Geraghty, captain in 1999, left the pitch and was not expected to return.

It would be interesting to see how these developments would impact on Meath's bid to make progress in the qualifiers.

Back to Football

With Meath dealing with their internal difficulties, the remainder of the Championship was pretty mundane with little to get excited about.

Following their three-game saga with Wicklow, Louth looked in good shape as they faced Wexford, who were playing their first game, in the quarter-final.

Wexford, with Mattie Forde impressing once again, were in command at half-time as they led by 0-12 to 2-2 and Louth were struggling as John O'Brien and JP Rooney scored the two Louth goals.

The second-half was a dreadful affair. Wexford lost their shape. Louth finished strongly and for all their difficulties only lost by 2 points, 0-16 to 2-8.

Reports emerged after the game of a row in the Louth dressing-room at half-time. Several members of the panel refused to travel home on the team bus and were subsequently dropped from the panel for the qualifiers.

After their exploits against Meath, Dublin were back in action with a semi-final clash with Offaly, who if they were to avoid playing in the Tommy Murphy Cup, would need to win and gain not only a place in the Leinster Final but also an extended run in the Championship. Offaly had earlier defeated Carlow in their quarter-final by 2-19 to 3-7 in a match of poor quality, despite producing 5 goals.

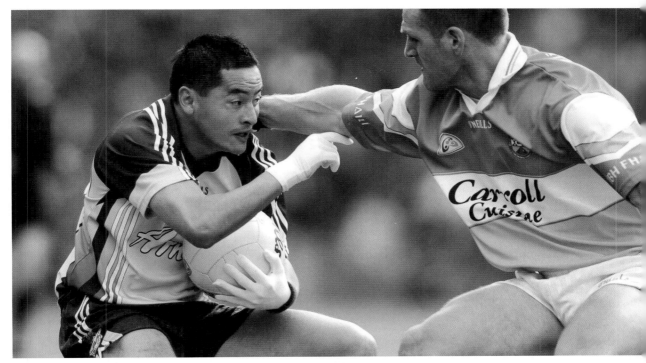

**Jason Sherlock, Dublin, attempts to get past defender Scott Brady, Offaly.
Dublin v Offaly. Leinster Football Semi-Final. Croke Park 24 June 2007**

Dublin were always in control and never looked like losing a disappointing contest that was once again played before a sell-out Croke Park crowd.

It was 1-7 to 0-4 at half-time but there was a touch of good fortune about the Dublin goal scored by Alan Brogan, whose fisted effort for a point was deflected to the net by Offaly full-back Joe Quinn who was trying to clear the danger. At one stage it was 0-5 to 0-0 and long before the finish the game was over as a contest as Dublin marched comfortably into another Leinster Final by 1-12 to 0-10.

Dublin	1-12
Offaly	0-10

Laois and Wexford contested the other semi-final and despite their obvious progress in recent years, Wexford, even with Mattie Forde, were not expected to deny Kearn's men a tilt at Dublin. It was the quintessential game of two halves and Laois won the one that counted most – the second-half, but overall it was another poor contest.

Wexford looked in a strong position at half-time as they led by 0-10 to 0-6, but amazingly they added only 3 points to their tally in the next 35 minutes as a reshaped Laois team seized the initiative.

A goal from Paul Lawlor in the 46th minute brought the sides level and Wexford's problems were compounded when they had David Murphy sent off 2 minutes later, with a second yellow card.

The 14 men were never going to deny Laois in the closing quarter and in the end the men from the O'Moore County were more convincing winners than the full time score of 1-13 to 0-13 would indicate.

Laois	1-13
Wexford	0-13

It all meant that apart from the two Dublin v Meath games, and to a lesser extent Micko's stint with Wicklow, it was a low-key Championship. The hope now was that the final, a repeat of the 2006 semi-final between Dublin and Laois, would at least produce some degree of entertainment.

Three-In-A-Row for Pillar's men

Dublin were hot favourites not only to complete a hat-trick of provincial titles but in the process to extend their unbeaten run over Leinster opposition in both league and Championship that now stretches back to June 2004.

As usual when Dublin are playing, it was another sell-out crowd in Jones Road and a good start to the day for Laois as they defeated Carlow to win the Minor title. But could they make it a double?

It was a strange game. Laois made a good start in what was their fourth final appearance in 5 years but in reality they were unable to match the physical strength of the champions.

Eight minutes gone and Ross Munnelly got in for a Laois goal when Dublin full-back Ross McConnell was caught badly out of position. However, Dublin took control in the vital areas of the field, while tactically Paul Caffrey also got it right. In defence Paul Griffin put the shackles on Michael Tierney, while Barry Cahill's capacity to win breaking balls complemented his strong running game. Ciaran Whelan was the dominant player in midfield while in attack Jason Sherlock pulled the strings on the '40' and Bernard Brogan enjoyed another good 70 minutes.

The pivotal moments in the contest arrived just on the 30-minute mark when Dublin struck for 2 goals. Bryan Cullen created the first for blond bombshell Mark Vaughan to finish neatly. Vaughan eventually bagged 1-6 of Dublin's total. Laois had barely time to draw breath when the second hammer blow was delivered.

Sherlock and Conal Keaney had done the spadework and Bernard Brogan did not hesitate to drill the ball to the net. It put the champions in a strong position heading for the half-time break – in front, and deservedly so, by 2-7 to 1-7.

Dublin got a third goal in the 40th minute. Again it was well constructed with Whelan, Sherlock and Keaney involved before Alan Brogan emulated his brother Bernard by effectively finishing the game as a contest.

Laois were now desperate for goals in an effort to bring them back into contention but all to no avail and the contest petered out in the last quarter as the Dublin defence dealt capably with whatever came their way.

Unfortunately the game ended on a sour note when a number of Dublin forwards got involved in some unnecessary off-the-ball incidents – and the sight of Alan Brogan trying to whip up the crowd did little to calm the situation.

However, it should not detract from another impressive display by a Dublin side with one objective on their mind, a date back here in late September. A few minor matters need to be ironed out before that becomes a reality, but for now they can relax and await their fate in the quarter-final draw.

It was a proud captain, Collie Moran, who accepted the Delaney Cup and their winning margin of 3-14 to 1-14 was a true reflection of their dominance and control.

| Dublin | 3-14 |
| Laois | 1-14 |

'3 in-a-row' – Mark Vaughan, Dublin, scorer of a crucial goal in the game, lifts the Delaney Cup as Dublin become Leinster champions for the third successive year. Dublin v Laois. Leinster Football Final. Croke Park 15 July 2007

James Masters, Cork, attempts to kick a point as Marc Ó'Sé, Kerry, attempts to block him. Kerry v Cork, Munster Final, Fitzgerald Stadium, Killarney. 1 July, 2007

6

Kerry Retake Title

MUNSTER FOOTBALL CHAMPIONSHIP

Kerry and Cork's domination of football in Munster continues, despite the efforts of Waterford, Clare, Limerick and Tipperary. The only question left was which of the two would lift the cup. In a fantastic final, Kerry answered that question.

6 Kerry Retake Title

Munster Football Championship

'As You Were' in Munster

The advent of the open draw in the Bank of Ireland Munster Football Championship some years ago hinted at an end to the dominance of the big two, Cork and Kerry.

Some counties briefly lifted their head above the parapet, especially Clare who actually won the title in 1992. Limerick promised a lot but never managed to get over the finishing line, narrowly failing to beat Kerry in successive finals. Tipperary, even with one of the country's best forwards – Declan Browne – in their side, also slipped back, while Waterford were still awaiting their first Championship win in 19 years as the 2007 campaign got underway.

In fact at the conclusion of the league, three of the six Munster counties were facing Division 4 football in 2008, which also meant unless they reached the provincial final, it was the Tommy Murphy Cup and not the All-Ireland qualifiers that would occupy their thoughts for the summer.

The Championship did provide us with one of the first big shocks of the year as the Páidí Ó'Sé-managed Clare were undone by Waterford who, on a balmy afternoon in the Fraher Field in Dungarvan, won a poor tie by 1-6 to 0-7. Clare actually led by 0-6 to 0-4 until Ger Power's 58th minute goal set Waterford up for a sensational win. John Kiely, the Waterford manager, was thrilled at the victory as it set up a clash with reigning All-Ireland champions Kerry. The game would be played in Dungarvan exactly 50 years after the Decies had shocked the Kingdom in a Munster semi-final, a feat they have been unable to repeat since.

| Waterford | 1-6 |
| Clare | 0-7 |

As for Clare, it was a chastened Páidí who left Dungarvan refusing to comment to the waiting media as speculation mounted that his tenure in the Banner County would come to an end and he would not be in charge for the Tommy Murphy Cup.

In the other first-round tie, Cork faced Limerick for the third time in the space of a few months and with home advantage were expected to win – and they duly did. In the corresponding clash in 2006 the counties had contrived to produce arguably the worst game of the entire Championship. This year's clash was better, but the outcome was still the same. Cork started in whirlwind fashion and an early goal from James Masters put them in control. For a while they lost their way and failed to score for almost 20 minutes. Then their second goal by Noel O'Leary just before half-time finished the game as a contest.

The second-half was a non-event. Limerick battled away but limitations in attack did little to help their cause as Cork ran out comfortable winners.

| Cork | 2-14 |
| Limerick | 0-7 |

All-Ireland champions Kerry took their Championship bow in the Fraher Field with new boss Pat O'Shea fearful of a repeat of the 1957 result, and in front of the RTÉ cameras as well. It was also a new look Kerry team who were without Seamus Moynihan, who retired after the 2006 All-Ireland final win over Mayo as did full-back Mike McCarthy. In fact manager O'Shea was taking no chances as Kerry took the precaution of staying overnight in a Cork hotel for the 2pm throw-in.

As it was, the pre-match hype – it was

Darragh Ó'Sé, Kerry, leaps high to prevent Nicholas Murphy, Cork, from fielding the ball. Kerry v Cork, Munster Final, Fitzgerald Stadium, Killarney. 1 July, 2007

the first time that Waterford footballers featured in a televised clash – affected the Decies who were soundly beaten. Eoin Brosnan drilled in two first-half goals. Waterford took 29 minutes to open their account and long before the finish the small crowd had lost interest in the one-sided nature of the proceedings. Kerry eventually won by 2-15 to 0-4.

Kerry	2-15
Waterford	0-4

Cork were in Limerick the same afternoon for their semi-final clash with Tipperary before a paltry crowd in the vast concourse that is the Gaelic Grounds, which made for an eerie and unreal atmosphere. There was never a hint of a shock in this game. Tipperary's best player Declan Browne was struggling with an injury and their attack suffered as a result.

Cork effectively put the game beyond Tipp's reach with two goals in a three minute spell before half-time. James Masters scored both. He finished with 2-7, and the Munster champions led 2-9 to 0-5 at half-time.

It was all one-way traffic in the second-half as Billy Morgan once again emptied the bench as he prepared for yet another Munster final against All-Ireland champions Kerry on the first Sunday in July. As it was, Cork ran out comprehensive winners by 2-18 to 0-10.

Cork	2-18
Tipperary	0-10

A familiar pairing in the Munster final then – Cork v Kerry – and on the evidence of the games to date, it's a situation that is unlikely to change in the immediate future, as the other counties have slipped back into the pack.

Beauty's Home Beckons

Having won the title after a replay in Páirc Uí Chaoimh in 2006, it meant a now familiar trip across the county bounds for champions Cork on the first Sunday in July and a date with their old rivals in scenic Fitzgerald Stadium, Killarney.

It was a unique decider in many respects as it would be the first time ever that Cork as the Munster champions and Kerry as the All-Ireland champions would meet in a Munster Final.

As usual with these age-old rivals the place was buzzing with anticipation and a huge crowd descended on the town with Cork in the majority. Business people were not complaining, especially after a wet and miserable June. They were glad of the influx of so many on what is always a special day.

A strong wind though would be a factor in the game, and despite the fact that Kerry are the reigning All-Ireland champions, many pundits had Cork as favourites. There was also an added incentive for the Rebels, having won the minor final convincingly over Kerry by 1-16 to 2-8, the county now stood on the cusp of a grand slam of provincial football titles – a feat rarely achieved by the Rebel County.

In April a fourth successive Under-21 crown had been collected and a few days before the trip to Killarney the juniors had beaten Clare. Could the mighty Kingdom end the year without a Munster title? The coming 70 minutes would decide, and also shape the season for the winners and losers. For the winners it was a place in the quarter-finals and for the losers the qualifiers that had in them some big hitters.

Last season Kerry transformed their team by placing Kieran Donaghy at full-forward and now Billy Morgan was adopting a similar tactic with Glanmire's Michael Cussen wearing the number 14 shirt. How they perform could decide the destination of the Munster title.

Cork won the toss and to the surprise of many elected to play with the wind. It's a tactic that is favoured by Morgan.

Mike Frank Russell and James Masters traded early points, but it was Kerry who settled quicker and despite playing into the wind looked lively in attack.

Team captain Declan O'Sullivan drilled over 2 points and Donaghy was proving a handful for Graham Canty, while at the other end Cussen was seeing little of the ball.

Cork, though, improved as Masters kicked 2 points. Kevin McMahon gave them the lead and on 23 minutes it was 0-5 to 0-4 for the champions and now Kerry were struggling.

Cussen then made an impact. In quick succession he won a great ball and kicked over 2 quality points to extend Cork's lead. Kerry hit back almost immediately when Russell and Donaghy had points and it was now developing into a good contest.

Cork got the next 2 scores from Nicholas Murphy and Donnacha O'Connor, but Kerry's capacity to hit back was a factor and on the stroke of half-time Eoin Brosnan knocked over a neat point created by Donaghy. Now Cork's lead of 0-9 to 0-7 at the break did not look enough, given the strength of the wind.

On the resumption O'Connor missed a relatively easy free and it would be some time before they scored again.

Kerry then enjoyed their most productive spell of the game and proceeded to rip Cork apart. In the space of 9 minutes, they scored 1-5 without reply. Colm 'Gooch' Cooper and Russell between them shared 4 points, while Declan O'Sullivan had another.

In the same period 'Gooch' showed his class with a cracking goal. Hesitancy in the Cork defence allowed him gain possession of the ball and in a flash it was nestling in the net. Kerry were in control 1-12 to 0-9.

Cork were staring a heavy defeat in the face and how they responded is a measure of their progress as Morgan reshaped his team. Cussen went to midfield and he helped break Dara Ó'Sé's dominance, while the introduction of Conor McCarthy and John Miskella brought an immediate improvement and it sparked a Cork fightback.

Pearse O'Neill scored a point, before a quickly-taken free by McCarthy set up a great goal. McMahon's pass put O'Connor clear and his powerful drive gave Diarmuid Murphy no chance. Now it was 1-12 to 1-10 and it was 'game on'.

O'Connor was having an excellent match and he followed his goal with 2 points to tie the game at 1-12 each with 6 minutes remaining. Kerry were on the rack. Roared on by their huge support Cork came in search of the winning scores. Then came a pivotal moment.

With the game moving into injury time, Cork won a free and Masters floated the ball in the direction of the Kerry goal. It broke to team captain Derek Kavanagh in splendid isolation and a chance to win the game. Just as he was about to pull the trigger and possibly give Cork victory, defender Tomás Ó'Sé tugged his jersey and the off-balance Kavanagh's shot sailed wide, much to the relief of the Kingdom supporters directly behind the town goal.

It seemed a blatant penalty but referee Martin Duffy ignored the appeals from the incensed Cork players. It was a huge let-off for Kerry and they took full advantage.

Kerry won possession from the kick-out and when the ball landed in Donaghy's direction he kicked a fabulous point, to restore their lead.

Cork now needed to win the kick-out to try and force a replay. They did but a poor pass led to a Kerry breakaway and once again they paid the ultimate price.

Kerry swept downfield and substitute Sean O'Sullivan matched Donaghy's earlier effort with a great point to finally kill off Cork's challenge and seal victory by 1-15 to 1-13.

Kerry	1-15
Cork	1-13

It was Kerry's first win over Cork in a Munster Final in Killarney since 1986. It was a special day also for coach Pat O'Shea, a native of the town, as he delivered a title in his first season at the helm as Kerry bid to become the first team since Cork in 1989 and 1990 to retain the Sam Maguire Cup. They now have one game less in which to achieve that feat.

As for Cork they head for the qualifiers buoyed by their display against the All-Ireland champions in their own backyard. The possibility that these two great rivals will meet again before the season runs its course is a live one.

So the blinds are pulled down on yet another Munster Football Championship. It produced an excellent final but it also raised a number of worrying issues.

There is a clear sign that the big two are once again a step ahead of the rest and little indication that the gap can be narrowed in the immediate future. Munster Council Chairman Jimmy O'Gorman has decided to set up a sub-committee to look at ways of bringing about an improvement. That though is

Nicholas Murphy, Cork, jumps highest to field the ball from Michael Quirke, Kerry, closely aided by Pearse O'Neill, Cork. Kerry v Cork, Munster Final, Fitzgerald Stadium, Killarney. 1 July, 2007

an argument for another day.

Right now it's the men in green and gold who are celebrating winning the Provincial Championship as Declan O'Sullivan lifted the Munster Cup into the Killarney sky in the shadows of the 'Reeks'. It was the 72nd time that a Kerryman had performed such a ritual.

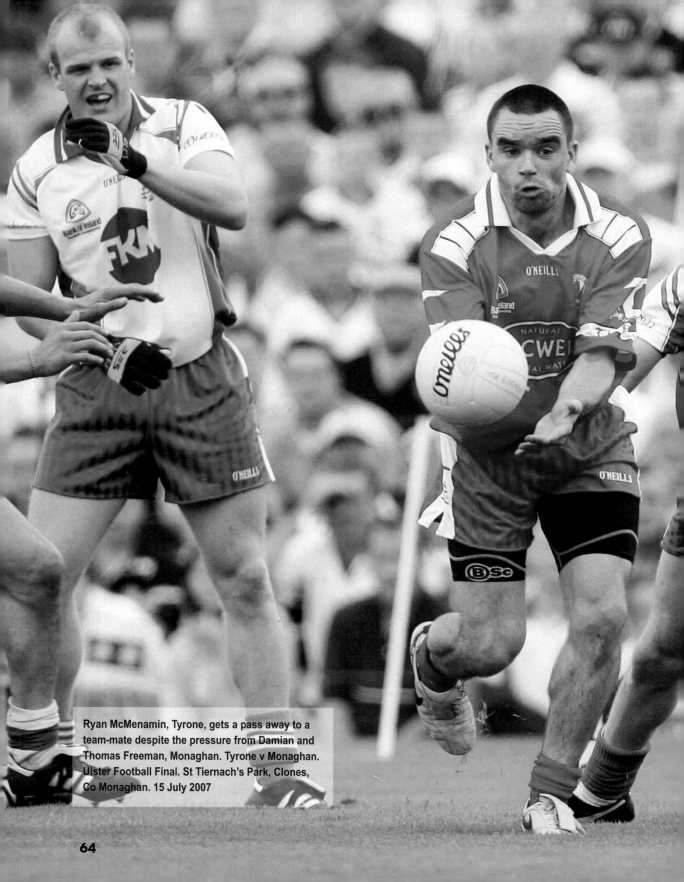

Ryan McMenamin, Tyrone, gets a pass away to a team-mate despite the pressure from Damian and Thomas Freeman, Monaghan. Tyrone v Monaghan. Ulster Football Final. St Tiernach's Park, Clones, Co Monaghan. 15 July 2007

Tyrone
Edge Out
Monaghan

ULSTER FOOTBALL CHAMPIONSHIP

*A re-energised Tyrone appeared
unstoppable in their campaign to win the
Ulster football title. But league
champions Donegal and an impressive
Monaghan were determined to make their
mark as Championship contenders.*

7 Tyrone Edge Out Monaghan

Ulster Football Championship

Ulster throws up its usual shocks

The non-availability of Croke Park ensured that for the first time in four years the Ulster Football Final would return to its spiritual home of St Tiernach's Park, Clones. However, but as has been the case in the province for the last few years, the route to the final would be as rocky as ever for the participants.

Tyrone, favoured by many for the All-Ireland title, the Ulster champions Armagh and newly-crowned league champions Donegal were all bracketed together in one half of the draw, opening the way for one of the so-called 'lesser counties' to claim a place in the 2007 decider.

Time was when Down and Cavan were the big two in the province. Now they are way back in the pack, with Down facing Division 3 football in 2008, not an endearing prospect for a proud county. Their clash in the first round evoked memories of the distant past for these two counties, but the game itself and subsequent replay did little to suggest they would have a major say in the destination of the big prizes come the autumn.

The drawn encounter produced a glut of goals that masked a poor contest. Down got the first goal from Ronan Sexton and their second goal arrived in the 20th minute courtesy of Benny Coulter. Poor defending was the order of the day as Cavan got their first goal from Larry O'Reilly. It all meant Down were ahead 2-3 to 1-5 at the end of a frenetic first-half.

Down's first attack of the second-half yielded a third goal – Sexton again the scorer as the contest entered a drab third quarter with scores a rarity. With 8 minutes remaining, Down held a slender 1-point lead, but Sean Brady's introduction brought about an improvement from Cavan. Down, despite their limitations, edged 3 points ahead and Coulter failed in his attempt to make it 4. That miss very nearly cost them the game.

A dreadful error by Down goalkeeper Mickey McVeigh allowed a shot from Jonathan Crowe to slip from his grasp and over the line. In stoppage time Dermot McCabe gave Cavan an unlikely lead and possible victory. However, Down did not deserve to lose and justice was done when a late free by Ronan Sexton earned them a replay in Newry a week later. It ended Down 3-8 Cavan 2-11.

The replay was another dull affair which saw Down chisel out a 4-point victory on an afternoon that was perfect for football. The conditions could not be offered as an excuse for the poor quality of the game. This time there were no goals, but the half-time score of 0-3 each is an indication of the substandard play from both teams.

Cavan were dealt a blow in the 43rd minute when Michael Lyng was sent off. In the intense heat the 14 men could not sustain their efforts. It was still level at 0-8 apiece with 15 minutes remaining but a strong finish by Ross Carr's men produced 5 points without reply to propel them to a meeting with Monaghan in the next round on a 0-15 to 0-11 scoreline.

Down	0-15
Cavan	0-11

Fermanagh were not expected to trouble Tyrone in their first round game and while they went close there was a sense that they lacked the self-belief to win what proved to be a dour contest. Mark Murphy got a Fermanagh goal in the fifth minute but they failed to build on it and Tyrone led 0-6 to 1-2 at half-time.

Fans gather along the Main Street in Clones, bedecked with the colourful flags of the red and white of Tyrone and the blue and white of Monaghan prior to the Ulster Football Final. Tyrone v Monaghan. St Tiernach's Park, Clones, Co Monaghan. 15 July 2007

Tyrone moved up a gear in the second-half and looked like building a commanding lead, but Fermanagh battled away and actually drew level with a Tom Brewster free. But an injury-time free from 40 metres by Ger Cavlan gave Tyrone a narrow but deserved 0-13 to 1-9 win.

Tyrone	0-13
Fermanagh	1-9

Derry's opening game with Antrim was postponed owing to a waterlogged Casement Park, but it only put off the inevitable as a week later Derry were never troubled in a 1-13 to 0-10 victory.

Derry	1-13
Antrim	0-10

Down, despite the benefit of two games, were still dispatched by Monaghan in the next round. Ciaran Hanratty got 2 goals in a 2-15 to 1-15 win. It was a sign of things to come from the Farney County men.

Monaghan	2-15
Down	1-15

The first really big clash was shrouded in controversy before a ball was kicked in anger as holders Armagh had to travel to Ballybofey for a clash with newly-crowned league champions Donegal. This attractive tie was originally fixed for Ballybofey but the Ulster Council, fearful that development work on the ground would not be completed in time, switched the match to Clones.

Donegal were angry at this decision and were confident that the ground would be ready. In fact this game was always their completion date target – the Officers of the County Board stressed this. On appeal the Council reversed their decision and the game was then switched back to Ballybofey. Armagh manager Joe Kernan was angry with this move as he felt the ground would not cope with the huge crowd who would want to see this clash.

The match itself produced a dramatic conclusion but for long periods it was typical Ulster football – a dour physical encounter. Armagh were bidding for a fourth successive title but Donegal boosted by their league success were confident of winning, especially with home advantage. It was a new-look Armagh team as the McEntee twins had retired and Francey Bellew was absent with a long-term injury, but an All-Ireland under-21 title win in 2005 had given Joe Kernan good options to build for the future.

There was little between the sides in the opening half and Armagh led 0-5 to 0-4 at half-time but a failure to convert a raft of chances would ultimately come back to haunt them.

Oisín McConville got a quality goal in the 43rd minute after which the sides shared the next 4 points. Armagh looked in control. As the game moved into the last quarter there was little to suggest that a lethargic Donegal could mount a comeback. But the wides continued to mount up for Armagh and Donegal sensed they still had a chance to win the game. Colm McFadden pointed his sixth free for the league champions and as the game moved into injury time only 2 points divided the sides.

Then came the final dramatic twist that altered Armagh's season. Brendan Devenney's lobbed effort for a point hung in the air and Kevin Cassidy appeared to be in the square as the ball dropped into goalkeeper Paul Hearty's arms or so it seemed. Whether distracted by Cassidy or not, Hearty spilled the ball and it trickled into the net to give Donegal victory at the death by 1-9 to 1-8.

| Donegal | 1-9 |
| Armagh | 1-8 |

It was a sweet win for Donegal who had suffered 3 Ulster final defeats and 1 All-Ireland semi-final loss to Armagh since 2000. Afterwards Kernan was critical of the stay-away Armagh supporters and also felt the winning goal was 'dubious'.

Worryingly for Donegal, the swagger was gone from their play and the warning signs were there and what happened in the semi-final re-inforced that view.

Semi-finals

Monaghan's graph continued to rise and the manner in which they disposed of Derry's challenge marked them out as genuine Championship contenders. A highly rated Derry side were unable to cope with the work rate and feverish tackling of a Monaghan side that were far superior in all aspects of the game.

The only mystery was that the winning margin of just 2 points certainly did not reflect Monaghan's dominance which was evident from the start. With 18 minutes played it was 0-6 to 0-2 before a late Derry rally saw them reduce the deficit to a point at half-time.

In the second-half a brace of points each from Thomas Freeman and Stephen Gallogly gave Monaghan a cushion for the anticipated Derry rally. Paddy Bradley did get a goal but even that failed to inspire those around him and Monaghan sealed a thoroughly deserved win, 0-14 to 1-9, with points from Rory Woods and Gallogly and they were back in a final – their first in 19 years.

Monaghan	0-14
Derry	1-9

The second semi-final between Donegal and Tyrone had all the makings of a classic, but the opposite materialised as the league champions were literally blown away by Mickey Harte's men. It sent a clear signal that Tyrone were back as a force as they produced their best performance since the summer of 2005. Donegal capitulated in the face of a relentless onslaught that they were powerless to stop.

Yet it looked so different after the opening 10 minutes. They scored an opportunist goal from Kevin Cassidy, had a goal disallowed and even missed a penalty. Tyrone played themselves into the game and a neatly-taken penalty by Colm McCullagh sent them on their way and they were in front by 1-6 to 1-3 at the break. The signs were ominous for Donegal – it would prove to be a long second-half.

Midfield was a no-go area for Brian McIver's men and with Brian Dooher in splendid form Donegal were put on the backfoot with some splendid off-the-ball movement. By the end of the third quarter Tyrone had extended their lead to 1-11 to 1-5 and Donegal's challenge had disintegrated even before Raymond Mulgrew finished off a tremendous move with a classy goal.

By the end Donegal were a ragged outfit and it left manager Brian McIver with a lot of soul-searching to do before the league champions enter the qualifiers. Tyrone cruised into the final. It finished 2-14 to 1-7. It was also an afternoon when Brian Dooher announced his return to the 'big time' notching 5 points with a top class display, after an injury-hit season. Mickey Harte withdrew him before the end. Dooher received a standing ovation from the crowd and a warm embrace from his manager. A rare show of emotion from Harte, but his respect for the captain is well known.

Tyrone	2-14
Donegal	1-7

Tyrone were back in the final and on the evidence of this display Monaghan faced a huge task, even if it was being played on their home ground in Clones.

Final returns Home

It was only fitting that on its return to the familiar confines of Clones, Monaghan

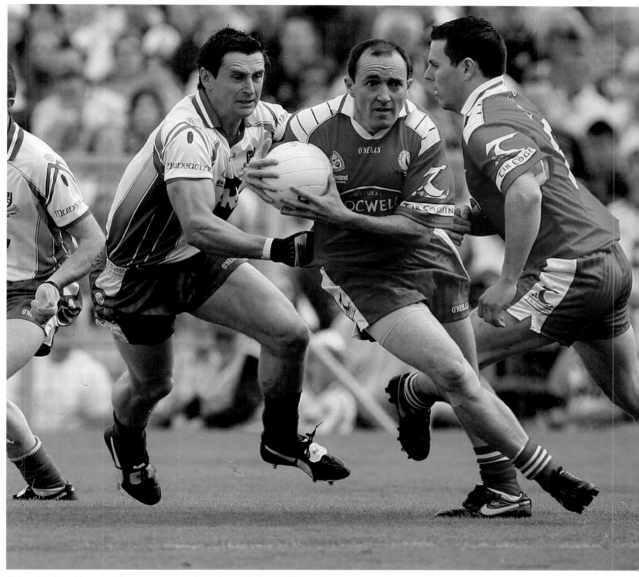

Brian Dooher, Tyrone, tries to get away from Gary McQuaid, Monaghan.
Tyrone v Monaghan Ulster Football Final. St Tiernach's Park, Clones, Co Monaghan. 15 July 2007

should take centre stage on Ulster final day. With Tyrone in the opposite corner it had the makings of an exciting clash.

Tyrone for all their dominance of football were seeking to win the Anglo-Celt Cup for the first time since 2003, the first year of Mickey Harte's tenure as manager. The wait was even longer for

71

the men from the Farney County who were making a return visit to the decider, a trip they had not made in all of 19 years.

But under astute manager Seamus McEnaney, a brother of top inter-county referee Pat, the signs pointed to Monaghan as an emerging force in Ulster. Yet with 46 minutes played it looked as if they were about to be on the wrong end of a heavy defeat as Tyrone, displaying all the smartness and experience gained over the last few years, built up a commanding lead of 1-13 to 0-8. Monaghan were making simple mistakes, turning over possession and missing goal chances that came their way, Tyrone were also making errors but less of them, crucial in a tight contest – as it turned out to be.

Clones was packed for the 'homecoming' and a crowd of 33,832 were present as favourites Tyrone raced into an early lead. With just 16 minutes gone they had 1-6 on the board. Philip Jordan got the goal after taking a pass from Gerard Cavlan and palming the return pass to the net. Owen Mulligan was troubling full-back Vinny Corey. Mulligan bagged 2 points before Corey was switched to the corner. At one stage in the opening half, Tyrone had a 7-point lead and looked set for an easy win.

Monaghan, though, for all their difficulties in certain areas, were hanging in and only trailed by 4 points, 1-8 to 0-7, at half-time but immediately after the break came the defining period in the game.

Tyrone opened up a considerable gap with some excellent football and with an 8-point lead (1-13 to 0-8) the expectation was that Mickey Harte's men would coast to victory. However, Monaghan had other ideas, as they thundered back into the game.

McEnaney had re-shaped his team at half-time even sending full-back Corey to full-forward in what appeared at the time to be an act of desperation. In fact it proved to be the switch of the match.

Monaghan's challenge was re-ignited in the 51st minute when Thomas Freeman lashed in a goal, created by Corey. A minute later the duo combined again this time for a point by the same scorer.

Monaghan were now in full flight. Corey was causing all sorts of problems for the Tyrone defence and with just 16 minutes remaining the gap was down to 3 points, 1-13 to 1-10, and the early swagger was gone from Tyrone's play.

Sean Cavanagh, who was outstanding all afternoon, gave Tyrone breathing space with his fourth point from play, but

Tyrone players make their way back out into the sunshine for the second half of the Ulster Football Final. Tyrone v Monaghan. St Tiernach's Park, Clones, Monaghan. 15 July 2007

Monaghan refused to go away and their determined play kept them within striking distance. It was helter skelter stuff in the closing 10 minutes as the game lost its shape. While Tyrone were still in front, they were living dangerously – especially when Corey had possession.

Just 2 minutes from time and Monaghan came again. Corey drove at the heart of the Tyrone defence and with only goalkeeper John Devine to beat, he frustratingly saw his effort come back off the butt of the upright. A collective sigh of relief could be heard from the Tyrone bench. As the game entered injury-time Mulligan pointed a free to push Tyrone 3 ahead again. Safe at last? But there was one final twist and it very nearly brought the levelling goal, from you've guessed who – that man Corey again.

In the very last minute of injury-time the converted full-forward sent a screamer in the direction of the Tyrone goal but it flew over the bar for the final act of a thrilling second-half. In a welter of excitement Tyrone hung on to win by 2 points 1-15 to 1-13.

Tyrone	1-15
Monaghan	1-13

It was a match of many twists, not least the wonderful contribution of 'man of the match' Sean Cavanagh with 4 points from play. The switch of Corey to full-forward which almost swung the game for Monaghan; Tyrone's goal scored by Philip Jordan, whose pace and ball-carrying ability made it possible, helped by a wonderful pass from Cavlan; the midfield battle between a quartet of quality footballers which saw Dick Clerkin and Eoin Lennon for Monaghan with their relentless and abrasive play shade it over Kevin Hughes and Joe McMahon. Mulligan's free taking was also exceptional, he bagged 4 from varying angles.

So yet another exciting Ulster Football Championship comes to an end, Tyrone just about deserved their win and their duopoly of the Anglo-Celt Cup with Armagh (no other county in the last 9 years has inscribed their name on its base) continues, as their extra experience told in the end.

As for Monaghan they will regret bad starts to each half, but on the overall evidence McEnaney's charges will shape the Championship before the biggest prize of all is finally dished out in September.

Ja Fallon, Galway, tries to retain possession as he is tackled by Paul McGovern, Sligo. Galway v Sligo. Connacht Football Final. Dr Hyde Park, Roscommon 8 July 2007

8

Sligo Ends Long Wait

The 2007 football campaign in Connacht signalled a shake-up in Gaelic football in the west. Galway and Mayo may have dominated in the past few years, but in 2007 Sligo had something to say about that.

8 Sligo Ends Long Wait

Connacht Football Championship

Long wait ends for Sligo

The draw for the 2007 Bank of Ireland Connacht Senior Football Championship ensured that there would be a new pairing in the final, as old rivals Galway and Mayo were due to play in a preliminary round game as early as May 20th. For the losers it meant a long wait for the qualifying rounds to begin. For two counties who have long been the dominant teams in the province this would not sit well with their respective supporters. The flipside of course was that it opened the door for other Connacht counties to claim a place in the final, and for one particular county it was an opportunity they were not going to let pass.

With the 5 home teams – Sligo, Galway, Leitrim, Mayo and Roscommon – being joined in the race by London and New York, the Connacht Council employ a rota system whereby each team visits these big cities for a first-round game. This year it was the turn of Sligo and Leitrim to pack the bags and bring the passport for a Championship encounter far away from the green fields of Connacht.

These games generally result in wins for the visitors and while there has been the odd scare or two along the way, a shock result is a rarity in a Championship that is often overshadowed by events in the bigger provinces. All eyes were focused on the Galway v Mayo clash as John O'Mahoney made his long-awaited return with his native county a few days before he faced the electorate on General Election day in his bid to become a member of the 23rd Dáil.

In between this game, Sligo and Leitrim recorded their expected wins. Sligo went to the 'Big Apple' and on the newly-laid surface of Gaelic Park in the Bronx easily saw off the challenge of New York, who offered only token resistance. It finished 2-18 to 1-3 and Sligo with the business done could enjoy a few leisurely hours in the city that never sleeps, before concentrating on their semi-final clash with Roscommon.

Sligo	2-18
New York	1-3

Leitrim had it a bit harder on a rain sodden surface in Ruislip as London made them fight all the way for a win.

Michael Meehan, Galway, attempts to kick a point as he is tackled by Keith Higgins, Mayo. Mayo v Galway. Connacht Football Championship. Pearse Stadium, Galway 20 May 2007

While it never looked in doubt, the 2-point margin tells its own tale. It was, in fact, Leitrim's third trip across the Irish Sea this year. A league game was called off late in April owing to heavy rain, and on a day borrowed from February, Leitrim won by 1-11 to 2-5, too close for comfort for boss Dessie Dolan.

Leitrim	1-11
London	2-5

Pearse Stadium was the venue for the latest clash between the big two in Connacht, just a few short weeks after Mayo had defeated their great rivals in a league semi-final. Generally, games of this nature produce good quality football, but on this occasion and before a huge and expectant crowd, they failed to deliver. Indeed as Galway v Mayo games go, it will not linger long in the memory bank, especially for Mayo folk.

The trend of the contest was set as

early as the second minute when Cormac Bane lashed in a goal. He repeated the dose in the 20th minute and Mayo were in shock.

In fact it was these two goals that divided the sides at the short whistle, Galway 2-5 Mayo 0-5, and already there was an air of inevitability about the outcome.

This was confirmed by the 45th minute when Mayo's Pat Harte saw yellow for the second time, followed by red and the champions were down to 14 men and on the way out of the race for the Connacht title. Ciaran McDonald, a folk hero in Mayo, was introduced but he made little impact, although to be fair he did strike the post with a good effort. It summed up Mayo's afternoon.

Galway coasted to an easy win. Indeed Mayo only scored 2 points from play over the 70 minutes. In a one-sided contest the final result is an accurate reflection of the dominance enjoyed by Peter Forde's team, 2-10 to 0-9. It left Mayo boss John O'Mahoney with a huge task on his hands if he was to save his side's season, as Galway looked forward to a trip to Carrick-on-Shannon for a semi-final meeting with Leitrim.

Galway	2-10
Mayo	0-9

Consolation for O'Mahoney came a few days later when he won a Mayo seat in the General Election for Fine Gael. The next time Mayo would take the field, the letters TD would be after his name.

Semi-Finals

Dr Hyde Park, Roscommon, was the venue for the clash of Sligo and Roscommon and it pointed to a win for John Maughan's home side. Sligo's best displays in recent years have come in the qualifiers and they were also playing at a venue that has not been kind to them in the past.

Initially this trend looked like it would be maintained, despite a good start which saw them score 3 points before Roscommon opened their account. However, Seamus O'Neill began to outplay Eamonn O'Hara in midfield and after drawing level Roscommon then struck for the first goal. It arrived in the 28th minute when Ger Heneghan and Gary Cox combined to set up Karl Mannion and the 'Rossies' were ahead 1-3 to 0-4 at half-time.

Early in the second-half Heneghan was involved again, this time setting up Cathal Gregg for Roscommon's second goal and at 2-4 to 0-4 it seemed as if the scriptwriters were correct after all.

But someone forgot to tell the Sligo lads who instead of folding, as many expected them to, responded with tremendous spirit and determination and no little skill.

O'Hara regained control in midfield and with good support from Paul McGovern they took over. The key to the game though was the Sligo half-forward line of Brian Curran, Mark Breheny and Sean Davey who between them kicked 9 points and some of them were of the highest quality.

The gap was down to 3 points on 43 minutes and Roscommon were struggling. Even when Cox got a point in the 46th minute, it was to be their last score as by now their challenge was in freefall. With 12 minutes left, substitute Kenneth Sweeney levelled the game and there was then only going to be one winner.

Breheny put Sligo in front and the insurance point arrived in injury-time from Curran. For the first time since 1975 the men from Yeats County were back in a Connacht final, and deservedly so on a 0-13 to 2-5 scoreline.

Sligo	0-13
Roscommon	2-5

Roscommon were stunned and their supporters made little attempt to conceal their anger having watched their side lose a 6-point lead and score only 1 point in the last half-hour of a game they were expected to win.

Manager Maughan had little to say except 'we are shattered, it's a difficult one to accept as it was a horrible performance.'

Contrast that with Sligo who could now plan for a Connacht Final, on a day when old ghosts were laid to rest.

Leitrim v Galway

It was a special day in Páirc Sean MacDiarmada, Carrick-on-Shannon, as GAA President Nickey Brennan officially opened the brand new stand and before a packed partisan home crowd Leitrim fancied their chances of causing an upset.

Galway, without ever producing their best, always looked capable of winning and their capacity to score points when needed most was a crucial factor in an absorbing contest.

In the eighth minute Leitrim's Gary McCloskey was at the end of a quality move to finish neatly to the net to give the home side the lead. However, the Galway attack repeatedly troubled the Leitrim defence and with all six forwards scoring in the first-half they were ahead

0-9 to 1-5 at half-time.

Galway were still struggling to kill off the home side. With 20 minutes left only 2 points separated the teams, and that after Leitrim's Donal Brennan had a goal-bound effort stopped by Paul Doherty. Leitrim were to miss another couple of chances that they would regret as Galway finally moved into a winning position. They even had a late goal wrongly disallowed but it made little difference as the Tribesmen had 4 points to spare 0-17 to 1-10 in a performance that had all the hallmarks of a side with designs on a long and rewarding campaign.

Galway	0-17
Leitrim	1-10

But first things first – it's another Connacht Final and a meeting with a Sligo side that were not there just to make up the numbers.

Historic occasion in Hyde Park

Any notion that the provincial championships have no future was firmly suppressed as Sligo ended one of the longest-running famines in the GAA by defeating Galway in a Connacht final

that apart from the result had little else to offer.

Consider the facts. It was 1975 since the JJ Nestor Cup found a resting place under the shadow of Ben Bulben. Not one member of the present panel was born when that feat was last achieved. Little wonder then that Championship specialists Galway were overwhelming favourites to once again land the title.

However, Sligo had come a long way since the spring of 2006 when they sacked their then manager, Dominic Corrigan. In the build up to the game they, and in particular the players, felt 'the ambush was on.'

Galway had peaked for Mayo in the first round back in May and struggled against lowly Leitrim in the semi-final so while Peter Forde's men may have been favourites, Sligo sensed that they were on the cusp of a famous win.

The match itself before a huge crowd started brightly enough but degenerated into a poor contest in the second-half as both sides lost their nerve for differing reasons – Sligo with victory in sight, Galway fearing a second successive defeat in a final.

Sligo actually got the opening 2 points from Kieran Quinn and Mark Breheny but Galway settled and with Joe Bergin dominant in midfield they surged

Kenneth Sweeney, Sligo, celebrates after scoring a second-half point.
Galway v Sligo. Connacht Football Final. Dr Hyde Park, Roscommon 8 July 2007

into a 0-5 to 0-2 lead, with their marquee names of Meehan, Savage and Fallon all on the scoresheet. So far it was going to script, Galway ahead as Sligo's possession game was making little progress and too often they found themselves heading into cul-de-sacs.

However, Sligo steadied and by the 20th minute another Breheny point had the sides level, their patient build-up slowly beginning to pay dividends.

Galway went back in front before the game's decisive score arrived and fittingly it came from Sligo's best player of recent years, veteran Eamonn O'Hara but it was the product of the teamwork that was the hallmark of their game.

Michael McNamara and David Kelly combined to send O'Hara galloping through the Galway defence, who then picked the right time to unleash a powerful drive past goalkeeper Doherty and it nestled in the net. It's a goal that will definitely be a contender for 'goal of the season'.

It was a significant score as it put Sligo, despite a hesitant start, in front at half-time 1-7 to 0-9 and the feeling was growing among the large crowd that something special was about to happen.

Galway now had to chase the game but they struggled as several of their big names weren't performing despite the assistance of a stiff breeze. Fallon faded after a bright start. Meehan was making little impact on a resolute Sligo defence while Pádraig Joyce's reputation probably kept him on the field for the 70 minutes.

Sligo, though, made hard work of winning a game they had in their grasp from early in the second-half. Poor shooting was a worry. In fact they employed 4 freetakers over the 70 minutes, with little success. With the game heading for injury-time a McNamara point pushed Sligo 2 ahead but there was a nervousness in their supporters and it affected the players as Galway came in search of the levelling scores.

By now Sligo's talisman O'Hara had departed the scene with an injury that forced him to watch the final 18 minutes from the sideline which was sheer agony for the 31-year-old. Galway did manage to reduce the margin to a single point, after

Joyce pointed a free. A draw looked to be on the cards especially as Fallon manoeuvred space for himself to shoot what would have been the equaliser. Had he done so it would have been a travesty as Sligo were clearly the better team.

But in keeping with the afternoon, his shot leaked wide and Sligo's relief quickly turned to joy. The final whistle brought an outpouring of emotion as the players were engulfed in a sea of black and white as their supporters invaded the pitch to acclaim their heroes and celebrate what was only the county's third Connacht title.

| Sligo | 1-10 |
| Galway | 0-12 |

Captain Noel McGuire accepted the JJ Nestor Cup on behalf of a proud team in the presence of GAA President Nickey Brennan to set in train a wave of celebrations that would last for days. But first the homecoming – and what a homecoming they received.

As the Sligo team bus, followed by a cavalcade of cars made its way home, bonfires blazed along the route. It was a long wait and they were certainly going to enjoy bringing the cup home, and then a special moment arrived. The team disembarked from the bus and with captain Noel McGuire clutching the most precious piece of silverware they walked across the county boundary at a disused railway line at Charlestown/Bellaghy to the cheers of thousands of supporters who had gathered to witness this symbolic gesture.

It also signalled a shift, for the time being at any rate, in Gaelic football power in the West. The party in Yeats County was well and truly under way.

Sligo captain Noel McGuire lifts the Nestor Cup as Sligo become Connacht champions. Galway v Sligo. Connacht Football Final. Dr Hyde Park, Roscommon 8 July 2007

The Cork and Clare teams come out of the tunnel at the same time. Frank Lohan, Clare, and Diarmuid O'Sullivan, Cork, clash, flanked by a guard of honour of young hurling fans – boys and girls. Cork v Clare. Munster Hurling Quarter-Final. Semple Stadium, Thurles. 27 May 2007

9

Turbulence In Thurles

CORK V CLARE

The Cork v Clare Munster Hurling Quarter-Final became 'that game' of the 2007 GAA calendar – the game that everyone remembers not for the fine skills of the players but for the off-the-pitch shenanigans. In this case, a pre-match brawl meant several players had to pay a very high price.

9 Turbulence in Thurles

Cork v Clare

The Melee

'I did not see what happened but it was not how I expected the Munster Hurling Championship to start, other than that I have no comment to make as the matter is now subject to the disciplinary process,' – the words of GAA President Nickey Brennan on the incident before the Cork v Clare first-round clash in Semple Stadium, Thurles.

The incident occurred as both teams left their dressing rooms at the same time. As they reached the end of the tunnel together something sparked the unsavoury scenes that followed.

Players from both sides became embroiled in the melee, while others attempted to restore order. It eventually calmed down and the teams went to opposite ends of the ground to commence their normal pre-match routine.

While this was going on referee Pat O'Connor from Limerick had not yet left the dressing room. The teams arrived on the field ahead of schedule, particularly Cork who should have allowed Clare out first. The referee did not witness the incident, but was advised it had occurred. The fact that O'Connor did not see what

happened was crucial in the subsequent investigation.

It should be pointed out that unsavoury though it may have been, no player received an injury that required treatment and all took full part in the game.

The respective managers, Gerald McCarthy (Cork) and Tony Considine (Clare), when asked for their views on what happened said they had not seen anything as they were in the dressing room at the time.

Before starting the match, referee O'Connor called the captains Kieran Murphy (Cork) and Frank Lohan (Clare) to him and issued a stern warning that was conveyed to both teams.

The game itself was a tame affair as Cork won in a canter, but the pre-match incident made all the headlines the following day and for several days and weeks afterwards.

As the game was being televised live it was the main talking point for the remainder of the afternoon and received a further airing on that evening's *The Sunday Game* programme. Much was also made of the fact that the incident occurred within metres of young boys

Diarmuid O'Sullivan and John Gardiner, Cork, clash with Colin Lynch and Andrew Quinn, Clare. Cork v Clare. Munster Hurling Quarter-Final. Semple Stadium, Thurles. 27 May 2007

and girls who had formed a guard of honour to welcome both teams onto the field.

Opinion was divided on the seriousness of what happened. Some saying it was 'handbag stuff' while others were of the view that it was disgraceful and called for severe penalties on all participants.

Within 24 hours referee Pat O'Connor submitted his report to the Central Competitions Control Committee (CCCC). As he had not seen

the melee he did not refer to it in his report. The fact that the referee did not mention the incident allowed the CCCC to view the video and based on the evidence they proposed sanctions on eight players and both county boards.

Cork County Board were fined €10,000 while Clare were fined €5,000.

One-month suspensions were proposed for 4 players from each team. They were Cork's Donal Óg Cusack, Diarmuid O'Sullivan, Sean Óg Ó'h-Ailpín and John Gardiner and Clare's Barry

Nugent, Colin Lynch, Alan Markham and Andrew Quinn.

The bans would have serious repercussions for Cork as they were due to face Waterford in the Munster semi-final on June 17th, while Clare's next game was a qualifier against Antrim.

The severity of the sanctions shocked both counties, but there was real anger in Cork when Sean Óg was suspended, as his role in promoting hurling in recent years has made him an iconic figure in the game, with a previously unblemished record.

Both county boards indicated they would be appealing all aspects of the suspensions, with the Cork Board adding that they would be making no further comment until that process was complete.

It was the first serious test of the recently reconstructed appeals procedure within the GAA and the outcome would be watched with interest. The CCCC also sought the identity of a fifth Cork player who they felt was also involved, but even with the use of video evidence they were unable to establish his identity.

Throughout the whole process, this player was never identified and as a consequence was not suspended. Clare were also annoyed at the suspension imposed on Barry Nugent as they claim he was mistakenly identified by the CCCC.

Because of the upcoming game with Waterford, the Cork players had their appeals heard first on June 7th by the Central Hearings Committee (CHC). Led by County Secretary Frank Murphy they put up a robust defence. During the course of the lengthy hearing, Murphy who is an acknowledged expert on GAA rules argued strongly that the phrase 'contributing to a melee' did not apply in this case. The hearing eventually adjourned, so late in the night that the Cork players missed their flight home and had to hire a car to make the return journey, without any decision having been reached.

The CHC issued a statement the following day saying that their findings would not be released until they had heard the Clare appeals. It was felt that to issue findings on the Cork players would render the appeals of the Clare players meaningless, as all eight players had been charged with contributing to a melee.

On Monday June 10 the appeals of the Clare players were heard in Croke Park and two days later the findings were released to the media after both county boards were first informed.

Suspensions were confirmed for

seven of the eight players, while Cork's John Gardiner had all charges against him dropped. The fines on both counties were reduced. Cork would have to pay €5,000 for leaving their dressing room before the instructed time, while Clare were fined €2,500 for their part in the incident, that had by now been dubbed 'Semplegate' – and 3 weeks after the game it was still dominating the headlines.

Cork were now in a race against time to clear their players for the Waterford game and were considering another appeal. County Secretary Frank Murphy told a Cork county board meeting 'that discussions were ongoing with the board executive, players and team management and no public announcement would be made until that process is finished with.'

In the event Cork did appeal to the Central Appeals Committee, and it was received by Croke Park at lunchtime on Wednesday June 13.

Cork were preparing for a meeting on Thursday but were advised it could not take place on that day because of the unavailability of one member of the Committee, and it would now be held on Friday 15th. Ironically the same member was also unavailable on the Friday and the hearing proceeded in his absence. It was also pointed out that given the short notice, the Committee that imposed the initial suspensions would not have enough time to prepare their defence.

While all this was going on, Cork actually named their team to play Waterford on Sunday 17. It included John Gardiner but obviously the other 3 players were omitted. However, manager Gerald McCarthy had not given up hope that the trio of banned players would be cleared to play.

The second Cork appeal was then heard on Friday and following another lengthy hearing the appeals were rejected. Now Cork had only one more option open to them – to take their case to the Disputes Resolutions Authority (DRA). This was done and a hearing was set for Saturday 16 in Portlaoise. It would finally determine the players' fate. Clare had also decided to take their case to the CAC, but as they were not playing again until June 30 there was less urgency in having their cases dealt with.

After yet another hearing, the Cork delegation headed home to prepare their case for what was essentially the last throw of the dice in an effort to clear their players.

It was not to be. They returned to Portlaoise on Saturday and despite what they termed 'a very fair and balanced hearing' the appeal once again failed.

However, they must have made a very good case as the results of the appeal were not conveyed to the media until 10.30 that night.

So after an exhaustive appeals process that involved endless meetings and trips, Cusack, O'Sullivan and Ó'h-Ailpín would not play against Waterford the following day. That was the end of the matter . . . or so everyone thought! Cork minus their key players lost the Waterford game by 3 points in a thriller and after the match, coach Gerald McCarthy let rip to the waiting media and spared no one, even Nickey Brennan, in his criticism.

Manager's outburst

Having first of all paid tribute to his patched-up team for their outstanding performance, Gerald then voiced his concern. 'I think the GAA needs to look at its disciplinary method. We had 4 players with 10 years of an unblemished record in inter-county hurling. A committee, the CCCC met and proposed a month's suspension on each of them without a hearing – that is scandalous to begin with.' The normally mild-mannered McCarthy continued, 'the players were pilloried in the press. Some of it was an absolute disgrace. I think the

media actually surpassed themselves in this one, the way they hung the players out to dry.'

'When I see the back page of a sports section with "Semplegate 8" and eight small pictures of the players involved – like criminals – these are lads with family, jobs and friends; they did not deserve such treatment and a small section of the media do no justice to your trade.'

The late cancellation of one meeting in particular irked McCarthy and prompted a call to Nickey Brennan. 'I was very angry with that; so much so that I phoned Nickey to express my annoyance but all I got was a curt reply and a hang up. I feel the players of our association deserve better than that.'

Gerald did apologise for the incident, 'it's something I did at every hearing I attended but there was a lot of extenuating circumstances that allowed it happen here (Thurles) and that came out in the hearing; but to have the matter drag on for almost three weeks does not reflect well and to wait until late last night for an answer is not good enough.'

Clare appeals

Three of the four Clare players attended a hearing of the CAC – Alan Markham

Clare manager Tony Considine, left, shakes hands with Cork manager, Gerald McCarthy after the game. The pre-match clashes between players led to controversy involving players, suspensions, county boards and even the President of the GAA, Nickey Brennan. Cork v Clare. Munster Hurling Quarter-Final. Semple Stadium, Thurles. 27 May 2007

was unavailable – but just like the Cork players, the appeals failed and all three would miss the qualifier against Antrim.

Markham subsequently withdrew his appeal and accepted his one-month suspension, while the Clare county board did not take their case to the DRA. They decided to draw a line under the incident and concentrate on the remaining games.

Players' statement

Three days after the game against Waterford, the suspended Cork hurlers broke their silence and issued a lengthy statement in which they apologised for their involvement in the incident but also hit out at the manner in which it was dealt with by the GAA. Just like their manager on the Sunday, the trio included Nickey Brennan in their criticism.

They began by apologising – 'this apology is sincerely given and we regret our involvement, however it is difficult to resist the urge to defend yourself or your team-mates especially where there seems to be no one in charge.' Cusack, O'Sullivan and Ó'h-Ailpín also voiced their concern about the GAA's disciplinary process and expressed the view that there was an anti-Cork bias, an anti-GPA bias and an anti-Frank Murphy bias shown by both the GAA and the media.

The players were fulsome in their praise of Murphy, 'it is well known that in the past we have had our differences with Frank, however in this episode his work on our behalf from the very first meeting was outstanding and for that we are extremely grateful.' They were also critical of Tipperary's Sean Fogarty, a GAA presidential candidate for April 2008, who commented on the incident, and accused him 'of a cheap electioneering stunt.' The trio were also scathing in their criticism of GAA President Nickey Brennan – 'we do not endorse the findings or procedures used in the new disciplinary system and we find it absolutely extraordinary that the President of the Association would implicitly attack us and our County Board for staying within the GAA in an effort to defend ourselves and for using those very procedures set up to discourage players from going to the courts.'

The statement was greeted with mixed reaction but its content stunned many within the GAA. President Nickey Brennan initially refused to comment but did say that a detailed media briefing would be held shortly and he would then deal with the matter.

President's response

On Monday June 25 exactly one month after the game, Nickey Brennan faced the media in Croke Park and strongly refuted the contents of the Cork players' statement.

'I want to state quite categorically in relation to comments made last week in a press release that there was no GPA bias, no anti-Cork bias and certainly no anti-Frank Murphy bias. People are paranoid at this situation and many of the Cork players' grievances are without foundation.'

In relation to the cancelled meeting – 'there was insufficient time for us to prepare for the meeting and we conveyed this to the Cork County Board.

We are also aware that they had not left Cork and all our communication is with the Board, we do not deal directly with the players.'

'Cork were offered Thursday but it did not suit. It then went to Friday and it was only at 2.53am Saturday morning that they sought an arbitration hearing, which took place that afternoon.'

As regards the phone call from Gerald McCarthy, 'I was in London at the time and I realised from his tone that he was angry, but the President, whoever he may be, cannot be expected to take every call and be aware of every detail in the process and I certainly was not going to get involved while it was still ongoing.'

The President said 'that the process was well carried out and we are happy with it, fairness was applied and that they didn't get due process is completely ridiculous and doesn't stand up to scrutiny.'

Nickey Brennan concluded by 'acknowledging the players took time off, but people at all levels have worked extraordinary hours at this, our process has been seen to be very fair and effective.'

That statement by the President effectively ended the matter. Clare did not pursue their case and the Cork county board at its meeting on Tuesday June 26 decided to draw a line under the whole incident and move on to what they do best – playing hurling.

The Munster Hurling Championship of 2007 had many memorable moments on the field, but it is the one off the field that generated as many column inches and left a number of quality hurlers sitting in the stands when they felt they should have been out on the field.

Footnote

The day after the CCCC proposed the suspensions they did not name the players. However the media, print, radio and TV quickly established their identity and released the names into the public domain.

The naming of the players clearly annoyed Croke Park, the county boards and team managers Gerald McCarthy and Tony Considine.

In the wake of the whole affair the GAA tightened up its procedures and no player can now be named until they -

[i] accept their proposed punishment from the CCCC.

[ii] have a hearing with the CHC.

Mark Foley, Limerick, tries to get to the ball
as Dan Shanahan, Waterford, tackles him.
Waterford v Limerick Munster Hurling Final.
Semple Stadium, Thurles 8 July 2007

10
Waterford Claim Title

MUNSTER HURLING CHAMPIONSHIP

A three-game saga between Limerick and Tipperary, the 'Semplegate' incident, a blistering semi-final between Waterford and Cork – and all this before a top quality final. Who says the Munster Hurling Championship doesn't have it all?

10 Waterford Claim Title

Munster Hurling Championship

Magical Munster Championship

Down the corridors of time the Munster Hurling Championship has left a host of memories, but the Championship of 2007 surpassed all that has gone before, leaving players and officials drained by events on and off the field.

It produced the Tipperary v Limerick trilogy, the Cork v Clare tunnel incident and the fallout from same, the Cork v Waterford semi-final – and all that before yet another memorable final.

Is it any wonder then that those who cherish their hurling in Munster have no desire to see its format altered, and issue a strong 'hands off' warning? If there are problems with hurling, they will not be solved by tampering with the Munster Championship.

It may not have got off to the best possible start, with the Cork v Clare tunnel incident (see Chapter 9), but thereafter it produced some memorable encounters. In fact the Cork v Clare game was a poor affair with Cork, the champions, never in any real danger of losing after laying down an early marker.

Points from Gerry O'Connor, Niall McCarthy and Kieran 'Fraggy' Murphy along with a superb defensive display from Ronan Curran put the champions in control and at half time Cork led by 0-9 to 0-4.

It was obvious that without a number of players that had anchored their team for years, Clare were struggling and on the resumption there was little improvement. Kieran 'Fraggy' Murphy set up newcomer Patrick Cronin for a Cork goal and with 25 minutes to play it was 1-13 to 0-4 and the Banner were facing a drubbing.

To their credit they rallied, helped by a Niall Gilligan goal and to a degree a realisation by Cork that the game was won. Colin Lynch and Alan Markham had points and they did reduce the gap to 5 points at one stage – 1-15 to 1-10.

However, Cork steadied the ship and a few late points eased them to a comfortable 1-18 to 1-11 win to set up a semi-final clash with Waterford, but in advance of that match there would be plenty of drama, most of it off the field.

Cork	1-18
Clare	1-11

Diarmuid Fitzgerald, Tipperary, takes the ball while closely marked by Andrew O'Shaughnessy, Limerick.
Tipperary v Limerick Munster Hurling Semi-Final. Semple Stadium, Thurles 10 June 2007

Limerick v Tipperary trilogy

The Gaelic Grounds in Limerick was the venue for the meeting of Tipperary and Limerick as the home side went in search of a first Munster Championship win in six years.

It was a gloriously sunny afternoon as the city ground to a halt with over 26,500 supporters making their way along the Ennis Road to witness what turned out to be an epic encounter, as the Championship sprung to life.

The sides traded points as Tipperary, forced to make two changes to their selected side, were slow to settle and Limerick opened up a 0-5 to 0-3 lead. Very quickly though the game swung Tipp's way, helped by a number of incidents that almost proved costly. The first occurred in the 12th minute, when referee Diarmuid Kirwan booked Tipperary's Eoin Kelly and Limerick captain Damien Reale.

Three minutes later John Carroll flicked home a Tipperary goal and it was followed by the game's first major talking point. In the 21st minute a late challenge by Reale on Kelly, earned him a second yellow card and with it dismissal. Limerick were down to 14 men and still 50 minutes to play in the baking heat.

Tipperary stretched their lead as Limerick were in disarray following Reale's sending-off, but they settled and with Ollie Moran in fine form, they drew level and only 2 late points gave Tipperary an interval lead of 1-9 to 0-10.

Despite playing with a man short, Limerick more than matched Tipperary in the second-half and with 55 minutes played they were still in contention at 1-16 to 0-16.

Within 5 minutes they were level as substitutes Mike Fitzgerald and Pat Tobin had points, and now it was Tipperary's turn to struggle.

It looked as though they had done enough when Eoin Kelly, Willie Ryan and Lar Corbett knocked over points to go 1-19 to 0-19 ahead with just 5 minutes remaining.

Richie Bennis, though, has got this Limerick team playing with great self-belief. They refused to surrender and with the game heading for injury-time, they conjured up the equalising goal.

Ollie Moran made it with a great catch and pass to Pat Tobin who gave Brendan Cummins no chance in the Tipp goal. It was all square at 1-19 each.

Tipperary	1-19
Limerick	1-19

That meant a replay a week later in Semple Stadium, Thurles which would now house two major games in 24 hours, and with it plenty of excitement, glamour and no little drama.

Saturday afternoon in Thurles and the place was rife with rumours of discontent in the Tipperary camp. In fact, such stories dogged the Premier county for most of the year.

This time they centred on goalkeeper Brendan Cummins who it is understood had a fall-out with manager Babs Keating over the delivery of his puck-outs in the drawn encounter.

For once the rumour machine was right and there was shock and amazement when the Tipperary team was announced. Cummins was dropped, replaced by Ger Kennedy, while Willie Ryan who had scored 0-9 the first day was also omitted. A gamble by Babs? The next 70 minutes would tell.

In fact for almost 50 minutes Babs looked to have got it right as Tipperary were in complete control and seemed set for an easy win. Seamus Butler got a 12th minute goal and at half-time Tipperary were in control leading 1-12 to 0-5 and Limerick looking dead and buried.

On 50 minutes it was 1-17 to 0-10 with little indication of the drama that was about to unfold, as Limerick fought back.

A couple of quick points followed by a goal from Mike Fitzgerald and Tipp were on the back foot but still ahead. Six minutes remaining they still led by 4 points, but amazingly for the second week in a row they could not protect a lead.

Limerick landed 3 points and with the game deep in injury time they won a free. After missing an earlier glorious goal chance, Andrew O'Shaughnessy kept his nerve to pop over the levelling score and force extra-time.

So as the late summer sun shone brightly on Semple Stadium, two highly charged teams battled it out for a further 20 minutes and once again Tipperary held the upper hand. A goal by Lar Corbett in the first period of extra-time had them ahead at the break 2-21 to 1-22. Tiredness was now a factor as the players on both sides dragged their weary limbs around for another ten minutes of frenetic hurling. Tipp failed to add to their tally.

Limerick had scored just 1 point as

referee Brian Gavin of Offaly indicated 2 minutes of injury time. Could they save the tie and earn a second replay their heroics deserved?

The answer was 'yes' and with time almost up they won a '65', hotly disputed by the Tipp defenders who were adamant it was wide. For the second time in the match the responsibility fell on the young shoulders of O'Shaughnessy but the army officer displayed nerves of steel as he drilled the *sliotar* between the posts to level the match after an enthralling 90 minutes of hurling.

Tipperary	2-21
Limerick	1-24

It was back to the Gaelic Grounds seven days later, for Round 3 of a contest that had outstripped Dublin and Meath for drama.

After the game Babs was confronted by angry Tipperary supporters over his team selection, but he shrugged it off and told the waiting media 'that we are lucky we have two quality goalkeepers in our squad and we picked Kennedy for tonight and we are happy with that.'

Babs may have been happy but many Tipp fans were not at what they perceived as poor treatment for such an outstanding goalkeeper. Interestingly, the following day Brendan Cummins and another member of the panel, Michael Webster, played football with their clubs. Cummins reportedly picked up an injury which made him doubtful for the visit to Limerick. A strange move to play a football game a week before a Munster hurling semi-final, but then by all accounts it was strange times in Tipperary.

So for the second time in a week the Munster Championship had lived up to expectations, but what was to follow little over 12 hours later, would even surpass the events of that Saturday evening in June.

Cork v Waterford

Cork and Waterford have quickly developed the most intense rivalry of the last six years, with several high octane clashes at both provincial and national level with the 'Rebels' just ahead in terms of vital games won.

Waterford were the new league champions. Cork lined out minus three key players (see Chapter 9) who were central to their success in recent years. This meant Championship debuts for goalkeeper Anthony Nash and defender Shane O'Neill, while Cian O'Connor was named at full-back. Could they adequately fill the boots of Donal Óg, Sully and Sean Óg? An expectant crowd of 36,532 watched in anticipation.

Referee Barry Kelly got proceedings underway and within 15 seconds John Mullane had a Waterford point. It set the trend for a rollercoaster of an afternoon and a Munster Hurling Championship encounter that surpassed expectations.

Cork quickly drew level with a Ben O'Connor sideline cut. Then came the first of 8 goals. Nash bombed a free deep into the heart of the Decies' defence. Kieran 'Fraggy' Murphy plucked it from the air and Clinton Hennessy had no chance – Cork 1-4 to 0-3 ahead.

One minute later another goal, this time Nash was powerless as big Dan Shanahan drilled a powerful shot to the net.

A second Waterford goal arrived courtesy of Mullane who was outplaying Brian Murphy. It was later revealed that Murphy had been ill all week and was replaced at half-time, but the makeshift Cork defence was struggling as Waterford piled on the pressure.

Cork, though, are Cork and back they came. Jerry O'Connor and Patrick Cronin combined to set up 'Fraggy' for his second goal – level again 2-8 to 2-8, and with so much happening supporters had barely time to draw breath, and

Swedish hurling fans, Monika Korona, left, and Saga Mills, right, supporting Waterford and Limerick respectively – wearing the colourful headgear. Waterford v Limerick Munster Hurling Final. Semple Stadium, Thurles 8 July 2007

there was more to come.

Crucially Waterford struck for 2 goals in the closing minutes of a spellbinding opening 35 minutes. Shanahan got his second and then Paul Flynn lashed a 20-metre free to the net. Joe Deane, who was back to his best, closed the scoring with a quality point for Cork but Waterford were 5 points in front at the break – 4-8 to 2-9. As the teams left the field to a tumultuous reception from both sets of supporters, we wondered could it get any better. It could and it did.

Cork with Jerry O'Connor and Tom Kenny dominating midfield were level by the 54th minute after Patrick Cronin lashed in his second goal in Championship hurling – 3-15 to 4-12. Then came the crucial score. Poor defending allowed Eoin Kelly latch onto a breaking ball and with only Nash to beat, he made no mistake, Waterford back in front, but not safe yet.

By now Cork had lost Niall McCarthy and Tom Kenny through injury, further draining their resources. Kenny's departure was vital as he was dominant in midfield and central to Cork's fightback.

Ben O'Connor also missed a 50th minute penalty at a time when Waterford were finding it hard to shake off Cork, who for all their pre-match difficulties had produced a stirring display. However, Cork refused to wilt and points from Deane, Ben O'Connor and Cathal Naughton cut the gap to just 1 point with the clock inching towards the 70th minute mark.

Mullane with a point, his only score of the second-half, and another from Tony Browne pushed Waterford 3 points in front in injury-time, but there was to be one final act before this gripping contest ran its course.

Cork won a free. Ben O'Connor drove it hard at the Waterford defence. It took a deflection and fell to Cork substitute Shane Murphy whose powerful effort struck the crossbar with Hennessy well beaten. In the ensuing scramble Waterford cleared the danger and survived to advance to the Munster final, as the width of the crossbar denied Cork a replay and with it a financial bonanza for the Council.

On the sideline former team-mates Justin and Gerald McCarthy embraced and shook hands, but Gerald would soon vent his anger over the treatment of his players, as Waterford won another thriller by 5-15 to 3-18.

Waterford	5-15
Cork	3-18

Eight goals, 33 points, a couple of yellow cards and plenty of drama and excitement was enough to quieten those who say the Munster Championship does not mean a whole lot. Try telling that to the players from Cork, Waterford, Tipperary and Limerick who had just produced the most magical of weekends the fabled competition has ever seen – and it was not over yet.

In a post-match interview Cork boss Gerald McCarthy, surrounded by a posse of media people, let rip. He first of all apologised for their part in the tunnel incident in the Cork v Clare game on May 27 before stoutly defending the integrity of his players who all previously had an unblemished record. Because of the appalling handling of this incident, this record was now gone.

GAA President Nickey Brennan also came in for criticism owing to the curt manner in which he terminated a phone call from McCarthy, who also said he was 'tremendously proud of his side's effort in a fabulous match and while we are very disappointed at losing our Munster title we will look at our injury situation and regroup for the qualifiers.'

Cork may have been beaten but the events in the lead up to the game had unified the camp, and the coming games in the qualifiers would be watched with interest.

Back to Páirc Na Gael for Round 3

For the third weekend in a row Tipperary and Limerick went head-to-head in an effort to resolve their ongoing semi-final saga and once again it lived up to expectations. On this occasion over 30,000 fans made the trek to the Gaelic Grounds in Limerick and they left it with the reputation of the Championship further enhanced.

The weather gods were not too kind and the game was played on a heavy sodden turf. Once again the contest spilled into extra-time. The game may have lacked the sparkle of the previous encounters but it was laced with passion and drama and of course the inevitable controversial refereeing decisions that all seemed to go against Tipperary, especially late in the game.

Eoin Kelly scored 4 points for Tipperary early on but it was Limerick who led by 0-7 to 0-6, when Tipp's first

goal arrived. Limerick's Mark Foley was down injured but the referee allowed play to continue. Darragh Egan lashed the ball to the net and Tipp were ahead. But Limerick battled back and it came as no surprise that it was all square 1-6 to 0-9 at half-time.

On 60 minutes it was still level 1-9 to 0-12 – there was just no separating these two sides or so it seemed. With 67 minutes played, Limerick had chiselled out a 3-point lead that looked good enough to secure victory but Tipperary had other ideas and for the first time in the three games it was their turn to battle back, and they did.

With the game in injury-time Tipperary had cut the deficit to the bare minimum. The sense of anticipation around the ground that this was not yet over, proved correct. In one last act Seamus Butler swung over the levelling score and for the second week in a row extra-time beckoned. Tipperary should have had a close-in free but referee Seanie McMahon ignored a blatant foul on James Woodlock.

Limerick had the first score of extra-time – a point from Ollie Moran – but Tipp's reply was instant and one that should have given them huge momentum.

Eoin Kelly, who had a great tussle

with Seamus Hickey, created a goal for Willie Ryan. Andrew O'Shaughnessy replied with a Limerick point but they still trailed by 2 at the midway point of what would prove to be the final and decisive phase of a gripping contest.

The extra-time was taxing on the weary limbs of both sets of players, but somehow and from somewhere Limerick summoned the energy to kill off the Tipp challenge.

In the last 10 minutes they finished out the game with a string of 5 unanswered points, their passion and desire finally the difference between the sides.

Finally, 4 hours and 10 minutes after it all began, there was a winner. Limerick 0-22 Tipperary 2-13.

Limerick	0-22
Tipperary	2-13

The delirious hordes of green-and-white clad supporters invaded the pitch and their heroes were carried shoulder high from the field. Babs and Richie Bennis embraced, as they look to the next game.

In Tipp's case it's the qualifiers, for Limerick it's a Munster Final clash with Waterford – the first between the counties since 1934.

It was time now to draw breath and look forward to the unique sporting occasion that is the Munster Hurling Final.

A strange atmosphere in Liberty Square

The build up was frenetic, the search for tickets relentless, yet there was a subdued atmosphere in Thurles for the Guinness Munster Hurling Final. Despite the demand for tickets the attendance was almost 5,000 down on capacity and there was a distinct lack of colour on the terraces occupied by the respective supporters.

President Mary McAleese and Taoiseach Bertie Ahern were present as the teams took the field for the pre-match routine as the rain cascaded down, making for an unpleasant afternoon in the home of hurling.

In the minor final Tipperary denied Cork a fourth successive title with a 4-point win in a lively contest, Tipp winning by 0-18 to 1-11.

The stage was set for the big game. Waterford, appearing in their fourth final in 6 years, were favourites to win, while Limerick were chasing their first title since 1996.

Limerick started well helped by good play from Michael Fitzgerald and Donal

Eoin Kelly, Waterford, takes the ball and tries to escape the attention of Mike O'Brien, Limerick, and his flying hurley. Waterford v Limerick Munster Hurling Final. Semple Stadium, Thurles 8 July 2007

O'Grady and they were further boosted when full-forward Brian Begley flicked in an early goal.

Waterford, though, are a very experienced side and it showed. Slowly they played themselves into the game and a point from Seamus Prendergast edged them ahead at the break 0-9 to 1-5.

Limerick had shown in their three game saga with Tipperary that they would not be beaten easily and they displayed dogged resistance throughout the second-half. In fact by the 45th minute they had actually opened up a 2-point lead.

But as so often in the past the Munster Final throws up a hero. This time he was wearing the blue and white of Waterford, and his name – big Dan

Shanahan.

The Lismore man left an indelible mark on this decider with a hat-trick of second-half goals that sealed a memorable triumph for Justin McCarthy's men.

His first goal arrived after Limerick goalkeeper Brian Murray had made a great save to deny Paul Flynn. Shanahan was on hand to usher the rebound home, but there were question marks about the defence who were marked absent.

Still Limerick were hanging on and as the game reached the hour mark only 2 points divided the sides, Waterford in front 1-14 to 1-12.

In their previous games Limerick had produced driving finishes but on this occasion they were dealing with a more coherent opposition who had tremendous self-belief in their own ability, and it surfaced in the remaining minutes.

The turning point arrived on 62 minutes when Shanahan pounced for his second goal to put 5 points between the sides.

Limerick did get the next 2 points, but there was no stopping Waterford and in the closing minutes they killed off the brave resistance offered by Richie Bennis's men.

Shanahan completed his hat-trick. He finished with 3-3. Paul Flynn and the McGrath brothers, Eoin and Ken, added points as Limerick's Munster Championship odyssey came to an end but the winning margin of 9 points, 3-17 to 1-14, did not reflect their contribution to a marvellous contest.

Waterford	3-17
Limerick	1-14

Team captain Michael Walsh accepted the cup from a proud Munster Council Chairman Jimmy O'Gorman, himself a Waterfordman, and in his (O'Gorman's) speech praised all the counties for the part they had played in yet another spectacular Munster Senior Hurling Championship.

So Waterford claim their eight Munster title but they have eyes on bigger things. Already they are league champions but the one they want still awaits. As for Limerick they move onto the quarter-finals, their season still alive. It's the least they deserve, given their contribution to the hurling Championship so far.

Henry Shefflin, Kilkenny, tries to secure the ball ahead of Diarmuid Lyng, Wexford. Kilkenny v Wexford. Leinster Hurling Final Croke Park 1 July 2007

11

Kilkenny Outplay Wexford

No surprise that Kilkenny made it to the final of the Leinster Hurling Championship, raising the usual question of what can be done to break the Cats' stronghold on hurling in Leinster. Wexford, however, did not appear to have any answers.

11 Kilkenny Outplay Wexford

Leinster Hurling Championship

Little Excitement in Leinster

It contains the same number of participating counties (5) as Munster, but that is where the comparison ends, as the Leinster Hurling Championship produced little by way of excitement and drama. In fact in the view of many it is Kilkenny's to lose rather than others to win.

It was probably best summed up by Offaly manager John McIntyre when he said 'there is a big black and yellow umbrella over the Leinster Championship and it's called Kilkenny, and until the rest of us reach that standard it will always be the same.'

The competition got off to the worst possible start as an incident before the opening game was more exciting than the match itself.

Offaly and Laois met in O'Moore Park, Portlaoise on Saturday May 26 and as the teams lined up for the throw-in, a mini brawl broke out as players from both sides got involved.

Fists and hurleys flew in all directions as the match officials endeavoured to regain control. When they eventually did, referee Michael Haverty from Galway issued just 2 yellow cards, 1 to each team before re-starting the game. In the light of the incident in Thurles the following day it made for a poor opening, but the fact that the referee dealt with the incident meant that no further action was taken.

This annoyed many people, especially those in Cork and Clare who felt it was far more serious than what happened in Semple Stadium. That aside, it was the only excitement on a blustery night in the heart of the midlands.

It was level at 0-4 each after 10 minutes, but gradually Offaly pulled away and by the 25th minute it was 0-10 to 0-4 and they added 5 more points to lead 0-15 to 0-4 at the break.

The second-half was a long drawn-out affair with little to get excited about. Damien Murray got a goal to add to his 12 points and the final result is a clear indication of the one-sided nature of a poor contest which ended Offaly 1-26 Laois 0-10.

Offaly	1-26
Laois	0-10

David Curtin, Dublin, catches the ball despite the attentions of Keith Rossiter, No 6, and Richie Kehoe, Wexford. Dublin v Wexford. Leinster Hurling Semi-Final, Nowlan Park, Kilkenny. 9 June 2007

Afterwards Laois manager, Damien Fox, admitted 'we were out of our depth', while Offaly boss McIntyre said a big improvement was required for their semi-final clash with All-Ireland champions Kilkenny.

The focus then switched to the first of the semi-finals which featured Wexford and Dublin on a splendid sunny Saturday evening in Nowlan Park. Both teams had reasonably successful league campaigns.

Dublin consolidated their position in Division 1 for 2008 and had they won one more game they would have made the quarter-finals.

Wexford did make the semi-finals before they were well beaten by Kilkenny and the manner of that defeat was a setback, which hinted at the possibility of a shock result in the future.

The other factor of course was not only was there a place in the final of the

Leinster Hurling Championship on offer for the winners, it also put them directly into the quarter-finals of the All-Ireland Championship and away from the much feared qualifiers.

Dublin lost a couple of players to injury and were dealt a further blow when Nigel Higgins got a Wexford goal in the fourth minute to put his side 1-3 to 0-2 ahead.

Tommy Naughton, the Dublin manager, has worked hard with the team all season and they showed commendable character to bounce back and were rewarded when Kevin Flynn scored a great goal.

Rory Jacob and John Kelly then traded goals and Wexford despite the good start were only 2 in front at half-time, 2-9 to 2-7.

Twice during the early exchanges of the second-half the sides were level, but a flurry of Wexford points in a 5-minute spell pushed them 2-13 to 2-7 ahead and victory was in sight.

Dublin, though, battled back. Davey Curtin and Stuart Mullen both scored points and with just a minute remaining, Ross O'Carroll knocked in a goal that levelled the match and a replay looked certain.

However, there was a late sting in the tail for the valiant 'Dubs' and inexperience cost them. Firstly, Kevin Flynn scuffed a sideline cut and in the follow-up hauled down a Wexford player for a needless foul and the Dubs paid the ultimate price.

With the last puck of the match in the 74th minute, up stepped Barry Lambert and from all of 75 metres and practically on the sideline he dissected the posts for the winning point and in the process broke Dublin hearts. It ended Wexford 2-14 Dublin 3-10.

Wexford	2-14
Dublin	3-10

Afterwards Naughton was devastated for his players – 'if we had managed to get in front we might have won. But I am proud of their efforts and we can take a lot of positives out of this match going forward.'

Wexford boss John Meyler was just happy to win – 'look, we are in the final and we will prepare as best we can for that game, but if we shoot 17 wides the next day we will get hammered.'

That left just one more game before the final pairings were known. Once again O'Moore Park, Portlaoise was the venue as Offaly had the unenviable task of facing the All-Ireland champions Kilkenny.

Offaly were given little chance and were practically written off before the game began despite Kilkenny manager Brian Cody saying that they were expecting a tough battle.

To be fair it was tight in the first-half. Offaly's Damien Murray picked up from where he left off in the Laois game and was unerring in his free-taking. The young star bagged 1-7 out of 1-10, but Kilkenny still held a slender lead of just 1 point at the break. Was there to be a shock result on the cards?

Cody, whom Offaly manager John McIntyre described as 'a ruthless manager driving a ruthless team' was clearly unhappy with that first-half display, especially at the concession of so many frees. He withdrew midfielder Derek Lyng and reshaped his team for the second-half.

It was a different story for the next 35 minutes. Offaly added just 3 more points to their total as Kilkenny shifted up a gear.

Henry Shefflin lashed over a few points, James 'Cha' Fitzpatrick was energetic in midfield and Martin Comerford drove the champions on as the Offaly challenge faded.

Eoin Larkin ushered in a goal and in the end the winning margin was an impressive 14 points, 1-27 to 1-13, but Cody was far from happy.

'It was a struggle the whole way. Offaly have good young players and made us work hard, and we will need to improve for the final.'

Late in the game Offaly were reduced to 14 men when Derek Molloy was dismissed for a second yellow card offence, and it prompted an amazing outburst from, of all people, Brian Cody. The Kilkenny boss defended the referees and lashed out at the referees' assessors who he said 'were being torn apart and slaughtered by some guy sitting in the stand with a pen and paper ticking boxes. It puts the referees under massive pressure and it leads to confusion. I have raised this several times in Croke Park but all to no avail.' Cody concluded, 'the referee's assessor – I would shoot him!'

The match was also significant for Henry Shefflin whose 12 points brought his Championship tally in 36 games to an impressive 18 goals and 264 points, surpassing the legendary Christy Ring in the all-time scorers list, but still stands almost 100 points behind the leading scorer, fellow Kilkennyman Eddie Keher.

Kilkenny	1-27
Offaly	1-13

So after a pretty uneventful series of

games the stage was set for the meeting of Wexford v Kilkenny [their 35th in all] in the Guinness Leinster Hurling Final. Could it rescue what had been a mundane Championship up to now? The hope was that it would.

In a funny way it had been a good week for the much maligned Leinster hurling. Offaly and Dublin would contest the Under-21 final, the first time in many years that neither Kilkenny nor Wexford would be involved.

Then as one of the curtain-raisers to the senior final, Dublin minors won their second title in 3 years with a comprehensive win over Kilkenny. Now a good senior decider would help but alas it was not to be.

In fact as a contest it was dead in the water after just 10 minutes as by then Kilkenny had bagged 2 goals, both scored by Willie O'Dwyer, the second created by a piece of Henry Shefflin magic.

It got worse as Wexford manager John Meyler withdrew veteran defender Declan Ruth and by half-time it was Kilkenny 2-11 to 0-6.

The watching dignitaries from many nations in the VIP section must have been wondering what it was all about.

Indeed it was all about Kilkenny as they strolled to their 10th title in 11 years with a comprehensive 2-24 to 1-12 over a Wexford side that were simply not at the races.

There was a strange and eerie atmosphere in the stadium as many in the attendance of 35,000 fans (Laois and Wexford met in the Leinster football semi-final which helped swell the crowd) began to drift away early in the second-half. So much so that at the end of a one-sided encounter, Kilkenny captain Henry Shefflin raised the Bob O'Keeffe Cup aloft to rows of empty seats.

| Kilkenny | 2-24 |
| Wexford | 1-12 |

Afterwards even Brian Cody was puzzled by Wexford's display – 'it was easier than I expected but all you can do is play what is in front of you and now all we can do is prepare for the quarter-final in a few weeks time.'

Wexford manager Meyler commented 'It was over at half-time and the fans voted with their feet. I apologise to them for that display – it's just not good enough. We'll meet up on Tuesday, perform some surgery on the team and try and pick it up for the quarter-final.'

So yet another Leinster Hurling Championship is over and the immediate reaction is that unless

Barry Lambert, Wexford, is first to this ball, closely marked by Jackie Tyrrell, Kilkenny.
Kilkenny v Wexford. Leinster Hurling Final, Croke Park. 1 July 2007

remedial action is taken, it has no future in its present format. Moving Galway and possibly Antrim into the Leinster championship was once again mooted but Liam O'Neill, Leinster Council chairman, was adamant that matters will improve – 'it may not happen in the short-term but the measures that the Council have put in place will bear fruit. Offaly and Dublin are in the under-21 final and Dublin won the minor title on Sunday, and while I accept the senior grade is disappointing we have to be patient and it will turn around.'

Right now that looks a long way off as both Kilkenny and Wexford prepare for their next assignment – ironically enough they were both in the quarter-finals – but for the men from Slaneyside the road back is a much tougher one. As for Brian Cody, the prospect of once again hurling into September looks a good bet.

John Gardiner, Cork, ball in hand, goes past
Francis Devaney, Tipperary. Cork v Tipperary.
Hurling Qualifier, Semple Stadium, Thurles.
14 July 2007

12

'Big Four' Go Through

HURLING QUALIFIERS

The hurling qualifiers threw up many talking points: Would Dublin achieve the impossible and trip up Cork? Would Galway manager Ger Loughnane manage to avoid controversy for more than five minutes and let his team do the talking on the pitch? Would the 'usual suspects' make it through the qualifiers?

12 'Big Four' Go Through

Hurling Qualifiers

Hurling Qualifiers

With the provincial finalists in Munster and Leinster known, the way was now clear for the qualifiers to begin, and they were greeted with about as much enthusiasm as turkeys greet Christmas.

As in previous years it would consist of two groups of 4 with the top 2 in each group joining Limerick, Waterford, Kilkenny and Wexford in the last eight of the Championship.

Ger Loughnane's Galway would also take their Championship bow and much interest would focus on how the Tribesmen would fare, especially in their clash with Clare. It would pit Loughnane against his long time friend Tony Considine who was having his own difficulties in the Banner County.

Antrim, who won the Christy Ring Cup in 2006, were also back in the qualifiers, eager to build on their success in that competition and also on their easy win over Down in the Ulster final.

But it was the presence of big hitters Cork and Tipperary in the qualifiers which was being keenly observed. Would they recover from the drama of the Munster Championship and be ready for the more mundane fare that these games would offer? Dublin and Offaly were the remaining teams in the series and the groups were as follows:

> **Group A**
> Clare, Galway, Antrim and Laois
>
> **Group B**
> Cork, Dublin, Tipperary and Offaly.

These counties would battle for the four places on offer to complete the line-up for the quarter-finals of the Championship.

There was general agreement that there would be few shocks in the series of games. The bookies were suggesting the big four, Cork, Tipperary, Galway and Clare would emerge, and the bookies are rarely wrong.

Round 1

Cork are well accustomed to going to the capital for hurling games in the summer, but on this occasion it was to Parnell Park in Donnycarney for their opening game against Tommy Naughton's Dublin, and not the more familiar Croke Park. In fact

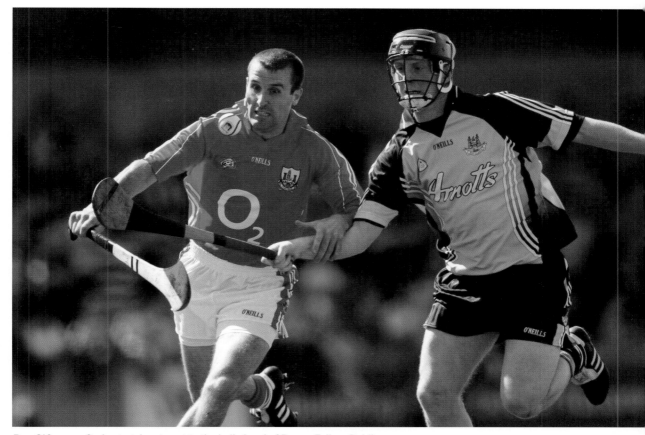

Ben O'Connor, Cork, stretches to get to the ball ahead of Ronan Fallon, Dublin.
Dublin v Cork. Hurling Qualifier, Round 1. Parnell Park, Dublin. 30 June 2007

it was the first Championship meeting between the counties since the 1952 All-Ireland Final. There was the slight possibility of a shock – Gerald McCarthy's men minus a few key players with injury and the tight confines of the Northside venue might limit Cork's renowned passing game. It was the perfect setting for a game – a full house including An Taoiseach Bertie Ahern getting a rare opportunity to watch his favourite hurling team, Cork, against his beloved Dubs.

Dublin matched Cork score for score in the opening 20 minutes. Cork lost both corner-backs Shane O'Neill and Brian Murphy through injury, but they had the previously suspended trio of Donal Óg Cusack, Diarmuid O'Sullivan and Sean Óg Ó'h-Ailpín back in the ranks. The game swung in Cork's direction after Dublin's wayward shooting began to let them down. Then came the turning point.

Cork captain Kieran Murphy latched onto a breaking ball and he drilled home the first goal. It gave his side an interval lead of 1-10 to 0-8 and the wind at their backs for the second-half.

In that second-half Cork were well in control. Joe Deane was in superb form and his delightful pass set up Murphy for his second goal and the job was complete when Patrick Cronin flicked in goal number 3 with the match in injury-time. Dublin battled away especially Ross O'Carroll, Ronan Fallon and goalkeeper Gary Maguire but in the end Cork had safely negotiated a tricky-looking hurdle to run out convincing winners by 3-20 to 0-15.

| Cork | 3-20 |
| Dublin | 0-15 |

There was a lovely atmosphere in the ground and as the Taoiseach departed just before the end he was given a nice send-off by the Rebel supporters, who sang 'cheerio, cheerio, cheerio'. To his credit he responded with a wave and a nice smile. It was that kind of an afternoon.

If there was a hint of a shock in Dublin, there was an even bigger chance of an upset in Thurles as Tipperary were in action for the fourth week in a row against an Offaly side who felt this was a game they could win. And they should have.

After their heavy schedule, Tipperary boss Babs Keating shuffled his pack and an Eoin Kelly goal left it all square 1-8 each at half-time, Sean Ryan getting the Offaly goal.

Keating made further changes for the second-half but they were still unable to pull away from a tenacious Offaly side on the cusp of a famous win. Kelly bagged 12 points for Tipperary, and it was his 12th score that pushed his side in front with time running out, but Offaly had one last chance for victory.

However, Shane Dooley's effort was blocked by Tipp goalkeeper Gerry Kennedy and Offaly paid the ultimate price when at the other end full-back Paul Cleary coughed up possession and the ever-alert Lar Corbett tapped the ball into an empty net. Offaly's inexperience, poor decision-making, indisipline at the back and rank bad shooting had proved very costly.

'We left it behind us and the players know it', said Offaly manager John McIntyre.

There was an audible sigh of relief around the old ground as Tipperary eked out a narrow win, 2-17 to 2-13.

Tipperary	2-17
Offaly	2-13

In Group A, Clare were making their first appearance since their defeat to Cork and all that went with that game. They travelled to Casement Park to face Antrim, minus their 4 suspended players, a spate of injuries and a county once again embroiled in controversy over the scheduling of club games that upset their preparation.

Clare made an excellent start with Diarmuid McMahon proving a handful for the Antrim defence. The sides were level 4 times in the opening 12 minutes before Clare opened up a 6-point lead thanks to a Brian O'Connell goal, leaving it 1-13 to 1-7 at half-time.

Antrim got a couple of early second-half points. The sides then exchanged goals, Derek Quinn for Clare and Brendan Herron for Antrim, and there was still 6 points separating the teams.

Backed by a vociferous home following, Antrim, scoring some lovely long-range points, cut the deficit to 4 points, 2-17 to 2-13 with 15 minutes remaining. But that was as good as it got.

Two-year old Dublin supporter [and future hurling star?] Diarmuid O'Dulaing from Rathcoole, Co Dublin, gets in a little practice during half-time in the Dublin v Cork Hurling Qualifier, Parnell Park, Dublin. 30 June 2007.

Clare raised the tempo again and a third goal from Niall Gilligan eased the visitors to a 3-21 to 2-15 win with boss Tony Considine admitting afterwards that he was glad to hear the final whistle.

Clare	3-21
Antrim	2-15

Meanwhile O'Moore Park in Portlaoise was the venue for Ger Loughnane's return to Championship hurling after more than half a decade away from the coalface, with Laois providing the opposition to his adopted county, Galway.

It was expected to be an easy outing for the Tribesmen but Loughnane was far from happy at the end of a scrappy encounter.

'Terrible, absolutely terrible' was his blunt assessment of his side's latest attempt to put themselves back in the frame for All-Ireland honours. 'If we play like that again we might not even make the quarter-finals and even if we do we will not be contenders.'

Laois had a very young team on duty comprising mostly teens and 20-year-olds and they braced themselves for the expected drubbing that never came. Galway got 2 early goals from Damien Hayes and Niall Healy but they failed to build on this advantage and Laois improved as the half progressed. Tommy Fitzgerald got a lovely point from a difficult angle but they really gained confidence when James Young rattled a 20-metre free to the net, and when he landed a long-range point, Laois were ahead 1-10 to 2-6 at half-time.

It was tempting fate to suggest that Laois would win as Galway had plenty of time to redress the situation and that's exactly what happened in the second-half.

Gradually they worked their way into a winning position. Iarla Tannion, Ger Mahon and Eugene Cloonan all had points and the win was finally secured when Hayes had his second goal to give Galway victory by 3-20 to 1-14.

Galway	3-20
Laois	1-14

Next up for Galway was Clare a week later in Ennis. Asked about that game, Loughnane replied, 'Well, I have no problem patrolling the sideline in Cusack Park but if we play like that I will be looking for the nearest exit.'

However in the days leading up to that game Loughnane would once again stir controversy in his native county, and an already tense occasion was now almost at boiling point.

Lar Corbett, Tipperary, tries to gain possession despite the attention of Tomás Brady, Dublin.
Dublin v Tipperary. Hurling Qualifier Round 2. Parnell Park, Dublin. 7 July 2007

Round 2

Little to get excited about in Group 1B as Cork and Tipperary had their expected wins over Offaly and Dublin respectively, highlighting once again the gap in standards between some of the teams participating in these qualifying rounds. Dublin at least were competitive in Parnell Park and only 2 points separated the teams at half-time, 0-8 to 0-6. Tipperary's Eoin Kelly went off with a groin injury. Dublin actually took the lead with a Peadar Carton goal on 44 minutes. Tipperary recovered and a goal by Lar Corbett and a 10 point contribution from Willie Ryan gave them a 1-20 to 1-11 win and a place in the quarter-final.

One controversial incident emerged from the qualifiers and its implications clearly angered prominent people within the Association.

Tipperary hurler Paul Curran received a serious injury in the game against Dublin. As a result, Dublin player Peadar Carton received an 8-week suspension that threatened his involvement in the All-Ireland Under-21 hurling final.

The case was then the subject of several protracted hearings at the end of which the Centrals Appeals Committee (CAC) cleared Carton on a technicality.

Then in an unprecedented move the GAA's most powerful body, the Central Council, referred the matter to the Disputes Resolution Authority (DRA), in effect challenging a decision of one of its own committees.

However, the DRA refused to become involved, Carton played in the final – a decision which still rankles with those in authority in Croke Park and has led to tensions between the CAC and the Central Council.

Tipperary	1-20
Dublin	1-11

Over 15,000 turned up in glorious sunshine to Páirc Ui Chaoimh and watched Cork demolish Offaly, still annoyed at their failure to beat Tipperary in the first round.

The men from the Faithful County were outclassed as Cork ran riot. Niall Ronan lashed in a fifth-minute goal, Joe Deane and the O'Connors, Ben and Jerry, were scoring some sublime points and at half-time it was 1-11 to 0-6 and the game was on life support.

The second-half resembled a mere training spin. Cork emptied the bench. Offaly waved the white flag and at the end the scoreboard tells its own tale – Cork 1-27 Offaly 0-11.

Cork	1-27
Offaly	0-11

So, as expected, Cork and Tipperary emerged from the group with a game to spare and they were to meet a week later in Thurles with nothing at stake but pride. However, a short few hours later all that would change.

Attention now switched to Group 1A. In the first game Antrim proved too good for Laois and in the process gave themselves an outside chance of a quarter-final spot. Their winning margin was 10 points, 1-23 to 1-13, Karl McKeegan got the Antrim goal. Laois were not helped by the dismissal of Shane Dollard at a time when the match was still competitive.

Antrim	1-23
Laois	1-13

However, that was only the sideshow. The real action was being played out before a full house in Cusack Park, Ennis as Loughnane and Considine locked horns after another dramatic week in the Banner County.

It was always going to be a crunch game as the winners would almost certainly top the group, but it was given added spice by comments made by Loughnane in *The Clare Champion* in the days before the game. Loughnane let rip at the Clare County Board, Chairman Michael McDonagh and Anthony Daly – even the humble club delegate felt the brunt of the Feakle man's tongue. However, his good friend Tony Considine was exonerated from criticism. He (Loughnane) labelled delegates as 'village idiots', said McDonagh was not fit to hold office and should have stepped down last year and Anthony Daly was not the right man for the manager's job when he got the position three years ago. As for Considine, Loughnane maintained that he was not getting the support he deserved from people within the county board.

Those that were at the receiving end of Loughnane's comments refused to be drawn into the controversy, although Daly did say 'that it's time now for Ger to forget about Clare and concentrate on his job in Galway.'

McDonagh sidestepped the issue by travelling with the Clare footballers to Ardfinnan for a Tommy Murphy Cup game against Tipperary, thus avoiding possible contact with Loughnane in Ennis on the night of the game. Considine himself had little to say only alluding to the fact that 'Ger and myself play golf once a week and we will do that next week as usual, irrespective of the result on Saturday. We are friends and will remain friends.'

The comments, though, caused a stir in the county with opinion divided on Loughnane's intervention in the week of such a crucial game, but what it did do was ensure a full house in Cusack Park for a match that had now assumed greater significance.

Unfortunately for the 14,551 spectators crammed into the compact ground, the match never lived up to the pre-game hype. Indeed confusion reigned prior to the throw-in as to the exact composition of the Galway team. It emerged later that the players were only told of their positions when they gathered for the now ritual pre-match huddle, another miscalculation by the manager.

Clare emerged winners by 2 points but even that did not reflect their dominance. But for a vital intervention by Colin Lynch, they could have lost, which on the night would have been a travesty.

Galway did get the opening score but were forced to play second fiddle to Clare for long periods of the first-half. A succession of wides undid a lot of their good work. Declan O'Rourke did get a goal which meant it was level at half-time Clare 1-5 Galway 0-8 – a scoreline that flattered the visitors.

On the resumption Galway rattled over 3 unanswered points and showed a brief hint of their undoubted potential, but that was as good as it got as Clare displayed great heart to fight back. Gerry Quinn went off injured but Clare were still battling hard. However, their efforts to gain parity was not helped by poor shooting.

Then came the defining moment in an error-ridden contest and it arrived right on cue, from a key player in 'saffron and blue'. Alan Markham's long delivery dropped in the danger zone. Niall Gilligan latched on to it and with a powerful drive drilled the ball into the back of the net to send the Clare supporters into raptures. After that there was no way back for Galway and it was Loughnane who had lost the battle, 2-10 to 0-14, with his friend in a crucial game for both manager and county.

| Clare | 2-10 |
| Galway | 0-14 |

Afterwards Loughnane was disgusted with Galway's performance saying, 'I may not be the man for this job if we cannot improve on that type of performance, our first big test and we failed'. As for Considine, 'it was a great result and we showed tremendous heart when it was needed most.'

You can guess who was the happier of the two on the golf course a few days later.

Quarter-final draw

With the 8 quarter-finalists known, as predicted, the GAA took the unusual decision to hold the draw for the last 8 of the competition before the final round of group games were played. This was done, it is understood, to allow counties time to prepare for the game itself and also to make provision for club fixtures which had taken a back seat in recent months. It also put a different emphasis on the last games as counties knew exactly what lay in store for them, depending on the outcome.

The draw itself was guarded in that the group winners would play the

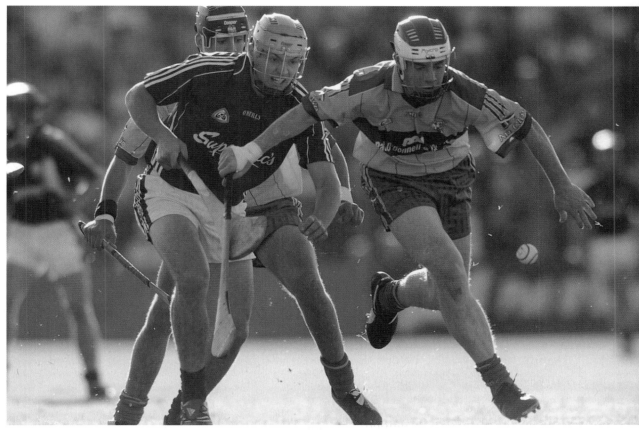

Kevin Dilleen, Clare, wins the race to get to the ball ahead of Iarla Tannian, Galway.
Clare v Galway. Hurling Qualifier, Round 2, Cusack Park, Ennis. 7 July 2007

provincial runners-up, which also meant Championship favourites Waterford and Kilkenny were kept apart.

It produced the following pairings. The winners of the Cork v Tipperary clash would play Wexford, while the losers would face newly-crowned Munster champions, Waterford. This ensured that the Cork v Tipperary game had an extra edge to it as the winners would in theory have the easier draw. Kilkenny as Leinster champions would

meet either Clare or Galway, and Galway's defeat in Ennis, which guaranteed Clare the top spot, was now making the road to ultimate glory that bit harder for Ger Loughnane's side. Limerick as Munster runners-up would meet neighbours Clare in the last of the quarter-finals.

Round 3

This was to all intents and purposes a

meaningless exercise, with one exception, as all the permutations had been sorted out the previous week. As a consequence – the Cork v Tipperary game apart – it was routine stuff.

Prior to the game with Antrim, Loughnane, in a reaction to the loss to Clare, had hinted that unless his side produced an emphatic performance he might just decide to head back to Feakle on the basis that he was not the man for the job.

No such worries though. Galway demolished the men from the Glens in a one-sided contest. Galway won as they pleased as the final scoreline of 2-31 to 1-9 indicates. However, before they faced All-Ireland champions Kilkenny, Loughnane would once again stir up a hornet's nest with some comments to the media.

Galway	2-31
Antrim	1-9

Clare and Laois completed their programme at a wet and windy Portlaoise. It was tougher than anticipated as Laois tested Tony Considine's side. Clare led at half-time by 0-7 to 0-4, but second-half goals from Barry Nugent and Colin Lynch saw the men from the Banner County emerge

winners by 2-14 to 1-11.

Clare	2-14
Laois	1-11

In the other group, Offaly and Dublin brought their summer and season to an end in an almost deserted O'Connor Park, Tullamore. With no relegation this year from the Championship, it was a non-event which Offaly won easily 2-25 to 2-13. At least both counties had the Leinster Under-21 final to look forward to and an opportunity to salvage something for all their hard work.

Offaly	2-25
Dublin	2-13

Cork and Tipperary rarely disappoint when they meet and while all the pre-match talk was about Tipp's approach to this game, the men from the Premier County showed they meant business. Yet after just 20 minutes they were in real trouble as Cork lorded proceedings and opened up a 5-point lead, 0-8 to 0-3. It was a damp and dreary night in Semple Stadium and only 12,903 supporters were present as Cork, with their half-back line in control and the O'Connors hitting points for fun, looked set for an easy win.

However, the game then underwent a

major transformation, when Willie Ryan knocked in a 21st minute goal and it sparked a Tipperary fightback, even without the highly talented Eoin Kelly.

Lar Corbett hit over a couple of points. Cork had a brace themselves but for all their early dominance only led by 1 point, 0-11 to 1-7 at half-time, but the momentum was with the home side. Within 15 minutes of the restart they had extended the advantage. Ryan got a second goal and a string of points left them 2-14 to 0-14 ahead.

Cork were shocked at the ferocity of Tipp's challenge and for a period had no answer, but in true Rebel fashion they battled back, helped by the introduction of a couple of substitutes. The Cork attack was struggling but they were thrown a lifeline when Niall Ronan's overhead flick produced a stunning goal.

It left just 1 point between the teams. John Carroll a second-half substitute gave Tipperary breathing space with a lovely point. Joe Deane cut it to 1 with time running out. Cork applied strong pressure but all efforts to get the levelling point failed. With the Tipp supporters waiting with baited breath, referee Barry Kelly finally brought a gripping contest to a close with Tipperary winners by 2-16 to 1-18.

| Tipperary | 2-16 |
| Cork | 1-18 |

It was a first win for Tipperary over the 'old enemy' in the Championship or a qualifier since 1991 and they celebrated in style as 'Slievenamon' was sung with gusto as the rain cascaded down from the darkening skies.

Babs, the villain a short few weeks ago, was now the hero, but as ever the realist he urged caution – 'we have nothing won yet and ourselves and Cork are heading for exactly the same stage of the Championship. It's all to play for still.'

So the qualifiers once again ended as expected with the 8 predicted counties making the quarter-finals, some by a longer route than others, but the overriding theme from all counties was 'the Championship really begins now.'

The dates and venues were then announced and on Sunday July 21 in Croke Park, Tipperary v Wexford would get proceedings underway at 2pm, followed at 4pm by Galway v Kilkenny.

A week later Limerick v Clare at 2pm, and that would be followed by Cork v Waterford at 4pm. A feast of hurling action and no little drama then to lift the gloom of a summer blighted by rain and more rain.

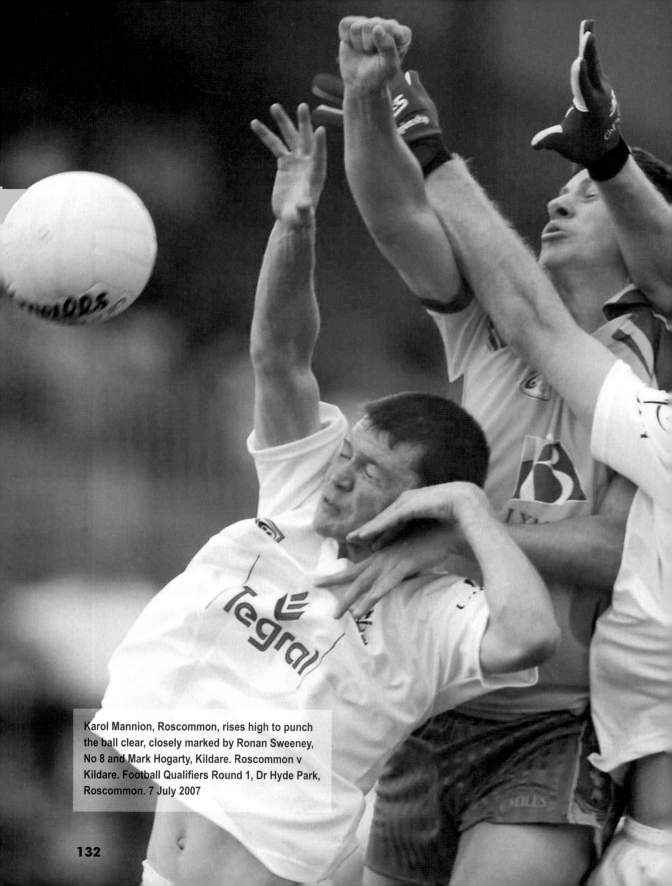

Karol Mannion, Roscommon, rises high to punch the ball clear, closely marked by Ronan Sweeney, No 8 and Mark Hogarty, Kildare. Roscommon v Kildare. Football Qualifiers Round 1, Dr Hyde Park, Roscommon. 7 July 2007

13
A Few Surprises

FOOTBALL QUALIFIERS ROUND 1

The heat is on now as each team in Round 1 struggles to take a step closer to Sam. Even the big guns like Mayo, Meath and Fermanagh find that in football, as in life, things do not always go according to plan.

13 A Few Surprises

Football Qualifiers Round 1

Football qualifiers

There was a change in format for the 2007 football qualifiers with one round of games removed to allow more time for club matches. It essentially amounted to a decision to eliminate eight counties from the series. This was based on league standings – the 8 counties that would constitute Division 4 in 2008 will instead participate in the Tommy Murphy Cup.

This move was initially passed without objection but when reality dawned, some of these 8 counties who had supported the move now expressed annoyance at not being allowed contest the qualifiers.

It also ruled these counties out of the race for the Sam Maguire Cup and among those who voiced their disapproval was new Wicklow boss, Mick O'Dwyer. However, it was all to no avail.

Round 1		
Derry	v	Armagh
Down	v	Meath
Limerick	v	Louth
Wexford	v	Fermanagh
Donegal	v	Leitrim
Mayo	v	Cavan
Longford	v	Westmeath
Kildare	v	Roscommon

St Tiernach's Park in Clones has witnessed many a shock result in the Ulster Championship and this time it saw another one. It was between two Ulster teams and it was the first big game of the qualifiers. Armagh were warm favourites to account for rivals Derry but Paddy Crozier's men had other ideas. It may not have been the best of games with the football of a poor standard but the result is all that counts at this stage.

Derry started brightly. Barry McGoldrick and Mark Lynch could have had goals before Paddy Bradley opened the scoring with a free. Collie Devlin increased their lead with a point from play. In fact by the 16th minute Derry were 0-4 to 0-1 ahead. Gradually Armagh improved. Diarmuid Marsden and Steven McDonnell both got points and after Bradley had notched another free, Derry led 0-6 to 0-4 at half-time.

Armagh were a rejuvenated team on the resumption and they were quickly level with points from McDonnell and Stephen Kernan. A couple of minutes later they had the lead for the first time in the game with McDonnell getting the point. Oisín McConville stretched their advantage to 2, 0-8 to 0-6. At this stage

Paul McGrane, Armagh, outjumps Fergal Doherty, Derry, to clear the ball.
Armagh v Derry. Football Qualifiers Round 1. St Tiernach's Park, Clones. 8 July 2007

Armagh looked likely winners but for the remainder of the game they scored only one more point. Bradley gave Derry hope with another free but with Armagh's increased intensity the Oak Leaf County were visibly tiring or so it seemed.

Once again Bradley's free-taking was keeping Derry in touch even after Stephen Kernan had an Armagh point, but as a disappointingly low quality affair neared its end the gap was down to a single point. Time was running out and Armagh were hanging on. They missed an opportunity to go 2 points ahead and were immediately made to pay. Aaron Kernan fouled Devlin and the ever-reliable Bradley duly pointed the free. Extra-time loomed large on the horizon but in the third minute of added time, rookie Colin Devlin became the Derry hero with the match winning point, 0-10 to 0-9.

So Armagh's Championship ambitions were over, two 1-point defeats was their lot in 2007. A few days later their manager, Joe Kernan, announced his decision to step down, ending a wonderful era for the Orchard County.

Down's season also came to an abrupt end when Meath, even without the enigmatic Graham Geraghty, made the trip to Newry and in a lacklustre encounter had an easy win.

There was a big crowd present and hopes were high that Down could get their season back on track, but alas it was not to be. Over the 70 minutes the crowd had little to shout about. Apart, that is, from a penalty claim when Benny Coulter appeared to be fouled in the square. Meath, though, were always in control and a Peadar Byrne goal had

them 1-4 to 0-4 ahead at the break.

By the third quarter Meath had extended their lead 1-9 to 0-5 and Down were staring defeat in the face. A flurry of points took the bare look off the scoreboard but with captain Anthony Moyles driving them on, Meath ran out comfortable winners by 1-10 to 0-8.

Louth made the trip to the Gaelic Grounds for a clash with Limerick. Louth were beset by problems after a tame exit to Wexford in the Leinster Championship. Six players who had featured in that game had left the panel, three of them headed to the US, while the other three for varying reasons were no longer involved. However, manager Eamonn McEneaney made light of the absentees, 'we have 32 on our panel. We had a meeting on Friday last and we are ready for the game with a very committed group of players'. To be fair his players displayed that commitment in a cracking match.

Louth were in front by 0-5 to 0-3 after the opening quarter but Limerick battled back and it was all square 0-7 each at half-time. There was a slight skirmish as the sides left the field at the break but it only added to the excitement for the second-half.

Ger Collins edged Limerick ahead at 0-9 to 0-8, but Shane Lennon brought the sides level again as the tempo of the game increased and the large band of Louth followers urged their side on. But as the game entered a critical phase, Limerick took control and 3 pointed frees from Michael Reidy pushed them into a 0-12 to 0-9 lead with 10 minutes remaining and it looked good enough for victory.

McEneaney then played his ace and it came up trumps. Darren Clarke was introduced and made an immediate impact to turn the game on its head. Another substitute, Sean O'Neill, began the Louth comeback with a point. Clarke scored one and then Mark Stanfield brought the sides level on 0-12 each with 5 minutes remaining. Clarke fired Louth ahead, but another Reidy point squared the game again as injury-time arrived.

Both sides missed chances, but in the fourth and last minute of the additional time, Stanfield became the hero of the Wee County with the winning point 0-14 to 0-13.

The home support were annoyed at the end of a gripping contest but it was a joyous band of loyal followers from Louth who began the journey home, content that their season was still alive.

Cavan were visitors to Castlebar as Mayo made their re-entry to the Championship under newly-elected TD John O'Mahoney. It was also an important day for Ronan McGarrity who made a welcome return to action after his recent illness.

In truth there was never much doubt about the outcome, even if at times Mayo were vulnerable to the visitors' 'route one' tactics that saw them concede 3 goals.

It was 0-6 to 0-5 to the home side after 30 minutes but by the short whistle Mayo had gone 0-9 to 0-6 ahead. However, an early second-half penalty by Dermot McCabe kept Cavan in touch and they had a second goal from Larry Reilly. Mayo did not panic. A Barry Moran goal and a succession of points, particularly from Alan Dillon, eased the Connacht side into a comfortable position. Rory Gallagher, the former Fermanagh player, got a third goal for Cavan before a brace of Conor Mortimer points saw Mayo run out comfortable winners on a 1-19 to 3-7 scoreline.

When Longford and Westmeath met in the Leinster Championship back in May, a stunning second-half comeback by Luke Dempsey's side had consigned Westmeath to the qualifiers where over the years they had enjoyed some notable wins.

On this occasion Westmeath had revenge on their minds and they made no mistake. Having built up an interval lead of 0-10 to 0-3, this time there was no way back for Longford. Westmeath finished with 14 men. Dessie Dolan's 6 points helped them to a comfortable 0-18 to 0-9 win.

John Crofton took his Kildare side to Hyde Park for a clash with Roscommon who were still reeling from their Connacht Championship loss to Sligo. A huge crowd were present to witness an exciting contest with the outcome in doubt right to the end. Kildare looked the livelier side early on and led 0-3 to 0-1 after just 7 minutes, with the contrast in styles an interesting sidebar. Roscommon backed by the wind were employing the long ball tactic while Kildare were using the short ball to good effect.

Roscommon were sloppy in their play and conceded needless frees. They were dealt a further blow when John Doyle blasted a fierce shot to the net for the game's opening goal, after good work by Mark Hogarty. Kildare were now in a strong position. Having played against the wind in the first-half, the Lily Whites had a 3-point lead at the end of 35 minutes and Roscommon needed a big improvement if they were to extend their season.

John Maughan reshaped his forces for the second-half and Gary Cox got an early point. The placing of Karl Mannion at full-forward also brought about an improvement. John Tiernan cut the deficit to a point before the 'Rossies' went in front and it was Mannion who drilled in the goal. Kildare's John Doyle, who finished with 1-8, had a point but Roscommon went 2 ahead again when Gary Cox scored a lovely point. They were dominant at midfield, they had momentum and were in a winning position. Kildare though fought back and 2 long-range points brought them level, but Roscommon regained the lead before the defining score of an exciting contest arrived.

With 65 minutes played Pádraig O'Neill lashed in a goal and suddenly Kildare had a 2-point lead. However, when the fourth official signalled 8 minutes of added time, Roscommon could still save their season. Ken Reilly extended Kildare's advantage to 3, quickly reduced to 2 when Ger Heneghan replied for Roscommon but the clock was inching ever nearer the 43rd minute. Kildare's victory was sealed when in the final minute 'man of the match' John Doyle scored an exquisite point and the Lily Whites were safely into Round 2 of the qualifiers, by 2-13 to 1-13. As for Roscommon, it's another case of 'what might have been'. Two home

Eamon Maguire, Fermanagh, gets his kick away despite the close attention of Niall Murphy, Wexford. Fermanagh v Wexford. Football Qualifiers Round 1. St Tiernach's Park, Clones. 8 July 2007

defeats ends their year and heaps more pressure on under-fire manager John Maughan.

It had not been a great year for the footballers from Fermanagh and as they faced Wexford they were seeking to win their very first competitive match of the year in league or Championship. Yet the qualifiers had been good to the men from the Erne County, who have never won the Ulster Championship.

Remember they reached the All-Ireland semi-final a few short years ago, knocking Armagh out along the way.

Wexford were poor in losing to Laois in Leinster and they showed they had not recovered from that loss in this game. There was a surreal start to the game as both sides scored goals in the opening minutes – James Sherry for Fermanagh while Redmond Barry replied for Wexford.

After the initial burst the game settled down and it was Fermanagh who took control and by the 11th minute they were 1-3 to 1-1 ahead.

Charlie Mulgrew had his Fermanagh side in great shape and while they were in front 1-7 to 1-4 at the interval it did not reflect their overall superiority. The Ulster side continued to dominate and extended their advantage on the resumption, helped also by a strong defensive showing that kept Wexford dangerman Mattie Forde in check, although it did take a great block by Shane Goan to deny Forde a goal at a vital stage in the second-half. In Forde's defence he was clearly unfit and was eventually withdrawn and his departure signalled the end of the Model County's challenge.

Fermanagh were never in any danger of losing, running out winners by 1-12 to 1-8. In a season when things did not exactly go according to plan, at least after this outing the season was still alive.

The final game in Round 1 saw league champions Donegal face a tricky-looking tie in Carrick-on-Shannon against a Leitrim side that were somewhat unlucky to lose to Galway in the Connacht Championship at the same venue. Donegal were slowly recovering from the hammering they had received from Tyrone in Ulster but the early season form they had displayed in winning the league was gone and this was a potential banana skin. Leitrim played with great energy and passion and sensed a shock as points from Ciaran Duignan and Fintan McBrien helped them to a 24th minute lead of 0-6 to 0-2.

With 33 minutes gone, Leitrim were awarded a penalty but much to the dismay of the large home crowd Donegal goalkeeper Paul Durcan made a great save from Michael Foley.

To compound Leitrim's woes, in the very next attack Donegal got a goal from Michael Murphy and instead of being 5 ahead, had they scored the penalty, Leitrim were now 1-5 to 0-6 behind at the break – against the run of play it must be said.

The sides shared 4 points on the resumption but this thrilling contest was now swinging Leitrim's way and when James Glancy knocked over a point the gap was down to 2, 1-10 to 0-11, with 10 minutes left on the clock. Donegal restored their 3 point lead, but Leitrim got a boost when it was announced that 6 minutes of additional time would be played. It signalled an all-out assault on the Donegal goal in an effort to gain parity but it looked in vain as time was running out.

However, there was one late twist when in a dramatic conclusion Glancy drove the ball to the net to square the match at 1-11 each and force extra-time.

In the opening half of extra-time Donegal powered in front when Rory Kavanagh and Christy Toye had points. It was 1-14 to 1-11 at half-time in extra-time.

Leitrim reintroduced Ciaran Duignan for the last 10 minutes of what had now developed into a gripping contest and he repaid manager Dessie Dolan's faith in him with 2 lovely points. Donegal were still in front with 1-14 to 1-13.

Not one of the 12,000 crowd in the beautifully appointed Páirc Sean MacDiarmada left as Leitrim came in search of the levelling score. Stephen McDermott edged Donegal 2 in front again with 5 minutes left. Michael Duignan cut it to 1 as this enthralling match entered the last minute – but there was to be no fairytale ending for Leitrim.

With practically the last kick of the game Eamonn McGee hit over a point to give Donegal breathing space and it finally killed off Leitrim's brave effort as they exited the qualifiers by 2 points, 1-16 to 1-14. A narrow win for Brian McIver's men to get their campaign back on track. For Leitrim the agony goes on.

Ken Donnelly, Kildare, tries to shrug off the
marking of Peter McGinnity, Louth.
Kildare v Louth. Football Qualifiers Round 2.
St Conleth's Park, Newbridge. 14 July 2007

42

14

Louth Spring Surprise

The pressure continued to build during Round 2 of the football qualifiers. Could Mayo salvage their season or would Derry crush their hopes? Would Fermanagh halt Meath's advance? Could Louth continue their winning streak against Kildare? And who would emerge victorious from a Donegal v Westmeath encounter?

14 Louth Spring Suprise

Football Qualifiers Round 2

Football Qualifiers Round 2

Meath	v	Fermanagh
Louth	v	Kildare
Derry	v	Mayo
Donegal	v	Westmeath

With the 4 provincial runners-up still waiting in the wings, Round 2 of the qualifiers would whittle the participants in the race for ultimate honours down to 12, and as usual a few surprising results emerged.

Meath v Fermanagh

Páirc Tailteann in Navan was the venue for this clash and a good crowd turned out. The home side were still without Graham Geraghty who had not yet rejoined the squad after his training ground bust-up a few weeks earlier. Fermanagh entered this game on the back of a good win over Wexford in the last round but never really looked like extending their season, yet they were never far away in a closely contested encounter. Meath led by 0-7 to 0-4 at half-time with Stephen Bray and Brian Farrell among the scorers for the Royal County.

In the second-half Fermanagh cast aside any inhibitions they might have had about facing Meath and took the game to their more fancied opponents. Barry Owens and Shane McDermott led the charge but the fact that they hit 10 wides in 35 minutes tells its own tale. Meath moved into a commanding position early in that second-half but Fermanagh battled back and with 7 minutes remaining had reduced the deficit to 2 points, 0-10 to 0-8.

Then came a crucial moment when a powerful Mark Little effort came back off the crossbar and with it went Fermanagh's last chance of victory. Both sides added a point to their tally but the goal Charlie Mulgrew's men needed never came and it is Meath who move on to the next round, narrow but deserving winners by 0-11 to 0-9.

The game also marked the end of Mulgrew's tenure at the helm in Fermanagh after 4 years in charge. The Donegal native had worked wonders with the squad which during his reign saw them reach the All-Ireland semi-final of 2004, but it was time he said 'for someone else to take this group of players a step further.'

Barry Owens, Fermanagh, tries to get his kick away despite the tackle of Anthony Moyles, Meath.
Meath v Fermanagh. Football Qualifiers Round 2. Páirc Tailteann, Navan. 14 July 2007

Derry v Mayo

Runners up to Kerry in 2006, Mayo appeared to have got their season back on track with a win, albeit not a very convincing one, over Cavan in the last round. Mayo were once again expected to account for another Ulster side in this round. Derry, though, had other ideas and at rain-lashed Celtic Park they unceremoniously dumped John O'Mahoney's men out of the Championship with a performance that suggests they will trouble a few more teams before the season is over.

Having beaten Armagh in Round 1, Paddy Crozier's side entered this game in confident mood and they left it with morale boosted further, leaving Mayo with a lot of soul-searching to do in advance of the 2008 Championship. The winning margin was a convincing 2-13 to 1-6, yet with 12 minutes remaining Mayo were still in with a chance. Derry started the game brightly and with Fergal Doherty giving them an edge in midfield they scored 3 points in the opening 8 minutes. Effective forward Paddy Bradley stretched their lead and they looked set for an easy win. Then as so often happens, a goal altered the shape of the contest.

It arrived in the 15th minute and Derry goalkeeper Barry Gillis was at fault. He spilled a routine delivery into the path of the inrushing Barry Moran who gratefully side-footed the ball to the net. A minute later Conor Mortimer pointed a free and somewhat against the run of play Mayo were level. Derry, though, quickly recovered their composure and points from Conleth Gilligan and Colin Devlin gave them an interval lead of 0-8 to 1-3.

Mayo, sensing they needed a big second-half if they were to salvage their season, went on the attack almost immediately and were quickly level when Pierce Hanley and Aiden Kilcoyne had points. Mayo's David Brady was dominant in midfield and his forceful play kept his side in touch before the direction of the contest swung Derry's way.

With 48 minutes played, a huge leap allowed Colin Devlin fist the ball to the Mayo net. Derry then switched Enda Muldoon to midfield and he, more than anyone, broke Brady's grip on the game. In the remaining minutes Mayo scored just 1 more point from Andy Moran, before Derry finally drove their advantage home.

The 10,000 plus attendance had plenty to shout about as the Oak Leaf County closed the game out. Paddy Bradley tacked on a couple of points before Muldoon lobbed the ball to the Mayo net to send Derry confidently into the next round in buoyant mood.

An impressive display by Derry, but for Mayo it's team-building time and several players that have anchored their side in recent years may very well have played their last game in the 'red and green' jersey.

Louth v Kildare

Louth, who barely got past Limerick in the last round, really turned on the style in this game and literally blew Kildare away. This was a scintillating performance by the Wee County who have put their recent difficulties behind them and will fear no one in the next round.

Kildare, despite hitting 5 early wides, were in front by 0-3 to 0-2, but Louth soon took over. In 17 minutes they tacked on 6 unanswered points to lead 0-8 to 0-3 after 30 minutes. Louth were a rejuvenated side with Mark Stanfield, Colin Judge and Brian White among the scorers. By contrast Kildare were struggling for scores.

Indeed it was left to defenders Emmet Bolton and Eamonn Callaghan to come forward and pinch points, but Louth responded with similar scores from Paddy Keenan and White to go the dressing room at half-time with a commanding lead of 0-10 to 0-5. The home crowd in St Conleth's Park, Newbridge for the evening match scarcely believed what they had witnessed.

In keeping with the downbeat mood of the Kildare supporters, the heavens opened at half-time. It was a sign that it could very well be one of those nights for the men in white.

Kildare did make a good start to the second-half with points from substitute Mick Foley and John Doyle, but Louth were in no mood to let this one slip. It was they who got the next 3 points and giving an exhibition of spirited and passionate football, they opened up a lead of 0-13 to 0-7 by the three-quarter mark, and Kildare were struggling to stay in touch. In another breathtaking passage of play, Hoey, Shane Lennon and Ronan Carroll boomed over points and now Louth's lead was an intimidating 0-16 to 0-8 and Kildare's season was all but over.

There was, however, a slight twist as the game entered the closing minutes. Doyle converted a free that barely raised a cheer as the Kildare faithful were streaming out of the venue. Kildare won a penalty and it was expertly put away by Doyle and now amazingly for all the difficulties they were just 3 points in arrears, 0-16 to 1-10. Could they pull it off? They were further boosted when it was announced that there would be 5 minutes of added time.

But just as quickly as it came, the dream of a stunning comeback died when Lennon who was outstanding all through placed midfielder Paul Keenan for the clinching goal to send Louth to Round 3 of the qualifiers and ended Kildare's year.

It was no more then Eamonn McEneaney's men deserved.

Donegal v Westmeath

Having survived by the narrowest of margins against gutsy Leitrim in the last round, Donegal headed for Cusack Park in Mullingar for a meeting with Westmeath, hopeful of an improved performance. What they produced was a display that dispatched the Lake County men with ease and a signal that their indifferent form of recent weeks was behind them.

In fact there was never much doubt about the outcome as Westmeath never really showed up for this game which made Donegal's task that bit easier. Westmeath got an early boost when goalkeeper Gary Connaughton saved Michael Murphy's penalty. Shortly after, Murphy opened the scoring with a neat point.

Dessie Dolan was working hard for Westmeath and after a sustained period of pressure, they took the lead for the only time in the game when Fergal Wilson had a point. However, by the 12th minute Donegal had moved 2 points in front, 0-5 to 0-3. Gradually Donegal put daylight between the teams. Brendan Devenney, Ryan Bradley and Niall McGeady all had points and the Ulster side went in at half-time with a lead 0-9 to 0-6.

Westmeath were within touching distance but Donegal looked to have more in the tank, even when Dennis Glennon narrowed the gap with a point on the resumption. Then 2 further Donegal points eased them 4 in front and Westmeath were visibly slipping out of contention. Westmeath custodian Connaughton was certainly in top form making several good saves that gave his side a chance but they were being outplayed in too many key areas and were not troubling Donegal.

Then came the match-winning score. Rory Kavanagh carved through the non-existent Westmeath defence, passed to Devenney and his blistering drive nestled in the net to finish the game as a contest. Kavanagh tacked on a couple of points. Gary Dolan missed a Westmeath penalty. Ciaran Bonner was sent off for a second yellow card, leaving Donegal to play out the remaining minutes with 14 men.

Late in the game Martin Flanagan registered a goal for Westmeath but it only took the bare look off the scoreboard as long before the finish this match was decided and that is reflected in the winning margin of 1-13 to 1-8 for Brian McIver's men.

Round 2 of the qualifiers saw Donegal, Louth, Derry and Meath advance to the next series of games where they will be joined by the runners

Francis Boyle, Westmeath, attempts to gain possession as he is tackled by Rory Kavanagh, Donegal.
Westmeath v Donegal. Football Qualifiers Round 2. Cusack Park, Mullingar. 14 July 2007

up from the provincial Championships – Laois, Cork, Monaghan and Galway.

The marathon that is the Bank of Ireland Football Championship was slowly developing into a sprint with the finishing line in sight.

Christy Toye, Donegal, takes possession and
races past Damien Freeman, Monaghan.
Donegal v Monaghan. Football Qualifiers
Round 3. Healy Park, Omagh. 28 July 2007

15

Monaghan Deny Donegal

FOOTBALL QUALIFIERS ROUND 3

Round 3 of the football qualifiers had some of the most entertaining games of the year. Monaghan continued their Championship sprint, whilst Derry v Laois provided a top-class game of football. Cork v Louth proved to be a nail-biting contest and Galway v Meath had two teams giving it their all to continue their journey to Croke Park.

15 Monaghan Deny Donegal

Football Qualifiers Round 3

Football Qualifiers – Round 3

It was time now for the four defeated provincial finalists to re-enter the race for 'Sam' and once again it fell to GAA President Nickey Brennan and Bank of Ireland's Humphrey Kelleher to preside over the draw. In two separate pools you had Cork, Laois, Monaghan and Galway, with Derry, Donegal, Louth and Meath in the other.

In the previous rounds the first team drawn out of the pot enjoyed home advantage, but for this round – the last before the quarter-finals – neutral venues would be named for all four games.

After RTÉ's Michael Lyster had explained the format, the following pairings emerged – Cork v Louth, Meath v Galway, Laois v Derry and Donegal v Monaghan.

The fixture-makers decided on a double-header in O'Moore Park, Portlaoise for Cork v Louth and Meath v Galway. Healy Park in Omagh would host the all-Ulster clash between Donegal and Monaghan while Kingspan Breffni Park in Cavan would welcome the footballers of Laois and Derry.

Monaghan v Donegal

Donegal entered this game as favourites but Monaghan were confident that they could reproduce their form of the Ulster final in which they came close to beating Tyrone, so the underdog tag suited them perfectly. Such was the huge crowd that thronged the venue, the throw-in was put back by 10 minutes. Even the Monaghan team were delayed en route to the ground.

Despite the delay it had no adverse effect on Monaghan who raced into a 1-4 to 0-3 lead after 25 minutes, the goal coming from Vincent Corey, who as he did in the second-half of the Ulster final, took up his position at the edge of the square. The points were notched by Paul Finlay and Thomas Freeman as Donegal struggled to cope with the intensity of Monaghan's play.

Crucially, though, Monaghan briefly lost their shape approaching half-time as first Freeman, and then Finlay, missed chances before Colm McFadden fired over a Donegal point and it was Corey's goal that divided the sides at the break, 1-5 to 0-5 for Monaghan.

It had been a pulsating first-half and there was a dramatic start to the second-half when in the third minute Rory Kavanagh fired in the levelling goal and now the impetus appeared to be with the men from Tír Conaill. Worrying times for Monaghan – would their poor finish to the first-half return to haunt them? Not so, as this is a new breed of footballer that Seamus McEneaney has nurtured and how they responded was an indication of that.

Finlay's pointed free steadied the ship and it injected them with renewed vigour for the remainder of the game. As the confidence drained from Donegal's play, it became apparent that this was one game they were not going to win. Freeman found himself on a one-on-one with Donegal goalkeeper Paul Durcan. There was only going to be one outcome – a second Monaghan goal.

Ciaran Hanratty, Finlay and Tommy Freeman added points. With 60 of the 70 minutes played, Monaghan enjoyed a commanding 2-10 to 1-5 lead. Eamonn McGee got Donegal's first score in 28 minutes as there was no stopping Monaghan who had the final say when Shane Smyth tacked on a point in a convincing 2-12 to 1-7 win.

It booked Monaghan a quarter-final berth and with it a return trip to Croke Park for the first time in 19 years for a Championship encounter. Immediately after the game, Brian McIver resigned as Donegal manager, saying 'I will not be involved with an inter-county team again.'

Strangely he would change his mind in the following weeks and would have to be interviewed for a position he already had. McIver was eventually re-appointed for a 3-year term by the Donegal country board.

Derry v Laois

This turned out to be a thoroughly engrossing contest as both teams played their part in one of the best games of the qualifiers, watched by another bumper crowd. Laois were outplayed for long periods but battled their way back into a game that looked beyond them at various stages.

Conleth Gilligan and Paul Murphy had Derry points and when Paddy Bradley added another, the Oak Leaf County had made the best possible start. Brian McCormack opened Laois's account but 2 further Derry points gave them a 0-5 to 0-1 advantage after 13 minutes. Laois conceded another point but then got three in a row, cornerback Joe Higgins getting 1, and the gap was down to the bare minimum when Brendan Tierney got their fifth score in the 25th minute.

Derry were denied a goal when Laois goalkeeper Fergal Byron made an excellent stop from Mark Lynch. The sides then shared the next 6 points, but it was Derry who still led 0-9 to 0-8 at the interval.

Colm Parkinson tied the game within minutes of the restart, but Derry's response was excellent. They hit the next 3 points and it was 0-12 to 0-9 in their favour. Laois were furious at one of referee Joe McQuillan's decisions but they put it behind them to bag the game's first goal. It arrived in the 45th minute and it came from rampaging wing-back Pádraig McMahon whose powerful drive tied the game.

It was Derry, though, who took inspiration from the score. Devlin and Gilligan tapped over points and Crozier's men back in front. Derry now sensed victory and Bradley's vision picked out Paul Murphy who made no mistake by firing in a cracking goal. With three quarters of the game gone, Derry were in control at 1-14 to 1-9. Derry's response to the Laois goal was exceptional – a stunning 1-3 without reply including a classy point from Sean Marty Lockhart, the veteran of many a battle in the red and white of his county.

Although staring defeat in the face, Laois never gave up. Tierney tapped over a point and suddenly it was game on again when Billy Sheehan slammed in their second goal, 1-15 to 2-10. Bradley's sixth point gave Derry breathing space and after Bradley and Tierney swapped points from frees, Laois needed a goal to keep their Championship ambitions alive as this compelling contest moved into injury-time. Laois corner-back Gerard O'Kane did get a late point, but the 2 scores they required to force extra-time never came and in a welter of excitement Derry hung on to win by 4 points 1-18 to 2-11 at the end of a truly great game.

Since losing to Monaghan in the Ulster Championship, Derry have now beaten three teams with serious Championship ambitions – Armagh, Mayo and Laois. Their quarter-final opponents have been warned.

Cork v Louth

Fifty years after they last met in the Championship, in which Louth shocked the football world by defeating Cork in the 1957 All-Ireland Final, the largest and smallest counties in the country would renew their rivalry in O'Moore Park, Portlaoise.

Louth entered the game on the back

Pearse O'Neill, Cork, tries to field the high ball, under pressure from Paddy Keenan and Mick Fanning, Louth. Cork v Louth. Football Qualifiers Round 3. O'Moore Park, Portlaoise. 21 July 2007

of wins over Limerick and Kildare, while Cork came close to beating Kerry in the Munster final but the few weeks of inactivity were a worry for Billy Morgan. Cork were also without Noel O'Leary, who had received a month's suspension following an incident with Paul Galvin in the Munster final.

Cork got the opening point from Derek Kavanagh but quickly found themselves behind after Brian White and Aaron Hoey had pointed frees. There was great pace to the contest and certainly Louth were matching their more fancied opponents.

With 10 minutes gone it was all square at 0-3 apiece before Cork moved up a gear. Points from James Masters, Kevin McMahon and Nicholas Murphy eased the Rebels into the lead. Any notion, though, that Cork would have it easy was quickly dispelled as Louth displayed tremendous character to battle with an intensity that threw Cork out of their stride.

In the next 14 minutes they hit 5 unanswered points. Hoey had 2, Brian White, Ronan Carroll and Colm Judge 1 each and Louth now led 0-8 to 0-6 and deservedly so.

Cork had not scored in 18 minutes and there was a degree of panic about their play and some easy opportunities were missed. Conor McCarthy eventually found the target to end Cork's barren spell before Shane Lennon and Kevin McMahon traded points. Much to the delight of their large band of supporters, Louth left the field for the half-time cup of tea 0-9 to 0-8 in front.

Cork's tactics were poor and full-forward Michael Cussen was making little impression. Indeed Cork did not seem comfortable in how to best utilise the Glanmire man, with the delivery of the ball often being too high, sometimes too long and the Louth defence coped easily.

Just 2 minutes into the second-half and a Donnacha O'Connor point had the sides level. The feeling was growing that Louth could not sustain their challenge and that their strong running game would take its toll. Yet, as they did in the first-half, they produced another good spell that yielded 3 points in quick succession and they were back in front 0-9 to 0-6. The contest, which had developed into a very entertaining one, now entered a critical phase and Cork, sensing they were in danger of slipping out of the Championship, responded in style.

In the process they altered their game plan, abandoned the long ball route and their pacey and intelligent forwards began to run at the Louth defence. It paid huge dividends. Pearse O'Neill and McMahon had points, in between Masters also scored and were it not for the excellence of Louth goalkeeper Stewart Reynolds it would have been a goal. All of a sudden, from being 3 points behind Cork were now level and threatening to overrun Louth.

Cork also scored the next 3 points, all from frees, as in the face of increasing pressure the Louth defence coughed up some easy frees which were duly punished. It was now 0-15 to 0-12 for Cork and the Wee County were struggling. Hoey had their first score in 16 minutes quickly cancelled out by another Masters' effort. There followed a period in which both sides missed chances, particularly Cork, that would have put the game beyond Louth, who were still in touch and only found themselves 2 points behind when Darren Clarke pointed in the 67th minute.

Cork did not score in the last 12 minutes of the match as Louth laid siege to the Cork goal in an effort to snatch victory, but the cornerstone of this Cork team is its defence and it held firm. Heading into injury-time Louth came again but a vital and timely interception by Cussen proved the final act of a lively encounter as Cork secured a place in the last 8 of the Championship with a 2-point, 0-16 to 0-14, win.

For Louth the adventure is over. They played a total of 7 Championship games, and they leave their mark on the Championship. As a consequence they will be better equipped to mount a serious challenge in 2008.

Galway v Meath

Confirmation that Graham Geraghty had resolved his differences with Colm Coyle and rejoined the squad was a timely boost for Meath in advance of this match, although Geraghty would start this game on the bench.

Galway, stung by their loss to Sligo in the Connacht final, reacted by omitting Pádraig Joyce, Derek Savage and Declan Meehan from their starting line-up. Peter Forde also opted for a 2-man full-forward line with the twin threat of Sean Armstrong and Michael Meehan hoping to unhinge the Meath rearguard.

Essentially this game was decided by 2 Meath goals in the space of 3 minutes at a time when Galway looked threatening and just after the Royals had lost 2 key defenders with shoulder injuries. By the 23rd minute the sides were level on four occasions and Galway were rueing several missed chances. After another Galway chance went a-begging, Meath struck for the first goal.

A long delivery took a slight

deflection – just enough to guide it into the path of Stephen Bray who gratefully dispatched it to the net with a powerful shot. Meath should have had a second goal minutes later when Bray this time unselfishly tried to pick out Peter Curran, who slipped at the most inopportune moment and the chance was spurned.

Within 3 minutes Bray made amends once again – loose Galway defending allowed him clear on goal after a quickly-taken free and he planted a low shot into the corner of the net. Galway were stung by this double blow and did get the next 2 points, but a confident Meath replied with 2 similar scores and they enjoyed a 6-point cushion at half-time, Meath 2-6 Galway 0-6.

The Connacht side made a determined start to the second-half, kicked 2 early points and then watched as Meath goalkeeper Brendan Murphy made an astonishing save from Joe Bergin at the expense of a '45' which Michael Meehan converted. In fact Meehan was now beginning to trouble the Meath defence and he was given added support with the introduction of veteran Pádraig Joyce.

To a huge cheer from their supporters, Coyle introduced Geraghty and the prodigal son of Meath football was back in the action and it lifted his colleagues. With 48 minutes gone, Meath, whose shooting was spot on, were still in front 2-9 to 0-10. Galway needed something to get back into a game that was slowly slipping from them, and they got it.

Meehan contested a high ball in the square with two defenders, went to ground and to the anger of all Meath people in O'Moore Park, the referee awarded a penalty. Players and officials alike protested vigorously, but the decision stood, penalty it was.

After a brief delay Meehan himself stepped up to the plate. Showing remarkable composure he drove a fierce shot past Murphy. When Armstrong added a point, the bare minimum now divided the teams, Meath 2-9 Galway 1-11. Meehan continued to torment the Meath defence. He watched in dismay as Clancy missed a great chance to square the game, but it was level a minute later when Meehan himself drilled a '45' straight over the black spot and the comeback was complete.

Now it was Meath's turn to show their mettle and, in a manner always associated with this proud county, they were not found wanting. Brian Farrell knocked over a free, their first score in 10 minutes, and then to a crescendo of noise in the well-populated stadium, Geraghty angled a lovely left-footed shot over the bar to signal his arrival back on the big stage. Farrell converted another free – Meath's 3-point advantage restored and Galway's challenge gone.

In the closing minutes both sides added a couple of points, Meehan's tally rising to 1-5, Bray's for Meath reaching 2-2, but it was the Royal county who took their place in the last 8 with a deserved 2-14 to 1-14 victory and the old swagger was back in Meath football.

For Galway, coming on top of a devastating loss to Sligo, it could very well signal the end for this particular team who successfully brought 'Sam' across the Shannon twice in the modern era. It is the end for manager Peter Forde who shortly after this defeat stepped down after 3 years at the helm.

Michael Meehan, Galway, shows his determination to get away from the attention of Darren Fay, Meath. Galway v Meath. Football Qualifiers Round 3. O'Moore Park, Portlaoise. 21 July 2007

Jason Sherlock, Dublin, attempts to get past Michael McGoldrick, Derry. Dublin v Derry. Football Quarter-Final, Croke Park. 11 August 2007

16

'Big Guns' In Last 8

The football quarter-finals included the usual heavy hitters (Kerry, Cork, Dublin, Meath, Tyrone) but also some less familiar faces (Derry, Sligo, Monaghan). All these teams had one thing in common – the desire to progress to the semi-finals.

16 'Big Guns' In Last 8

Football Quarter-Finals

Dublin	v	Derry
Cork	v	Sligo
Kerry	v	Monaghan
Meath	v	Tyrone

Football Championship Quarter-Finals

Following the completion of the qualifiers, the draw for the quarter-finals was eagerly awaited. The provincial winners could at last begin their preparations for an assault on 'Sam'.

Kerry had a six-week break between games, not ideal. Sligo as Connacht champions, enjoyed their new-found status in the West but were chomping at the bit for a return to Croke Park, their first as champions since 1975.

Dublin having wrapped up their third successive Leinster crown were looking forward to another full house on Jones Road, while Mickey Harte's Tyrone, the Ulster champions, had gone about their business with their usual efficiency and were being fancied by many to go the distance.

These four teams were placed in one pool and could not meet each other, while in the other pool you had Cork, Derry, Meath and Monaghan. These four

had survived the rigours of the qualifiers – some with impressive credentials. Obviously the benefit of playing these games would give them an advantage against the sides that had been inactive.

Once again, high up in an empty Croke Park the draw was conducted by GAA President Nickey Brennan and Bank of Ireland's Humphrey Kelleher, a former Dublin hurling manager representing the sponsors. It was completed without fuss and the following pairings emerged – Cork v Sligo, Meath v Tyrone, Dublin v Derry and Kerry v Monaghan.

Because of their huge support Dublin had been granted a stand-alone fixture with improving Derry. All-Ireland champions Kerry were on the same programme as a hurling semi-final, with the remaining two games as double-headers on August 4.

Cork v Sligo

This was a special occasion for the recently crowned Connacht champions as they returned to Croke Park with a new-found confidence and backed by a large and colourful band of supporters

Eamon O'Hara, Sligo, tries to retain possession despite the tackle of Derek Kavanagh, Cork.
Cork v Sligo. Football Quarter-Final, Croke Park. 4 August 2007

who easily outnumbered those from Cork. To be fair Cork teams and fans had endured a lot of travelling in recent weeks, and their hurlers were back in Croke Park 24 hours later for a clash with Waterford. This scheduling incensed many Rebel supporters who felt, with some justification, that both games should have been on the one day.

The game itself was a poor one and Sligo for all their early enthusiasm lacked direction and had glaring weaknesses in attack. Indeed it looked at times like they had come to avoid a heavy defeat rather than to win the game. In the opening stages they troubled Cork, but for all their promise they only had 1 point on the board, that from John McPartland. It took Cork 10 minutes to open their account, a point from leading scorer

163

James Masters, and it quickly became evident that even playing below par, Billy Morgan's men would win. A second Masters' point edged Cork in front before John Miskella knocked in a 16th minute goal. Kevin McMahon added a point but Cork found it hard to break down the Sligo defence who at times had 12 men behind the ball. In fact McMahon's point was their first in 16 minutes.

Sligo were poor and lacked ambition, not helped by a below-par performance from their best player, Eamonn O'Hara. In fact they only scored 2 points in the first-half and Cork led 1-3 to 0-2 at the break.

Cork roused themselves on the resumption. In 5 minutes they knocked over 3 points and Sligo were struggling, even when Mark Breheny and Masters traded points. For the only time in the game O'Hara then showed glimpses of his potential and it sparked Sligo's best spell of an undistinguished contest. O'Hara, Breheny and Sean Davey all had points and there was a brief hint of a comeback at 1-7 to 0-6. Cork, though, sensing the danger quickly responded, helped by an outstanding display from midfielder Nicholas Murphy. They outscored Sligo by 4 points to 2 in the remaining minutes to ease into their

third semi-final in as many years by 1-11 to 0-8. However, the display did little to enhance their prospects of reaching their first final since 1999. Indeed they were dealt a blow later in the evening when news broke that ace forward James Masters would miss the rest of the campaign with a suspected broken jaw as a result of a heavy tackle, which earned Ross O'Donovan a yellow card.

Cork	1-11
Sligo	0-8

So Sligo's odyssey with the Championship came to an end. While they may have been disappointed with their display they can reflect with justifiable pride on a campaign that brought great joy to the football people of a proud county.

Meath v Tyrone

Tyrone's march to glory in Ulster, especially their demolition of Donegal, had many people thinking that the swagger was back in Mickey Harte's men and it would take a good team to beat them in their bid to regain the top prize. However, they had struggled in the Ulster final and now they were facing a Meath team on a roll, thanks to 3 wins in

Graham Geraghty, Meath, tries to halt the progress of Ryan McMenamin, Tyrone.
Meath v Tyrone. Football Quarter-Final. Croke Park. 4 August 2007

the qualifiers and also with Graham Geraghty back on board.

If the Cork v Sligo clash that proceeded this game was poor, the Croke Park crowd of 52,049 quickly forgot about it as this contest produced plenty of drama, scores and passion.

Meath made an excellent start and after 10 minutes led by 0-3 to 0-0. Tyrone's difficulties were compounded by their inability to win possession even from their own kick-outs. Ger Cavlan and Raymond Mulgrew eventually got points for Tyrone but the momentum was still with Meath who extended their advantage with points from the influential Stephen Bray and Peadar Byrne. The Tyrone full-back line was in real trouble. As a unit they conceded 4 points from play in the opening quarter. The failure of Brian Dooher and Sean Cavanagh to make an impact was also hurting the Ulster champions.

Meath almost had a goal in the 23rd minute but Byrne's shot was brilliantly saved by John Devine at the expense of a fruitless 45. Then in the very next move Cavanagh roused himself to produce a moment of magic. Grabbing a kick-out he soloed 40 yards under the Hogan Stand before unleashing a powerful drive that nestled in the net via the underside of the crossbar.

But it was Meath who took the initiative to kick the next 3 points, the third from Geraghty. It gave them an impressive interval lead of 0-10 to 1-5.

Tyrone's cause was not helped by an out-of-sorts Owen Mulligan who missed 2 good opportunites that would have tied the scores. Also, by now Brian Dooher, one of their key men, had departed with an injury that had made him a doubtful starter. Mickey Harte reshaped his team for the second-half and it worked to an extent as the Meath scoring rate dried up, and so this enthralling contest took another twist.

Cavlan's long-range free struck the upright but fell kindly for Mulligan who stroked a lovely ground shot to the corner of the net and Tyrone were back in the game. However, Mulligan continued to miss chances and these misses let Meath off the hook and they drew level when Brian Farrell pointed a free.

Then came the game's defining moment and it was provided by Geraghty who cheekily lifted the ball over Devine and into the net for a peach of a goal. As this absorbing contest entered the last quarter Meath led by 4 points but Tyrone were still battling away. Geraghty was lucky to escape with a yellow card for a tackle on Cavanagh. To some it warranted a red card. Mulligan once again missed the resultant free.

Tyrone kicked a succession of wides. They did reduce the deficit to 2 points when Ryan Mellon kicked a 70th minute point but their last chance of saving the game went when Stephen O'Neill drove a 45 wide in injury-time.

Meath, despite failing to score in the last 16 minutes, survived to reach the semi-final. Once again Tyrone's dreams are over as a combination of Meath's tenacity and their mounting injury list took its toll in a game in which the Royals emerged winners on a 1-13 to 2-8 scoreline.

Meath	1-13
Tyrone	2-8

Dublin v Derry

A stand-alone fixture before yet another full house and this time the Dublin supporters were in the ground reasonably early, allowing the game to get underway near enough to the appointed time of 3pm. Derry came into the fixture on the back of a number of impressive displays in the qualifiers, notably knocking out fellow Ulstermen Armagh, and manager Paddy Crozier has knitted a fine side together.

The Oak Leaf County also have in Paddy Bradley one of the game's best forwards with the potential to unhinge any defence while doubts still persist about the merits of the Dublin full-back line. But could Derry handle the cauldron that is Croke Park when the Dubs are in full flight? In fact it was Derry who scored first – a lovely point from centre-forward Paul Murphy, who carried an injury into the game. Mark Vaughan, with his blond hair making him easy to pick out, soon had Dublin in front with 2 points, one from a free followed by a sweetly-struck 45. Derry, though, were playing with a purpose. Moving the ball quickly out of defence and enjoying a slight edge in midfield they soon eased in front.

Bradley and his strike partner Conleth Gilligan shared 4 points. With 15 minutes played, Derry deservedly led by 0-5 to 0-2. However, just as quickly the game turned in Dublin's favour as Shane Ryan and Ciaran Whelan began to break Derry's grip in the middle of the park. Conal Keaney landed a free before the free-flowing Dublin attack cut loose. Jason Sherlock was excelling on the '40', probing and running in all directions while the Brogan brothers, Alan and Bernard, were also stretching the Derry rearguard.

The brothers had a point each and Keaney another before the captain Collie Moran put the Leinster champions 2 in front 0-7 to 0-5 on 23 minutes. Colin Devlin and Bernard Brogan exchanged points and despite been outplayed for a period Derry were by no means out of the game and they were quickly level at 0-8 each when Bradley and Murphy scored a point apiece. There was now great pace and energy to the game and the crowd of over 80,000 were captivated by the proceedings. Late points from Brogan (Bernard) and another well-hit 45 by Vaughan gave Dublin an interval lead of 0-10 to 0-8.

Interestingly, between the 17th and 35th minute there was 9 points scored, all from play, a clear indication that this was football of the highest quality and some of the points were just that, quality scores.

Derry were dealt a blow at half-time when a reoccurrence of a knee injury ruled Paul Murphy out for the second-half. It robbed their attack of a potent striker and certainly reduced their options as the game entered a critical phase in the closing stages.

Dublin posted their intent on the resumption by scoring 4 points in 10 minutes. Derry did get 2 but there was a sense that Caffrey's men were moving up a gear. This view was reinforced when Moran and Keaney extended their advantage to 0-16 to 0-10 with 56 minutes played. Derry were struggling to stay in touch.

Yet it could all have been so different were it not for Dublin goalkeeper Stephen Cluxton. Twice he denied Derry with brilliant saves at a time when the game was delicately poised. They both came within minutes of each other and on both occasions the chances fell to Eoin Bradley. Cluxton was brave and when the second chance was saved, the ball was quickly transferred the length of the field before Jayo landed a Dublin point to extend their advantage.

Paddy Bradley, having just missed an easy free, got a Derry point, their first in 11 minutes, but when Vaughan and Sherlock replied for Dublin, it was 0-18 to 0-11. Game over and with the strains of 'Molly Malone' and 'come on ye boys in blue' ringing out from the Hill, it looked just that. Caffrey then introduced a few substitutes, withdrawing Moran, Ryan and Bernard Brogan in quick succession, but it very nearly backfired. Derry had not gone away and they mounted a spirited fightback that had Dublin on the rails as the game entered the closing 10 minutes.

Fergal Doherty fired over a point. Gilligan knocked over a free and when Paddy Bradley landed his sixth point of a gripping contest, the gap was down to 4 points and the Hill was suddenly muted. A minute later they were almost silent when Eoin Bradley cut it to 3 with a fabulous score. Suddenly from a position of almost total control Dublin were on the ropes, and they almost paid the ultimate price.

Derry launched another assault on the Dublin goal. Paddy Bradley gained possession and lined up a shot. He looked destined to raise the only green flag in the game but a brilliant block by Barry Cahill saved his side. It was to be Derry's last chance.

In the minutes that remained Dublin showed good maturity to retain possession and frustrate their opponents and when the full-time whistle sounded, a semi-final spot beckoned, while for Derry they will reflect on the chances that slipped away. Over the 70 minutes they created several goal opportunities but converted none. Cluxton played his part in that, but it also raises questions about the Dublin full-back line that will need addressing if they are to reach the final for the first time since their last success in 1995.

That, though, is for another day as Dublin were back in the semi-final, thanks to an 0-18 to 0-15 win over a Derry side of whom a lot more will be heard of in 2008.

| Dublin | 0-18 |
| Derry | 0-15 |

Kerry v Monaghan

When these sides last met in the Championship back in 1985, Kerry were about to complete the 3-in-a-row, with a team many of whom had All-Ireland medals for loose change. Yet in the semi-final of that year they very nearly came a cropper at the hands of the men from the Farney County. Could they again repeat their heroics of that year, when they lost in a replay? Certainly manager Seamus McEnaney thought so, as he felt the Kingdom were vulnerable.

It was all of 6 weeks since Kerry's last outing, a 2-point win over Cork in the Munster Final, while Monaghan having come close to Tyrone in the Ulster final were boosted further by their win over Donegal in the qualifiers. McEnaney had them fit and rearing to go, focussed on the job in hand and quietly confident that they could spring a surprise. They also enjoyed huge support as the Kerry fans' reluctance to travel was clearly evident among the huge crowd in HQ.

Tomás Ó'Sé, Kerry, tries to reach the ball as Paul Finlay, Monaghan, attempts to restrain him.
Kerry v Monaghan. Football Quarter-Final, Croke Park. 12 August 2007

It may have been their first appearance in the last eight but Monaghan showed scant regard for Kerry's reputation and inside 3 minutes had the game's opening points from Rory Woods and Thomas Freeman. Kerry were showing the signs of their 6-week lay-off but eventually opened their account with a Mike Frank Russell free.

Monaghan, though, were impressive. They had Vincent Corey listed at full-back, but lining out at full-forward, repeating the move that almost won them the Ulster final. At the back they placed JP Mone in the number 3 slot and in the early exchanges he was getting the better of Kieran Donaghy. As a unit the Kerry attack was not functioning, and that is a tribute to the Monaghan defence.

It got better for Monaghan when Ciaran Hanratty was hauled down by a couple of Kerry defenders. Keeping his composure Freeman coolly slid the resultant penalty neatly to the net – 8 minutes gone, Monaghan 1-2 Kerry 0-1.

That score seemed to galvanise the Kerry challenge. Dara Ó'Sé won a couple of balls in the middle and in the space of 6 minutes they were level. Colm Cooper pointed 2 frees, Russell another while their only score from play was registered by Eoin Brosnan and now it was all square at 0-5 to 1-2. Monaghan had gone 16 minutes without a score and the omens did not look good, but they battled away, missing a couple of chances before they eventually found the target. Paul Finlay landed a free and in quick succession Rory Woods and Stephen Gollogley had them 3 ahead with 28 minutes played.

Kerry, though, are a seasoned outfit. They never panicked and their experience showed before half-time as they once again drew level. Killian Young and Russell scored from play and with 35 minutes on the clock Russell landed the equaliser with another free. While the football may not have been the best (not helped by the greasy conditions) it was all to play for in the second-half and Monaghan were right in there at 1-5 to 0-8.

Freeman and Cooper exchanged points on the resumption but Kerry were still not firing on all cylinders. The work of the Ó'Sé brothers was a significant factor as it kept the Kingdom in touch, particularly Marc Ó'Sé who was immense over the 70 minutes, while when it was needed most, Dara in midfield delivered. Monaghan still had the winning of the game and urged on by their fanatical supporters, they once again opened up a lead. Hanratty pointed twice, Woods also scored and they were back in front at 1-9 to 0-9, with 55 minutes played. Donaghy missed from close range and had what appeared to be a perfectly good goal disallowed and Kerry were still struggling.

Then came a defining moment with 57 minutes gone. Another high ball into Donaghy, it broke off the full-back and fell invitingly into the arms of Kerry captain Declan O'Sullivan. The Dromid man was ice cool and duly slipped the ball to the net, and for all their problems Kerry were level at 1-9 each. Now the champions would surely drive on and close the game out, but if the Monaghan goal in the first-half sparked Kerry into life, this time it was the turn of the Ulster side to respond and they duly did. Freeman, a constant thorn in the Kerry defence, had a point. Finlay had a similar effort and with 8 minutes remaining, Monaghan were back in front 1-11 to 1-9.

Kerry boss Pat O'Shea rang the changes. Galvin, Russell and Brosnan were withdrawn from the misfiring attack, even Cooper and Donaghy failed to score from play, and it was a substitute who re-ignited their challenge. Caherciveen man Bryan Sheehan entered the fray and with his first strike at goal he scored a point. He repeated the dose 3 minutes later and suddenly Kerry were level. They had also decided to move the ball through the hands rather than pump it high in to Donaghy. It was a tactic that worked and ultimately produced the match-winning point.

With 69 minutes gone and the sides level, Tomás Ó'Sé gained possession in his own half of the field and headed for the Monaghan goal. A couple of passes later he was on the 13-metre line. Cooper screamed for a pass, but Ó'Sé ignored him and coolly fisted the ball over the bar. Kerry were ahead for the first and only time in an absorbing contest.

Monaghan launched 2 late attacks in an effort to gain parity, but all to no avail and their heroic effort fell just short as Kerry's craft and know-how got them out of jail.

Kerry	1-12
Monaghan	1-11

The champions are back in the semi-final and what a clash awaits them – the 'old enemy' not from across the county bounds but the city boys from Dublin. What a prospect!

The stage was set now for two cracking semi-finals, Cork renewing rivalry with Meath and rekindling memories of some titanic tussles in the late 1980s. Meath manager Colm Coyle played in most of those games while then as he is now, Billy Morgan will be patrolling the sidelines.

And what can be said about Dublin and Kerry. In 1975 a young Kingdom team beat Kevin Heffernan's Dublin to set in train a series of matches that changed the face of Gaelic Football. Would the present generation do something similar? The coming weeks would reveal all.

Four counties are left in the race for 'Sam'.

The Cork and Waterford teams stand together during the playing of the National Anthem. Cork v Waterford Hurling Quarter-Final, Croke Park. 29 July 2007

17

Cork
v
Waterford

*A Waterford v Cork hurling
quarter-final was always going
to be a cracker of a game – so much so,
that they ended up playing it twice!*

17 Cork v Waterford

Hurling Quarter-Final

Drama on the Double

It has developed into hurling's greatest modern day rivalry, even surpassing Cork v Tipperary. So when Cork and Waterford were paired in the quarter-final, you were guaranteed excitement and two classy teams delivered on the double.

Waterford had won an epic Munster semi-final when Cork were without 3 key players. Now these players were back and it was a re-shaped and highly motivated team that faced the Munster and league champions. Joe Deane had taken over the captaincy of Cork and the long-serving star was looking forward to the challenge.

Waterford manager Justin McCarthy's task was to instil in his players the belief that they could beat Cork in Croke Park – something they had failed to achieve in two previous encounters. Waterford made the better start and with Ken McGrath shaping up to play the proverbial blinder, they raced into an early lead by 0-4 to 0-3. Then in the space of 2 minutes Dan Shanahan laid further claim to the title of hurler of the year. In the 10th minute he lashed in a goal followed by a lovely point. The Decies were in control by 1-6 to 0-4 and hurling confidently.

Cork though are an experienced side. They did not panic and slowly inched their way back into the game helped by a number of strong displays from key players. Among them was Sean Óg Ó'h-Ailpín who put his indifferent form of a few weeks earlier behind him to show his class with a quality performance. Tom Kenny landed a wonder point. Ó'h-Ailpín surged forward to score a beauty and when Ben O'Connor added another just 1 point separated the sides.

Cork were now in full flight and Waterford were struggling for scores. Indeed in the 17 minutes before half-time Cork outscored Waterford by 6 points to 1. Such were Waterford's difficulties that after 28 minutes they withdrew midfielder Jack Kennedy in favour of Eoin McGrath. However, it was all square as the two heavyweights of the hurling Championship headed for the dressing room, Cork 0-10 Waterford 1-7.

With an attendance in excess of 60,000 present what followed just added another chapter to the story of these two splendid teams. Supporters had barely settled back in their seats for the second-

Seán Óg Ó'hAilpín, Cork, tries to catch the dropping ball as John Mullane, Waterford, tackles him.
Cork v Waterford Hurling Quarter-Final, Croke Park. 29 July 2007

half, when Paul Flynn slipped his marker and drilled a low shot to the net. Shanahan tacked on a point, Waterford 2-8 to 0-10 in front. Could this get any better? It did!

Two minutes later Cork won a penalty. Up stepped Niall Ronan and his powerful shot almost ripped the net apart – goal. Sean Óg got his second point and the Rebels were back in the game.

Between the 12th and 21st minutes of the second-half the sides shared 6 points, 5 from play, one as good as the next,

before Flynn edged Waterford 2 clear, 2-13 to 1-14.

The final 10 minutes of this exhilarating contest surpassed anything these great rivals had produced in their last 6 clashes, and that is a measure of the standard produced. Cork were now playing with renewed confidence and sensing the winning of the game was within their grasp. This view was reinforced when Kieran 'Fraggy' Murphy surged through the Waterford defence to bat the ball to the net, Cork in the lead 2-14 to 2-13. In the next 4 minutes John

Gardiner had a Cork point, but Seamus Prendergast and Shanahan replied for Waterford and as the clock moved ever nearer the 70th minute mark it was level at 2-15 apiece.

The stadium throbbed with excitement in anticipation of the unfolding drama, and it duly arrived. Who would win it? Would there be a winner, as both sides missed chances, Waterford more than Cork as they hit 14 wides. While Cork were annoyed at some of referee Brian Gavin's decisions, he would make one more 'big call' before this game was over. Tom Kenny's powerful run left several Waterford defenders trailing in his wake. His shot was stopped but not dealt with adequately by goalkeeper Clinton Hennessy, and it fell invitingly into the path of Niall Ronan. The Cork attacker did not need a second chance and in a flash the *sliotar* was nestling in the net. In the next attack a Joe Deane pass put Kevin Hartnett clear and he shot over a point, Cork 3-16 Waterford 2-15.

Cork had one foot in the final. Would Waterford fail in Croke Park again? But this particular journey was not over yet. It had another twist with the referee at the centre of a dramatic incident in injury-time. Waterford were not beaten and back they came. Paul Flynn gained possession 20 metres from goal and hit a rasper of shot that looked destined for the top right-hand corner. Somehow Cork goalkeeper Donal Óg Cusack made a brilliant save and deflected the ball away, but in a flash Stephen Molumphy reacted and batted the *sliotar* into the net, 1 point between the sides and 1 minute of additional time to play.

Could Cork hold on? Could Waterford force a replay or even win?

Eoin McGrath found himself in splendid isolation 30 metres from the Cork goal. A simple chance to tap over the equaliser, but he went for glory, skipped around the challenge of Diarmuid O'Sullivan and angled a shot to the corner of the net. Again Cusack made a wonder save and as the ball broke Flynn reacted but a couple of Cork bodies got in the way and somehow they kept the ball out of the net. McGrath could scarcely believe he had missed. Would his miss cost Waterford a replay?

In the ensuing scramble the ball ended up with Cusack, who appeared to be fouled as the referee blew his whistle. Referee Gavin arrived in, nodded to his umpires and to the consternation of the Cork defenders he awarded a 20 metre free, as he deemed Cusack picked the ball off the ground. The Cork custodian was furious with the decision.

When it all calmed down, Eoin Kelly tapped the free over the bar, the sides were level. Cusack took the puck-out, still angry with the referee who then, to no one's surprise, brought proceedings to a halt. It was all square, Cork 3-16 Waterford 3-16.

Cork	3-16
Waterford	3-16

At the end of the game Cork boss Gerald McCarthy sprinted across the field to confront Gavin. So did Cusack and a number of irate defenders, but with a wave of his hand he dismissed their protestations. In the post-match media briefing McCarthy was still angry and expressed his opinions forthrightly, saying the 'referee made a wrong call and it cost us the game'.

What it did mean was that after another titanic battle for supremacy, there was very little between these two teams and the replay, fixed for Croke Park a week later, would be well worth seeing. A nation awaited another thriller.

Dan Shanahan, Waterford, celebrates after scoring his side's second and winning goal as John Gardiner, Cork, looks disconsolate. Cork v Waterford Hurling Quarter-Final, Croke Park. 29 July 2007

Replay

The crowd was down on the drawn encounter. It's an expensive business following successful teams. It was a cold afternoon in Croke Park as the hurlers of Cork and Waterford met for the fifth time in a major game. The winners would face Limerick a week later in the semi-final.

In contrast to the drawn clash, Cork made the better start and points from Jerry O'Connor, Niall Ronan and Kieran Murphy cancelled out 1 by John Mullane. Indeed Cork could have had 2 goals as twice in quick succession Tom Kenny and Timmy McCarthy breached the Waterford defence but Hennessy was equal to the task on both occasions.

Cork, with Jerry O'Connor and Tom Kenny dictating matters in midfield, were hurling authoritively and on 20 minutes were 0-7 to 0-5 ahead, but should have been more. Then the game's first goal arrived. Hesitancy in the Cork defence saw the hard-working Stephen Molumphy gain possession and his pass across the square found Dan Shanahan. Do you need to ask what happened next? Goal for Shanahan, his seventh of the Championship, and Waterford were in the lead 1-5 to 0-7.

Cork got the next 3 points, all from the majestic Ben O'Connor. Crucially in the few minutes before half-time, Waterford scored 2 to Cork's 1 and at the break the narrowest of leads for the Leesiders 0-11 to 1-7.

Waterford would have been the happier of the two teams as they headed for the dressing rooms as they had been outplayed for most of the opening 35 minutes, yet only 1 point separated two evenly matched teams.

Six times in the first 15 minutes of the second-half the sides were level, 10 times over the 70 minutes, as Michael Walsh and the effective Eoin McGrath had Waterford points, matched by similar quality scores from Cork's Tom Kenny and Jerry O'Connor.

With 57 minutes played the game now entered a crucial phase. Eoin Kelly edged Waterford ahead. Surprisingly, in the space of 4 minutes Cork replaced big hitters Joe Deane, Jerry O'Connor and Timmy McCarthy. A lift for Waterford, perhaps?

However, in the very next move of the match Waterford were boosted further when the game's defining moment arrived.

A long delivery dropped in behind the Cork defence and lurking for the loose ball was big Dan Shanahan and without breaking stride he drilled a low shot well beyond the reach of Cusack in the Cork goal. Paul Flynn and Eoin

Waterford supporters in suitable headgear, enjoying the atmosphere, the sunshine and the final result. Cork v Waterford Hurling Quarter-Final, Croke Park. 29 July 2007

McGrath had Waterford points, in between Ben had one for Cork, but the Decies were now 2-16 to 0-17 in front and looking likely winners.

Cork needed a goal, but the changes in attack had not worked and it was left to Ben O'Connor to tack on a few points – he finished with 0-9. The game ended on a distressing note with Cork's Niall Ronan carried off on a stretcher following an accidental collision with a Waterford defender. It all meant the second-half extended for almost 40 minutes and in the end there was no denying that Waterford were deserving winners of yet another cracking contest by 2-17 to 0-20.

So Cork's bid to make it a fifth successive semi-final failed at the hands of their keenest rivals of recent years, but gracious as ever Gerald McCarthy had no complaints – ' very disappointed, the lads are gutted, but thankfully Niall (Ronan) is okay, but the better team won and we wish them well in the semi-final.'

Waterford finally break the Cork hoo-doo in Croke Park. Now could they take one more step and end a long wait for a place in the final? We would know the answer in seven days.

Waterford	2-17
Cork	0-20

Lar Corbett, Tipperary, tries to grab the ball while under the close attention of Eoin Quigley, left, Richie Kehoe, No 5 and Darren Stamp, Wexford. Wexford v Tipperary. Hurling Quarter-Final, Croke Park. 28 July 2007

18

Three Games, One Shock

HURLING QUARTER-FINALS

As Babs controversially shuffled his Tipp team, Wexford prepared to take advantage. Ger Loughnane managed — yet again — to divert the media focus from his Galway team onto himself as they took on Kilkenny. Meanwhile, Limerick readied themselves to bring their hunger to win to a struggling Clare team.

18 Three Games, One Shock

Hurling Quarter-Finals

Tipperary	v	Wexford
Kilkenny	v	Galway
Limerick	v	Clare

Hurling extravaganza

In a change to the previous year when Thurles hosted two of the quarter-finals, it was decided that for the 2007 Championship all four games would be played in Croke Park. It was also agreed that the games would be played on separate weekends, thereby giving hurling two big high-profile days, a good promotional ploy.

However, when news filtered through of a tragic road accident in Thomastown, County Kilkenny that claimed the life of Vanessa McGarry, wife of Kilkenny goalkeeper James, there was immediate calls for a deferral of the games.

The first two games were Kilkenny v Galway with Tipperary and Wexford meeting in the opening game of an attractive double-header on Sunday July 22. After confirmation was received that the funeral would take place on the Sunday morning of the games, the GAA, following consultations with all four counties, immediately cancelled both matches.

It was the right decision and the many hurlers and GAA officials that attended the funeral is testimony to James's high standing within the game. The events of that fateful morning put sport and all it entails into perspective, as a young and vibrant life was snatched from a loving family. It was decided to reschedule the games for the following Saturday, making it a bumper weekend for hurling in Croke Park with the top 8 counties battling it out for the last 4 places as the race for the Liam McCarthy Cup gathered momentum or in the words of one manager, 'now the real action begins.'

Babs' gamble backfires [Tipperary v Wexford]

The circumstances may not have been what they wished for but the week's postponement seemed perfect for Tipperary who had endured a hectic programme in the last few months.

When manager Babs Keating announced his team for the original fixture, there was surprise at the omission of star forward Eoin Kelly.

Keating maintained that Kelly had not fully recovered from the groin injury sustained in the qualifier game against Dublin. Kelly, though, was adamant that he was fit, and with the extra week it was felt that Keating would include the Mullinahone man for the re-fixture. But Babs stuck to his guns and the country's top forward watched the opening 20 minutes of the game from the substitute's bench in the Hogan Stand.

Wexford on the evidence of their Leinster final collapse were rank outsiders, but Babs' decision not to start Kelly was viewed by many as a slur. It seemed as if Keating expected his side to win and would then have his man fully fit for the semi-final a week later. An insult to Wexford maybe, but for manager John Meyler it was the perfect motivation.

Tipperary also suffered from the omission of goalkeeper Brendan Cummins and his replacement Gerry Kennedy did not enjoy the best of afternoons. A couple of the Wexford goals might not have happened on Cummin's watch.

In a strange twist it was the Wexford goalkeeper Damien Fitzhenry who emerged as the hero from this joyous quarter-final. However, this game was more about Wexford's spirit, which they had in abundance as they put the heavy defeat to Kilkenny behind them, and they went for the jugular from the off.

But their old failing of shooting wides looked like undoing them. They shot more wides than scores over the 70 minutes and should have had 3 goals by half-time. As it was they had only 1, scored by Rory Jacob 2 minutes before Lar Corbett had one for Tipperary to give the Munster side an interval lead of 1-8 to 1-5. By now Keating had introduced Kelly but the Mullinahone man did not have the best of outings, at times trying the impossible when the simple option might have paid bigger dividends.

Keith Rossiter, Malachy Travers and Paul Roche impressed for Wexford, while in attack Rory Jacob and Barry Lambert tormented their markers. For Tipperary Benny Dunne and Darragh Hickey were picking off some nice points and the winning of the game was still within their grasp. In fact they should have put Wexford to the sword in the opening minutes of the second-half but Corbett and Dunne shot from over-ambitious positions, while Fitzhenry made a great stop to deny Kelly a goal at a crucial stage of the game.

Wexford's second goal arrived in the 43rd minute when Rory Jacob's diagonal pass found Barry Lambert who drilled the ball to the net. Momentum was now with Meyler's men, and Babs could do little to stop it. For all their difficulties Tipperary were still in the lead as the game meandered towards the 67th minute when Wexford won a free on the 20-metre line, but to the left of the goal.

Then came an incident that not only changed the direction of the game, but the hurling year and also the respective managerial careers of Meyler and Keating. A Tipperary defender protested at the decision to award the free, and Westmeath referee James McGrath moved the ball. Now the free was directly in front of the goal. Cue goalkeeper Damien Fitzhenry – he made the long journey from the other end of the field and cool as you like he drilled a powerful shot to the roof of the net. Wexford in front, Tipperary staring elimination in the face. They did have one chance to save their season but Kelly's free was almost 100 metres out and never looked like finding the range. The full-time whistle sounded a few seconds later. Wexford were in the semi-final winning a dramatic match by 3-10 to 1-14.

Wexford	3-10
Tipperary	1-14

A shell-shocked Babs spoke to the media and stood by his decision to omit Kelly from the start, and said, 'some players made the wrong choices when in possession, that is what cost us the game. Fair play to Wexford, we wish them well in the semi-final.'

Wexford boss John Meyler was breathless with excitement, 'a great result for the lads and it gives us an opportunity to redeem ourselves when we play Kilkenny in the semi-final.' But would they?

As for Tipperary and their charismatic manager, Babs Keating, another season ended without silverware, a season that was dogged by rumours of a divided camp. Within days of this defeat, the curtain came down on Keating's second stint in charge when Babs stepped down from his position and the hunt began immediately for his successor. Keating, if only for his frankness and willingness to speak to the media, will be missed.

Kilkenny v Galway

In the build-up to the original fixture (postponed owing to the death of Vanessa McGarry) Galway manager Ger Loughnane stirred up a hornet's nest with comments in relation to Kilkenny's style of play. In an interview he suggested, 'that while the present Galway team is one of the best I have worked with, I wonder will they be able to cope

Iarla Tannian, Galway, tries to solo past JJ Delaney, Kilkenny.
Galway v Kilkenny. Hurling Quarter-Final, Croke Park. 28 July 2007

with the "overzealous" defensive methods of this Kilkenny side.' Continuing he said, 'I hope we will get an open game, but are we ready for the savaging that Kilkenny will give us and I hope the referee will give us some chance.' Loughnane was now on a roll – 'this flicking and belting across the wrists can't happen next Sunday and if it doesn't, you never know.'

A few days later there was a further twist to the story when the original referee Pat O'Connor was unavailable and replaced by Wexford's Dickie Murphy. It only added to the intriguing nature of the contest. GAA President Nickey Brennan blasted rumours that there was a conspiracy theory in relation to Dickie Murphy's appointment. It had been suggested that the change was a reaction to Loughnane's outburst. Brennan dismissed the notion out of hand, 'absolutely nothing to do with it, in fact Pat O'Connor contacted the office to say he was unavailable owing to work commitments, it's as simple as that and there is no sinister motive behind the change.'

As for Kilkenny there was annoyance among their supporters but the official line was 'it has nothing to do with us'. County Board Chairman Pat Dunphy said, 'I am not getting involved in a meaningless debate, we are concentrating totally on the match.'

The match itself was an emotional day for James McGarry who, accompanied by his young son, took his place with the Kilkenny substitutes (he did not tog out), and looked uneasy as a minute's silence was impeccably observed in memory of his late wife.

The game itself was a smashing contest as Galway locked horns with the All-Ireland champions and gave them a severe test. Galway played with a controlled aggression and a gameplan that had been designed to create space for their lively forwards to operate in. One player who revelled in the space was Alan Kerins and he hit 3 points in the first 11 minutes. Their hurling was fast and stringent, gone was the needless running into trouble. Galway led by 0-5 to 0-2, but the champions displayed their usual composure to claw their way back into the game and some quality points by Eoin Larkin and Martin Comerford and the free-taking of Henry Shefflin broke Galway's momentum.

However, a lovely goal in the 24th minute created by Damien Hayes and Niall Healy and expertly finished by Richie Murray restored Galway's belief. From here to the break, Kilkenny rattled over 6 points as Tommy Walsh and Willie O'Dwyer produced some magical play and Brian Cody's side led 0-13 to 1-9 at the end of a sparkling 35 minutes.

The second-half was just as lively and it featured some quality scores, including a monster point by Galway goalkeeper Colm Callanan. For the best part of the next 25 minutes two evenly matched sides traded points before Niall Healy's brace pushed Galway into a narrow lead 1-14 to 0-16. Kilkenny then worked a goal chance and predictably availed of it. Eddie Brennan's run caught out the Galway defence and his offload to Richie Power made the task of finding the net easy.

Galway, though, were not beaten yet and 3 frees by the excellent Kerril Wade tied to scores at 1-17 each, which quickly became 1-18 as the outcome danced on the edge of a knife with 60 minutes played. There was little hint of what was to come and when it did Galway were stunned by the ferocity of Kilkenny's finish. Eoin Larkin gained possession under the Cusack Stand and spotted Eddie Brennan in splendid isolation near the Galway goal. The pass was inch

Brian Begley, Limerick, tries to hook Alan Markham, Clare, as they both struggle for possession.
Clare v Limerick. Hurling Quarter-Final, Croke Park. 28 July 2007

perfect and the subsequent goal matched the pass. Brennan and Power added points, 5 up with 5 to go, Galway shell-shocked.

Brennan again got possession twirled past Ger Mahon and stitched it. Incredibly Kilkenny scored 2-4 in the last 10 minutes while Galway failed to raise a flag of any colour in the same period.

Kilkenny	3-22
Galway	1-18

Kilkenny by virtue of their 3-22 to 1-18 win were safely through to their 11th successive semi-final where Wexford await. As for Galway and Loughnane the Johnny Logan song springs to mind – *What's Another Year?*

Limerick v Clare

A big game for under-pressure Clare boss Tony Considine as Limerick, even though they were disappointed at losing the Munster final, had shown enough throughout that campaign to suggest they were steadily improving.

In truth it was a poor contest in which Clare never led as Limerick's graph continued to rise with an impressive performance highlighted by an exceptional display from Andrew O'Shaughnessy. O'Shaughnessy was a star under-21 player but had yet to produce the goods on the big stage. However, in the 3-game epic with Tipperary, he delivered some classic scores, and now he was to do it again.

With 8 minutes gone Limerick were 0-4 to 0-1 ahead, 'Shaughs' had 3, and with Clare's weakness in attack once again proving to be their Achilles heel. It was an assured performance by Limerick. On the 31st minute they had stretched their advantage to 0-10 to 0-3, O'Shaughnessy now on 6. Clare rallied briefly with the next 3 points, but O'Shaughnessy's seventh point gave Limerick an interval lead of 0-11 to 0-7 at the end of a drab 35 minutes of hurling.

Clare did get the first point of the second-half, but when Donie Ryan bagged a Limerick goal in the 37th minute there was a sense of inevitability about the outcome. The game as a spectacle was slowly dying on its feet and any time Clare hinted at a revival with a couple of scores, Limerick had the capacity to respond even at a time when O'Shaughnessy's scoring rate had died down. With just 17 minutes remaining, the lead was a comfortable 1-17 to 0-12. Clare were thrown a lifeline when Diarmuid McMahon got in for a goal but it proved to be a false dawn, because just as quickly O'Shaughnessy once again found the range. In the closing minutes he rifled over 4 more points, bringing his tally to 11, as Limerick cruised into the semi-final.

A huge step forward for an emerging Limerick who might just be on the verge of fulfilling the promise shown as under-age players. They were now just 70 minutes away from an All-Ireland final appearance, on the back of this 1-23 to 1-16 win.

Limerick	1-23
Clare	1-16

For Clare another traumatic year once again dominated by off-the-field controversy. Manager Considine, so often at the centre of these events, said after the game, 'we have no complaints; we were beaten by a better team on the day. I will see what the future holds before I say any more.'

Little did he or the assembled press know that it would be his last time speaking as Clare boss. A short few weeks later a meeting of the Clare County Board summarily dismissed Considine from his post, at a time when he was out of the country on holidays.

It just about summed up Clare's season, while the popular Limerick boss Ritchie Bennis was – 'delighted to be in the semi-final and getting better all the time.' How right he was!

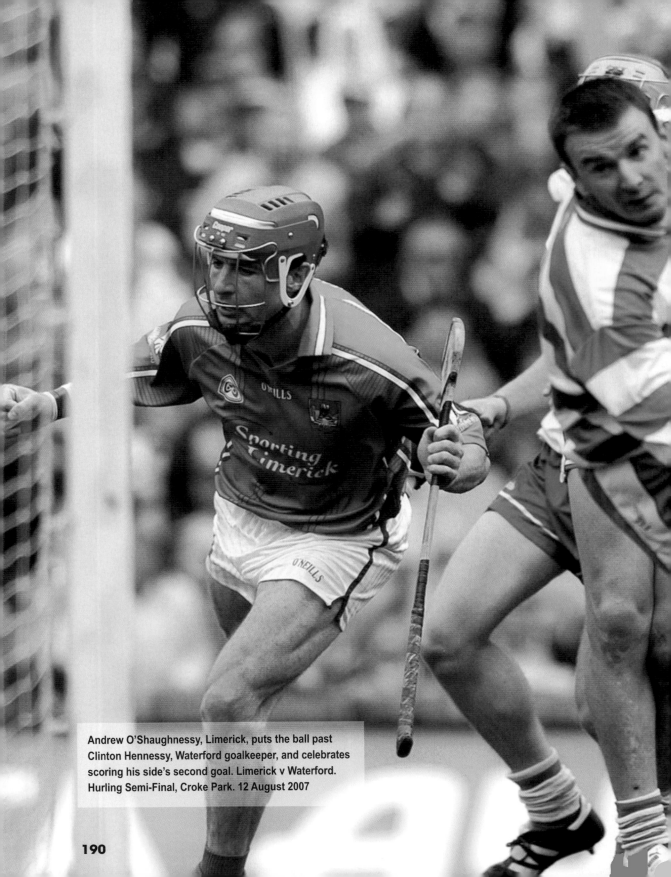

Andrew O'Shaughnessy, Limerick, puts the ball past
Clinton Hennessy, Waterford goalkeeper, and celebrates
scoring his side's second goal. Limerick v Waterford.
Hurling Semi-Final, Croke Park. 12 August 2007

19

Limerick Land KO

The two semi-final hurling matches were the polar opposite of each other. Whilst Kilkenny v Wexford produced a lacklustre 'going-through-the-motions' game, Waterford v Limerick provided an All-Ireland hurling semi-final to be remembered.

19 Limerick Land KO

Hurling Semi-Finals

> Waterford v Limerick
> Kilkenny v Wexford

Repeat pairings in semi-finals

The Cork v Waterford games apart, the quarter-finals of the Guinness Hurling Championship were mundane affairs. When the dust settled you had the unusual situation of repeat pairings in the semi-finals. Kilkenny and Wexford would meet for a third time in a big game in the space of a few months, while Munster rivals Limerick and Waterford would contest the second semi-final.

It afforded Limerick and Wexford the ideal opportunity to avenge their defeats in the provincial deciders, but there was general agreement that these pairings were not ideal and should have been avoided.

Wexford flop yet again

The decision to play the Wexford v Kilkenny semi-final as a curtain raiser to the Cork v Waterford quarter-final replay was a clear indication of the lack of appeal in this fixture.

Indeed had it been a stand-alone game, it's quite possible that it would have been played in a near deserted stadium as supporters from both counties were in the minority.

Kilkenny were confident of winning, while even after the morale-boosting win over Tipperary a week earlier there was little confidence that Wexford would halt the Cats' march to yet another final, their fourth in 5 years.

Yet Wexford started well and after 7 minutes led by 0-3 to 0-0. Barry Lambert had 2 points, while David O'Connor also scored and there was a hope that maybe, just maybe, they would trouble the champions.

Henry Shefflin and Martin Comerford had Kilkenny points, but Darren Stamp made it 0-4 to 0-2 for Wexford, before the tie swung decisively Kilkenny's way.

By the 16th minute Kilkenny were in front and Wexford went 14 minutes without a score before Lambert squared the match at 0-5 each on 25 minutes.

The game was being played at a pedestrian pace and lacked the real bite or intensity normally associated with an All-Ireland semi-final. It was as if everyone was waiting for Kilkenny to inflict further misery on their

Aidan Fogarty, Kilkenny, strikes the ball despite the close marking of Malachy Travers, Wexford. Kilkenny v Wexford. Hurling Semi-Final, Croke Park. 5 August 2007

neighbours.

Then it happened. They moved up a gear. Shefflin landed 3 points, Lambert one of the few Wexford players to impress scored his fourth to keep his side in touch. However, as if to emphasise their superiority, Kilkenny were to score 3 unanswered points to lead 0-11 to 0-6 at half-time and already there was a feeling this game was heading in only one direction.

There was little indication in the opening period of the second-half that Wexford would improve. In fact by the 46th minute Kilkenny had widened the gap to 9 points to 0-15 to 0-6, as Shefflin scored with ease. The points continued to flow over Damien Fitzhenry's bar and with 13 minutes remaining Kilkenny were in cruise control at 0-21 to 0-8. By now, with their place in the final long secure, Brian Cody had used the full complement of substitutes and it made little difference to the outcome.

To the relief of many, mostly Wexford people, the fourth official signalled just 1 minute of added time. In that period Michael Jacob bagged a Wexford goal, that did not even take the bare look off the scoreboard, but it was Kilkenny who were to have the final say.

Henry Shefflin rifled over his 14th point and Kilkenny's 23rd to draw the blinds on Wexford's season in emphatic fashion, by 0-23 to 1-10.

| Kilkenny | 0-23 |
| Wexford | 1-10 |

Kilkenny have now met and beaten Wexford in 3 major games this season. On each occasion the gulf in standards was plain to see. It's a long road back for the men from the Model County.

As for Kilkenny, well another final on the first Sunday in September beckons but would the lack of a serious test hinder their bid to retain the title? One thing is certain though, the training sessions in Nowlan Park in the coming weeks will be lively.

Waterford or Limerick to bridge the long gap

Having finally seen off Cork, Waterford were clear favourites to reach their first final since 1963 when they faced Limerick a week later to determine Kilkenny's opponents.

Limerick suffered agonising defeats in 1994 and 1996 but with a two-week gap since their quarter-final, they were that bit fresher and having ran Waterford close in the Munster final they had no fear of playing them again. They were also helped by the pundits who had written them off. The whole country, it appeared, wanted a Kilkenny v Waterford final. Waterford, though, had failed in their 5 previous attempts in recent years to reach the final. Could they finally bridge that gap?

Limerick were not there just to make up the numbers and they set their stall out from the start. The ferocity of their challenge completely stunned Waterford. Andrew O'Shaughnessy and Paul Flynn swapped points before Donie Ryan smashed in a great goal for Limerick and it imbued the team with confidence to hurl splendidly for 20 minutes. In that period they ripped the heart out of the Waterford challenge. Shaughnessy banged over 3 points before drilling in a fabulous goal in the 15th minute as the Decies' full-back line crumbled under intense pressure.

There was little Waterford could do and by the 22nd minute there was an

Richie Bennis, Limerick manager, being congratulated by Dan Shanahan, Waterford. Limerick v Waterford. Hurling Semi-Final, Croke Park. 12 August 2007.

unreal look to the scoreboard – Limerick 2-7 Waterford 0-3.

Justin McCarthy introduced Eoin McGrath and the diminutive midfielder helped ignite Waterford's challenge, which was given further momentum when Stephen Molumphy dived low to direct Dan Shanahan's cross to the net on 26 minutes – game back on again.

Waterford had sparked into life, and now it was Limerick's turn to struggle as scores were hard to come by. Shanahan who barely had a clear shot on goal managed to pinch 2 points and Ken McGrath landed a long-range free. The gap that at one stage was 10 points was now down to a manageable 4 at half-time – 2-9 to 1-8.

Both sides left the field with the cheers of approval from the crowd of

195

80,546 ringing in their ears. This was an All-Ireland semi-final at its best – a far cry from the mundane affair Kilkenny and Wexford served up seven days earlier.

Now the question being asked was – 'could Limerick maintain their grip or would the exertions of 3 games in 14 days take its toll on the Munster champions?'

There was a dramatic start to the second-half. Sean O'Connor was clear on goal but Waterford goalkeeper Clinton Hennessy stopped his poorly-hit shot. However, 2 minutes later the Ardmore man could do little to deny Limerick. Once again it was Ryan with the strike, his second goal, to extend their advantage. Limerick were playing with a ravenous hunger that Waterford just could not match. The much vaunted Waterford attack was making little impact as Seamus Hickey, Damien Reale and Brian Geary were superb and chances were few and far between.

By the 20th minute of the second-half scores had dried up somewhat, but the passion and intensity had not, as Limerick were still playing as if their lives depended on the result.

However, Waterford were due to hit a good patch and on cue it arrived. Limerick manager Richie Bennis, who expended as much energy as his players on the sideline, withdrew experienced but tiring Mark Foley from defence and almost immediately they conceded a goal scored by Eoin McGrath and now just 1 score divided the sides, 3-10 to 2-10 for Limerick. It was gripping stuff.

Eoin Kelly with a superb point cut the lead to just 2 points and Waterford were on the cusp of a sensational comeback. James O'Brien and Shanahan traded points. Veteran Tony Browne landed a long-range effort for Waterford and with just 6 minutes of an enthralling encounter left it was a 1-point game.

It was draining stuff and as the big screen in the stadium scanned the crowd the sheer emotion was etched on the faces of supporters from both sides. Waterford were trying everything to get back into the game. Justin gambled and withdrew marquee names Paul Flynn and John Mullane from the attack. Both had failed to score from play – a tribute to the tenacity of the Limerick defence.

Shanahan who had plundered goals for fun in his previous games, 3 against Limerick in the Munster final, 8 in total throughout the Championship, never looked like getting one this time, although to his credit he did score 4 lovely points.

Then, as so often in a big game, there comes a turning point and when it arrived, it finally closed the door on

Waterford's brave but ultimately failed bid for a final place.

Five minutes to go, Limerick full-forward Brian Begley was grounded in the square. Referee Seamus Roche awarded a penalty, with Limerick just 1 point ahead. A choice for Andrew O'Shaughnessy – do you take the soft option and tap it over the bar for a point or go for glory and finish the match? The young army officer was in no doubt and displaying nerves of steel he unleashed a powerful drive that almost lifted the net from the goalpost. Goal! Game over! Limerick in the final.

To their credit Waterford got 2 points from Eoin Kelly but with their crestfallen supporters heading for the exit, they turned back to see Begley himself lash in Limerick's fifth goal to put the issue beyond doubt, Limerick 5-11 Waterford 2-15.

Seconds later the full-time whistle sounded and Bennis was mobbed by players and officials alike as the men from the Treaty City celebrated a famous win at the end of a contest that once again displayed the very best of Munster hurling, even in an All-Ireland semi-final.

Limerick	5-11
Waterford	2-15

It had many highlights. Shaugnessy's tally of 2-7, Ryan's 2 goals, Shanahan's quality points, but most of all it was a game played in the best of spirits. Sure it was tough, but not once did either side cross the line and when it was over players shook hands and embraced, exactly what you would expect from two sporting counties.

Limerick may have only scored 5 times in the second-half but the fact that 3 of them were goals proved crucial in deciding the outcome. Waterford were devastated at yet another loss, and it is small consolation that their contribution to the hurling year of 2007 will not be forgotten. But reality dawns and the long wait for a final appearance goes on – but for how much longer can some of their players go on? A thought to ponder on in the weeks and months ahead.

The stage was set then for the 2007 All-Ireland hurling final, Kilkenny v Limerick on September 2nd – a repeat of their meetings in 1973 and 1974 which ended with one victory each.

Limerick have not tasted glory since their win in 1973. Kilkenny are bidding to retain the title and also join Cork at the head of the Roll of Honour with 30 titles. A huge incentive, then, for both teams as the countdown begins to hurling's biggest day.

Kieran Donaghy, Kerry, tries to shield
the ball from Ciaran Whelan, Dublin.
Dublin v Kerry. Football Semi-Final,
Croke Park. 26 August 2007

20

Cork - Kerry Prevail

FOOTBALL SEMI-FINALS

*As with the hurling semi-finals, the
football semi-finals produced two very
different games. Meath put up a fight
but it was never enough to stop the Cork
juggernaut. Meanwhile, Kerry v Dublin
was a battle to the death, with an old
rivalry vigorously renewed.*

20 Cork – Kerry Prevail

Football Semi-Finals

Cork	v	Meath
Dublin	v	Kerry

Top dogs battle it out in last four

Cork v Meath, Dublin v Kerry, Munster and Leinster, no Connacht representatives. Even more surprisingly, given their dominance in recent years, Ulster is once again fallow ground in the Bank of Ireland football semi-finals.

In the late 1980s and early 1990s, Cork and Meath enjoyed a rivalry that captivated the nation. They met in 4 successive finals and each one of them was shrouded in controversy. Indeed such was the ill-tempered nature of these games that when the teams ended up in the same location on an end-of-season holiday, the players barely nodded in one another's direction. Matters finally thawed out and it took the untimely death of then Cork goalkeeper John Kerins to bring sanity to the respective squads. The last meeting between the counties was the All-Ireland final of 1999 which Meath won and in fact this was their first ever meeting in a semi-final.

As for Dublin and Kerry, their rivalry ushered in a new era in Gaelic Football in the 1970s with some fascinating encounters, none better then the semi-final of 1977, generally recognised as one of the best matches of all times.

Dublin have not beaten Kerry in the Championship since that day. In fact not since 1995 have the 'Dubs' appeared in the final, while Kerry were bidding to reach their fourth successive decider.

One thing was certain, a team that had already lost in the Championship, Cork or Meath, would contest the final. Would it be a first ever Cork v Kerry decider or would Meath and Dublin renew rivalry. All will be revealed as the semi-finals took shape.

Cork v Meath

There was a strange atmosphere in the stadium as only 38,500 spectators attended this game and the pre-match routine did not include the parade as the GAA forgot to book a band. Meath, on the back of an impressive march through the qualifiers, including the win over Tyrone, were favourites to reach the final.

Cork were appearing in their third

Michael Cussen, Cork, rises highest in midfield to claim this ball despite the efforts of Nigel Crawford and Mark Ward, Meath. Cork v Meath. Football Semi-Final, Croke Park. 19 August 2007

successive semi-final but the wins over Louth and Sligo had done little to suggest they could beat Colm Coyle's revitalised side.

James Masters was an absentee from the Cork team with a broken jaw received in the win over Sligo. How the team would respond without the Championship's leading scorer was also a concern.

Donnacha O'Connor got the game's first point for Cork in the second minute but the Rebels also missed relatively easy frees in a nervy opening period. Tactically Cork were flying. Big full-forward Michael Cussen was given a roving role thus taking Meath full-back Darren Fay away from his natural habitat. As a consequence Fay had little impact on proceedings. In defence Cork deployed Graham Canty on Stephen Bray with Michael Shields marking Shane O'Rourke – moves that worked from the off. Anthony Lynch and Ger Spillane were both back to their best and had big games. It was round one to Billy Morgan in terms of strategy.

Meath got the next 2 points from O'Rourke and Brian Farrell but Cork soon settled, particularly as they gained an edge in midfield and dominated the next 20 minutes in which Meath failed to score. Daniel Goulding, Nicholas Murphy, John Miskella and O'Connor again all had points to put Cork into a 0-5 to 0-2 lead, as Meath still struggled.

One moment of tension arrived in the 10th minute when Cork wing-back Noel O'Leary, a tree surgeon by profession, appeared to land a blow on the chin of Graham Geraghty who hit the ground in dramatic fashion. After consultation with his linesman, referee Brian Crowe issued O'Leary with a yellow card but the Central Competitions Control Committee (CCCC) were certain to review the incident and the Cill Na Martra man could face further censure. The incident seemed to galvanise Cork and O'Leary emerged as one of their top performers. Cork then went on to score the next 3 points while Geraghty was practically anonymous for Meath for the remainder of the game.

At 0-5 to 0-2 Colm Coyle reacted. Meath had a goal chance in the 24th minute but Cork goalkeeper Alan Quirke made an excellent stop from Bray. Coyle switched O'Rourke to centre-forward and it brought about an immediate improvement in Meath's play. Having gone 17 minutes without a score, Meath then scored 3 points in 3 minutes, from Caomhin King, Farrell and O'Rourke and now it was all square at 0-5 to 0-5. This was a worrying period for

Noel O'Leary, Cork, clashes with Graham Geraghty, Meath.
Cork v Meath. Football Semi-Final, Croke Park. 19 August 2007

Cork. Would they fold under Meath's strong comeback? They answered in emphatic fashion.

In quick succession O'Connor, who was a constant thorn in the Meath defence, Goulding and Kevin McMahon

203

all landed points and it was Cork who were ahead 0-8 to 0-6 at half-time. Those 3 points were crucial as it gave Cork the confidence to take the game to Meath on the resumption and they did so in some style.

Strong running by Pearse O'Neill and O'Connor earned frees which Goulding and O'Connor converted and there was a feeling that Cork were about to move up a gear.

Meath did pull a point back from Stephen Bray but it was only a temporary blip as Cork proceeded to dominate the remainder of the contest. McMahon had a point before a flowing move that began on their own 20-metre line ended with corner-back Kieran O'Connor fisting over the bar. It was a statement of intent by a rampant Cork outfit. Now on 45 minutes gone, it was Cork 0-12 Meath 0-7.

Six minutes later came the score that nailed the Meath challenge. Cork won a sideline ball and the alert Daniel Goulding caught the Meath defence napping to put McMahon in the clear. The wing-forward with lovely balance slipped his man and his shot, although it took a slight deflection, dipped over goalkeeper Brendan Murphy and dropped into the net. There was no way back for Meath and there was a look of resignation on Colm Coyle's face as he surveyed the damage Cork were inflicting on his team. For once in their proud history there was not even the hint of a fightback, a trait always associated with the Royal County.

Cork ran in 3 more points, 2 from rampaging centre-forward Pearse O'Neill, before Meath finally added to their tally with a point, their first in 22 minutes. The closing stages saw Billy Morgan empty his bench giving his panel valuable game time in advance of the final. O'Connor brought his tally to 0-6, and when referee Crowe called time on the contest, the scoreboard did not lie. It was easy for Cork who ran out convincing 1-16 to 0-9 winners.

| Cork | 1-16 |
| Meath | 0-9 |

Coyle had no complaints, 'the better team won but it's been a good few months for us and we will be back stronger next year.'

As for Billy Morgan, when he finished having a dig at the 'RTÉ experts' and confiscating a reporter's dictaphone, he said he was delighted to be back in the final – 'yeah we're delighted. I have great belief in these players and right now I'm not too worried who we play in the final. I will think about that in a few days.'

It was an anxious couple of days for Cork defender Noel O'Leary after, as expected, the CCCC asked referee Brian Crowe if he was satisfied he took the correct action in the incident with O'Leary and Geraghty.

However, the Cavan official decided that no further action should be taken, and to the relief of Morgan, O'Leary was cleared to play in the final. In reaction to the decision, Cork selector John Corcoran said, 'it's the right decision – it was a thing of nothing really and we are delighted that Noel will be available for the final.'

One finalist known, now would it be old rivals Cork v Kerry in the final or would it be a battle of the city slickers to decide the destination of Sam in 2007?

Kerry v Dublin

By contrast with the Cork v Meath semi-final, this game was played before a full house of almost 82,000 and the atmosphere inside the stadium was electric. The Hill, as ever, was a sea of blue but a handful of 'green and gold' clad supporters joined them and were accorded a rousing welcome, as was the 'Dubs' most famous fan, An Taoiseach Bertie Ahern, wearing, appropriately for the occasion, a blue sports jacket.

Pre-match pageantry out of the way (this time the GAA did book a band), the clock moved nearer 3.30pm. The tension was palpable as the teams retreated to their respective positions.

There was an explosive start and it came from the champions. With 15 seconds gone, Eoin Brosnan kicked a point and when Paul Galvin knocked over 2 more, Kerry were in dreamland, while Dublin, a bit like boxer Bernard Dunne the night before, were on the canvass.

Dublin gradually regrouped but they were missing chances. Mark Vaughan kicked an easy free wide as a degree of cynicism crept into the game. Vaughan also missed a clear goal chance early on that would have settled his side and himself.

Referee John Bannon was having a difficult time as the first-half wore on. It was blighted by bad sportsmanship and the reaction of some of the Dublin players to Kerry misses did little for their reputations. Dublin eventually opened their account after Shane Ryan placed Barry Cahill for a 7th minute point. Cahill along with Bryan Cullen exerted strong pressure around the middle and began winning the breaking ball. It helped drag the Leinster champions back into the game as Kerry went 22 minutes without scoring.

Dublin were level on 19 minutes thanks to Alan Brogan, and Kerry were dealt a further blow when midfielder Dara Ó'Sé was forced off with a hip injury in the 21st minute, with Tommy Griffin taking his place. Ó'Sé's departure coincided with Dublin taking the lead for the first time with an excellent point from Vaughan. The scene seemed set for Dublin to ram home their advantage.

However, Kerry showed their resolve. Donaghy created 2 points, while Colm Cooper who had seen little of the ball up to then drilled over 2 superb points once again emphasising his class.

Kerry, like Dublin earlier, were now missing chances but team captain Declan O'Sullivan knocked over a beauty from an acute angle. At the break, Dublin, despite their poor start, had a lead at half-time, albeit a narrow one, 0-8 to 0-7.

The tension that was evident throughout the first-half continued as the teams left the field with a number of players becoming embroiled in a slight melee, as Dublin boss Paul Caffrey attempted to bring the matter to the attention of referee Bannon.

Thankfully it came to nothing, but Kerry's Paul Galvin, like Cork's O'Leary a week earlier, faced an anxious few days following an incident with Paul Casey. In fact over the 70 minutes referee Bannon dispensed 13 yellow cards, 7 to Kerry and 6 to Dublin. It's a tribute to his experience that he found it necessary to keep his red cards safely tucked away in his notebook.

As they did at the start of the game, Kerry were buzzing on the resumption. Indeed some Dublin fans, and Kerry ones for that matter, could hardly believe the score if they returned late for the second-half.

With 2 minutes gone a flowing Kerry move with Killian Young and Cooper involved, saw Declan O'Sullivan squeeze the ball past Dublin goalkeeper Stephen Cluxton for a crucial goal. It set in train a period of Kerry dominance. Defenders Tomás and Marc Ó'Sé were flying while in attack Cooper and Bryan Sheehan were directing operations with military precision and the Dublin defence was all at sea.

In the next 5 minutes they extended their lead to 5 points and enjoyed a monopoly of possession and should have been further ahead. Eoin Brosnan made it a 6 point lead, 1-12 to 0-9, and there was little hint of a Dublin recovery. But it came, helped by an improved performance from Ciaran Whelan in midfield as Caffrey reshaped his attack in an effort to prise open the rock-solid

Declan O'Sullivan, Kerry, tries to get to the ball before Bryan Cullen, Dublin.
Dublin v Kerry. Football Semi-Final, Croke Park. 26 August 2007

Kerry defence.

Jason Sherlock was withdrawn and one wonders is this the last occasion 'Jayo' will be seen in the 'sky blue' Dublin jersey. Whelan helped Dublin win 7 successive kick-outs, prompting Kerry boss Pat O'Shea to re-introduce Dara

Ó'Sé after the Gaeltacht man received a pain-killing injection at half-time.

Bryan Cullen also played his part as a centre-back. His defending at times may be suspect, but going forward he is exceptional and he helped himself to 2 points as the 'Dubs' battled back. They

207

reeled Kerry in with 5 unanswered points and should have had a goal in the 58th minute but substitute Ray Cosgrove dragged his shot wide from close range. It was to prove one of the game's pivotal moments in a nail-biting second-half.

With the minimum between the sides a dreadful error by Dublin goalkeeper Cluxton, gave Kerry breathing space at a time when they were under the cosh. Forty metres from his own goal he gifted the ball to Kerry, who responded with a fisted point by Sean O'Sullivan. Minutes later Declan O'Sullivan stretched the lead to 3 and Dublin looked gone. They were not – yet! Cullen's second point and another by Conal Keaney whittled it down to 1 again, heading for injury-time, of which there would be 4 minutes.

Crucially Kerry won the kick-out. Donaghy in a roving role gobbled up possession of the breaking ball and after a sequence in which they patiently kept the ball, frustratingly for the Dublin players, it was eventually worked across the field and it fell to captain Declan O'Sullivan, who had an outstanding match, to hit the clinching point and extend Dublin's wait for a place in the final for another year at least. Kerry won a cracker by 2 points, 1-15 to 0-16.

| Kerry | 1-15 |
| Dublin | 0-16 |

Caffrey was very disappointed – 'it will take a long time to recover from this. It's a pretty sore dressing room in there right now.' As for his own position Caffrey was non-committal, 'that is for another day, my term is up but look, not now.' Within weeks of this game Caffrey was reappointed for another term by the Dublin county board.

Kerry's Pat O'Shea in his first year at the helm was delighted with the win, 'naturally we're thrilled. It was tough going out there especially without Dara, but we got there and now it's Cork in the final – something to look forward to.'

Yes, it was Cork v Kerry in the All-Ireland final. More accustomed to meeting in Páirc Uí Chaoimh or Fitzgerald Stadium for the Munster title, they would now go head-to-head in Croke Park with the biggest prize of all at stake.

It would make for an interesting few weeks along the famed county bounds, as Kerry go for their 35th title and Cork only their seventh.

For the winners there would be bragging rights, and for the losers a winter of avoiding the neighbours.

Clare manager Tony Considine gives
support to Brian O'Connell, Clare. Clare
v Antrim. Hurling Qualifier Round 1,
Casement Park, Belfast. 30 June 2007

21

Considine & Clare Controversy

THE BANNER COUNTY
IN THE NEWS AGAIN

The Banner County is no stranger to controversy when it comes to hurling. However, given the shenanigans of 2006, the people of Clare would be forgiven for thinking 2007 would be a quiet year. How wrong they were . . .

21 Considine & Clare Controversy

The Banner County in the News Again

Fitzgerald quits, Considine sacked in Clare

Exactly a year on from the Ger Loughnane saga, Clare hurling was once again embroiled in a fresh controversy. This time the key players were long-serving goalkeeper Davy Fitzgerald and newly appointed manager Tony Considine.

Considine, who acted as a selector under Loughnane before joining the 'media game', had been critical of some of the Clare players in his articles in the *Irish Examiner*. Therefore his appointment, after a long drawn-out process, did not perhaps meet with universal approval from the Banner County hurling fraternity.

However, there was general agreement that he (Considine) had assembled a strong backroom team which was unanimously approved at a Clare County Board meeting early last November.

Joining as selectors were Pat O'Connor, Ger Ward, Tim Crowe and Ciaran O'Neill – all highly respected within Clare hurling. The inclusion, though, of Dave Mahedy as team trainer was seen as a major coup as Mahedy's reputation is widespread. Overall, it was felt that the backroom team was now well equipped to take the team forward. All appointments were for a two-year term.

That optimism quickly dissipated as rumours soon circulated that all was not well in the camp. Most speculation centred on the theory that the manager and his high-profile goalkeeper were on a collision course.

It soon emerged that Fitzgerald was about to quit, not long after Clare had begun their pre-season training.

The background? In January the panel trained collectively on four nights a week, while they had a programme to work on in their own time for the other three days.

Fitzgerald had no problem with the amount of work involved; his difficulty was the time in which he had to do it in. He also wanted to focus on specialist goalkeeping drills, rather than running long distances three times a week. At 35, Fitzgerald also felt he needed extra time to recover from these sessions. But he didn't have it all his own way. In the background, it was apparent that his commitment to other teams was creating a problem.

In 2006 he had trained Liam

Limerick IT's Austin Murphy hugs manager Davy Fitzgerald during the cup presentation.
LIT v NUI Galway, Fitzgibbon Cup Final [Hurling], Dr Cullen Park, Carlow. 10 March 2007

Mellow's in Galway and was reappointed for this season. He was also involved with his own club, Sixmilebridge, and was once more back with Limerick IT who were bidding to win the prestigious Fitzgibbon Cup. The team management felt that such commitments were interfering with his Clare commitments and felt this lay behind his objection to training with them four nights a week.

Some players began to resent the early season latitude that Fitzgerald had been afforded by previous management teams, and privately objected when he returned in March and then proceeded to lecture the panel on the need for full commitment.

Fitzgerald's high-octane approach on match days was also unsettling teams but it was never broached by the players as they felt the goalkeeper was incapable of change.

With the rumour machine now in overdrive, the hype reached a crescendo when Fitzgerald did not feature in a Waterford Crystal Cup game against Tipperary, which Clare lost, thus giving credibility to the rumours. After the game, Considine declined to comment. The situation showed no sign of improving and matters finally came to a head after a training session in Ballyline on a Wednesday night. Fitzgerald voiced his concerns and he was bluntly told by Considine that he could take or leave the system. The two-time All Ireland winner stormed out of the dressing room, jumped into his car, weighed up his options and then stormed back into the dressing room and told Considine he could leave it.

In hindsight, that was a mistake by Fitzgerald. He had chosen to walk away and as Considine has repeatedly said since: 'his decision, his choice'. So the worst kept secret in hurling was now out in the open – folk hero Fitzgerald was no longer part of the Clare senior hurling panel.

From his first day in the job, Considine had declined to discuss players who were no longer part of the set-up, in particular Brian Lohan and Seanie McMahon, who had retired after the 2006 Championship, preferring to concentrate on the players that he was now working with. And in an interview with the *Irish Examiner*, Considine played his ace card, stating: 'it was entirely Davy's own decision, made for his own reason and it's something he has got to sort out himself.'

The next move now was to bring about reconciliation between the parties, but before that could happen, another bombshell was dropped into Considine's lap in the week before the NHL got underway.

Team trainer Mahedy had decided to withdraw from the backroom team citing business and work commitments as his reasons for stepping down – a reason not accepted as credible by many.

Mahedy was expected to stay on board for the full two years, but Considine said 'his involvement was only going to be for a six-week period', despite earlier giving assurances that he would be with the team in Down for the league game. Mahedy was not there and had actually given his last session to the team. Meanwhile, behind-the-scenes moves were underway to try and resolve the impasse with Fitzgerald. Considine made a move through County Board Secretary, Pat Fitzgerald, Davy's father. At that meeting Fitzgerald was told that the way back meant any return would be under Considine's terms only.

The pair had met once, not long after

Fitzgerald left the panel, but nothing came of it. But with Mahedy's departure Considine found the urge to communicate. In the midst of this mess, the Clare players continued to train away and vice-captain Gerry Quinn was put forward to relay the clear message that they were staying out of the issue and were quite happy with the direction in which the squad was moving.

In Mahedy's absence the physical training was taken over by selector Tim Crowe, a PE teacher by profession.

This threw up another sub-plot. Two years previously in 2005, when Fitzgerald was training his home club Sixmilebridge, he dropped 5 players from the panel who went to the Galway races the day after a Championship defeat. Among them was Niall Gilligan, a current Clare star, but so too was Cyril Crowe, Tim's son. It caused a huge split in the club and some members are still not on speaking terms as a result.

Could Fitzgerald return to the panel and now train under Crowe, who was and still is particularly reticent with Fitzgerald? Unlikely.

The Clare County Board then opened official communication channels, appointing a 3-man delegation consisting of Vice-Chairman Michael O'Neill, Treasurer Bernard Keane and Sixmilebridge's John Corbett. They met both parties separately one night, and while Fitzgerald was open to a meeting with Considine, the manager allegedly refused.

At a subsequent County Board meeting Corbett raised the matter and 'challenged the Board to do everything in its power to resolve the impasse.' Even RTÉ's Marty Morrissey offered himself as a mediator as the crisis deepened with the departure of 2 more players, Brian Shalley and Colin Lafferty, but both players confirmed that they were unable to give the required commitment.

A few days before the opening league game, Considine announced his panel of 33 players. Frank Lohan would captain the side and, not surprisingly, Fitzgerald was out. By this stage All-Star nominee Tony Carmody and actual All-Star Tony Griffin had also withdrawn from the panel for different reasons. Griffin decided to cycle across Canada in a bid to raise funds for cancer research, while Inagh man Carmody left the squad for personal reasons. The writing was on the wall for Clare already. With two top class forwards gone, where would their scores come from?

In the first round of the league, Clare easily defeated Down but 2 days after this temporary respite came another defection. This time in the shape of selector Ger Ward, who did not travel north to that match. Again it was put down to that old chestnut 'business commitments' but Ward, like Mahedy, was gone and would not return. The row at this stage was pure national media fodder and kept the papers brimming with news during the normally slow stage of the season. It took yet another twist when selector Tim Crowe lambasted 'these people' who are carrying out a 'witchhunt' to force Tony Considine to resign. Crowe, who stood by Considine throughout the saga, was scathing in his criticism of certain sections, in particular Marty Morrissey for comments written in a local newspaper column, in which Morrissey claimed that 5 major issues of conflict have occurred since Considine took the helm.

Crowe maintained 'that six weeks into the job an orchestrated and cunning attempt is being made to get him to resign, by a small section with a huge vested interest.'

'Hurling is a team sport, we have our training regime which is accepted by the 33 players on the panel, and there is no place for individual prima donnas.'

February moved into March and the row rumbled on. Once again mediation was mentioned, and at a County Board meeting a proposal by Fitzgerald's club Sixmilebridge that prominent local businessman Martin Lynch be approached was accepted.

However, it's understood Considine favoured one-to-one talks and was not enamoured with the idea of sitting down with a third party. So that move was all in vain. No subsequent meetings between the parties involved took place.

Clare's league campaign produced mixed results. In fairness new goalkeeper Philip Brennan performed well and could not be faulted, a point that Considine was keen to reiterate. When again asked about Fitzgerald, his reply was interesting. 'Are people still talking about that? That's over with now; Davy himself said he would not be back until next year, his words . . . not mine.'

Continuing, Considine said: 'hurling survived when Christy Ring and DJ Carey retired, and will continue to survive. As for Philip Brennan he is an excellent goalkeeper and that is why we brought him into the panel.'

Clare's league campaign ended with a home defeat to Cork in the final game. A combination of other results meant that they failed to make the play-off stages and would instead have to concentrate on challenge games in advance of the Championship. One of these brought about another problem.

A game had been arranged with Tipperary which was meant to be played behind closed doors. Even some of the players were unaware of who they were playing as they assembled for the match.

A local newspaper, *The Clare Champion*, found out about the match and wrote a report on the game. As a consequence, Considine instructed the players not to speak to the newspaper. Team captain Frank Lohan told a local journalist he was not allowed to talk when an interview with the captain was sought.

The Clare County Board officers were also not made aware that the game was actually taking place and this did little for relations between the manager and the officials, in particular Pat Fitzgerald, who was also the team's liaison officer.

With the team preparing to play Cork in the Munster Championship, relations between the parties showed no signs of easing. At a board meeting on May 3rd the manager's fate was discussed. Just as the meeting was about to get underway the assembled media were advised that they would not be allowed in for the duration of the debate.

A vote of 'no confidence' was proposed by Tony O'Brien of the Smith O'Brien's club. The motion evoked a lengthy debate but was eventually withdrawn without a vote being taken.

On hearing this, Considine expressed surprise, 'I am mystified where all this is coming from, who is orchestrating this. All I want to do is manage and prepare the team to play Cork. Let us concentrate on that and no more of this nonsense'.

Of course the Championship game with Cork brought its own problems (see Chapter 9). Apart from the defeat, the subsequent suspensions left Clare with a depleted team for their opening game in the qualifiers.

This was a tricky-looking trip to Belfast to play Antrim in the All-Ireland qualifiers and in keeping with events surrounding the team, it created more problems.

A round of games in the Clare Club Championship was scheduled for the week before the game and Considine sought to have these matches postponed.

However, his request was unanimously rejected at a County Board meeting on June 12. Coming just a short few weeks after the same board had discussed a vote of no confidence in the manager, they had dealt him another blow.

Indeed there was still anger in Clare about the Semplegate suspensions and there was even talk about withdrawing from the Guinness Championship, although such talk was rubbished by Considine who said they would be competing.

However, he was still angry with the decision not to postpone the games, giving him just 8 days to prepare for the trip to Belfast, and there was even a suggestion he would resign. 'A lot of things have gone on in the last 6 months but this is the worst as it affects preparation, and when you affect preparation, you affect everything else. There is someone orchestrating this and you don't have to be a genius to work out who it is.'

This is taken as a veiled reference to county secretary, Pat Fitzgerald who throughout the entire saga only made one comment and it was a telling one 'I have nothing to say at this point but when I do, I will have plenty to say.'

As it was, Considine did not resign and Clare continued their season of uncertainty.

In fairness, Considine and his players ignored the sideshows and went through the qualifying group unbeaten, which included a hugely significant win over Galway on a pretty tight-looking Cusack Park pitch!

This ensured they topped the group and instead of facing Kilkenny in the quarter-finals, they had a game, quite winnable at that, against neighbours Limerick in Croke Park.

But Clare played poorly and Limerick won easily enough. The curtain came down on Considine's first Championship campaign as Clare manager. Leaving Croke Park that evening, little did he realise that it would also be his last. Or did he? Because it was felt by some that even if Clare won the All-Ireland, Considine would not survive.

Interviewed after the game the manager said: 'It's disappointing but we did not play well enough, and best wishes to Limerick in the semi-final.'

Asked about his future: 'Ah sure we will give it a few weeks; think about it and see what happens. I was given a two-year term and I would like to see that through.'

All that changed at the August meeting of the Clare County Board, when a recommendation from the Executive Committee that he be replaced was passed by 45 votes to 6.

Considine was out of the country on holidays and was only made aware of the decision when a friend phoned him. Naturally he was furious at the way the issue was handled and let rip at the officers, describing them as operating a 'Kangaroo Court'.

Clare manager Tony Considine shakes hands with Galway manager Ger Loughnane after the final whistle. Clare v Galway, Hurlilng Qualifier Round 2, Cusack Park, Ennis. 7 July 2007

'It was well set up and thought out. It's a mafia-style thing and there is no room for it in sport and definitely not in the GAA.'

'They had people to do the execution inside. They had told the people inside to do it or they would be executed themselves. It's a power thing.'

He found support in some quarters, among them former GAA President Sean Kelly, also writing in the *Irish Examiner*. Kelly said: 'Tony was abroad on holidays. Why wasn't he given an opportunity to put his case. Everyone is entitled to have his side of the story put. I am amazed that the Clare County Board didn't insist on hearing the man before dumping him.'

A few days after, outgoing selector Tim Crowe went further and called for the Clare County Board to step down and for GAA President Nickey Brennan to investigate the circumstances that led to Considine's sacking.

In a strongly worded statement Crowe was vitriolic in his criticism of the Clare County Board. 'Given what happened last week I think any fair minded Clare people need to know what happened in that kangaroo court, because it could have long-term implications for the future development of hurling in the county.'

Crowe went even further and called for the board officers to step aside, 'because the time is right for a change, the handling of this confirms that the GAA in Clare is in a shambolic state, and the people on top do not have the best interest of Clare hurling at heart. Tony's record is comparable with any manager since 1997, and we need a new beginning with people who have vision, ability and no allegiances, if we are to enjoy more glory in the years ahead', he concluded.

Considine himself said, 'life goes on and I will probably get involved with hurling again at some stage, but I tell you whoever takes over the job of Clare manager better "mind his back"' – a parting shot from a man who had a traumatic few months at the helm.

The County Board, for their part, were slow to comment, but Chairman Michael McDonagh did eventually answer some of the criticism directed at the officers. 'I backed the manager in all instances during the year but there was just one problem after another.' McDonagh insisted he acted properly all the way through. 'I made no phone calls to any club or anyone prior to last Tuesday's (Considine's sacking) meeting.'

So a saga that began on a cold Wednesday evening in Ballyline when Davy Fitzgerald walked away, ended in a room in Ennis with an inevitable conclusion: the sacking of Tony Considine.

At the September meeting of the Clare county board, Mike McNamara waas appointed as the new Clare hurling manager in succession to Tony Considine. At the same meeting Frank Doherty was appointed as football manager to replace Paidí O'Shea.

Roscommon's Alan Cunniffe leaves the field holding the Nicky Rackard cup as, in the background, the Dublin football team take to the pitch before their game with Derry. Roscommon v Armagh. Nicky Rackard Cup Final [Hurling], Croke Park. 11 August 2007.

22

The Cup Competitions

ROSCOMMON, WICKLOW,
WESTMEATH PREVAIL

*The Cup Competitions – Nicky Rackard,
Tommy Murphy and Christy Ring –
have varying levels of support among
GAA fans. Nonetheless, all three
competitions threw up some exciting
encounters – not least by teams looking to
regain lost pride after some harsh
Championship encounters.*

22 The Cup Competitions

Roscommon, Wicklow, Westmeath prevail

Glory for minnows in Cups

The recently-introduced cup competitions in hurling and football are a welcome addition to the GAA calendar, especially the Christy Ring and Nicky Rackard Cups in hurling.

The Tommy Murphy Cup in football has been greeted with mixed reaction and the reluctance of some players to play in the competition has called into question its continued existence.

This fact was acknowledged by GAA President Nickey Brennan in his programme notes for this year's final, when he felt 'the negative publicity generated was not good for the image of the Cup.'

It had also been decided early in 2007 that teams who will compete in Division 4 of the 2008 National League would have to play in the Tommy Murphy Cup and not the Championship qualifiers, which did little to generate interest among the counties affected. Offaly, for instance were Leinster finalists in 2006 and were now confined to the Cup, while Mick O'Dwyer, a man who enjoyed great days in the Championship, was also unhappy about Wicklow's exclusion from the qualifiers.

The apathy towards the competition is reflected in the fact that for their trip to Dungarvan, Carlow could only muster 17 players, while as soon as Clare exited the competition Páidí Ó'Sé immediately resigned as manager. Indeed there is a suggestion now that the competition will be axed next season in favour of a return to the qualifiers for all 32 counties, a possible short-lived existence then for the much maligned Tommy Murphy Cup.

By contrast the Ring and Rackard Cups have been an unqualified success, even if the gap between these and the Liam McCarthy participants still exists.

Nicky Rackard Cup

This competition is confined to teams in Divisions 3 and 4 of the National Hurling League and the format was unchanged from previous years. Four groups of 3, with the top 2 in each section to qualify for the quarter-finals. Among the 12 counties participating were Roscommon, who last year suffered a humiliating hammering from Antrim (9-39 to 0-5) and subsequent relegation from the Christy Ring Cup, and Warwickshire.

The group games were pretty clearcut containing no real surprises and when the dust settled, the quarter-finals were down for decision on July 14. Roscommon, competing at their own level once again, easily defeated Monaghan 4-19 to 1-8, while Warwickshire's season came to an end at the hands of Louth, who ran out easy winners 4-26 to 1-3. Donegal, runners-up in 2006, made it back to the semi-finals with a 2-14 to 2-8 win over Louth, while in the all-Ulster clash between counties more accustomed to meeting in football, Armagh got the better of Tyrone on a 2-19 to 1-9 scoreline.

The semi-finals were scheduled for a week later and there was no doubting the merits of the winners. Roscommon trashed Louth 2-13 to 0-5, while Armagh had an emphatic win over Donegal, running up an impressive 3-28 in the process while conceding just 2-10.

The stage was then set for a unique final and the hurlers of Armagh and Roscommon would get their day in Croke Park on Saturday August 11 as a curtain raiser to Dublin and Derry in football.

It produced a lively contest which was settled by the game's only goal which arrived in 43rd minute. Armagh made the better start and opened up an early 0-5 to 0-2 lead, but they also hit 6 wides in that period and also made life easy for the 'Rossie's' goalkeeper David Connell who dealt with a few weak efforts with confidence. Roscommon battled away and the free-taking of Shane Sweeney ensured it was all square 0-6 each at half-time.

David McConn has been responsible for the resurgence in Roscommon hurling and the manager made two big calls that shaped the outcome of the contest. For the second-half he introduced Gary Fallon and also switched Sweeney to midfield in an effort to break Armagh's grip, both moves worked.

The sides continued to trade points up to the 43rd minute, when John Moran's delivery wasn't dealt with by Armagh goalkeeper Joby Burke and up stepped Fallon who flicked the loose ball to the net. Roscommon were in front and there they stayed.

It was tough on Armagh who hurled well for the 70 minutes and in Declan Coulter and Ryan Gaffney they possess quality hurlers whose efforts deserved better.

Roscommon ran out winners by 2 points, 1-12 to 0-13, and in the process completed a nice treble of under-21 'B' Championship, National Hurling

225

League Division 3 and now the Nicky Rackard Cup – a far cry from 2006 when they were at rock bottom.

It was a proud captain Mervyn Connaughton who accepted the Cup from GAA President Nickey Brennan and an equally special day for Roscommon hurling folk, none more so than Athleague's Johnny Haughey who has dedicated over 60 years to the promotion of hurling in a county that is dominated by football.

It may be the lower tier of hurling but Roscommon and Armagh played their part in an entertaining final and also achieved their goal of qualifying for 2008's Christy Ring Cup and with it, respectability.

Nicky Rackard Cup Final	
Roscommon	1-12
Armagh	0-13

Tommy Murphy Cup

Eight teams in this competition meant it was easy enough to run off over a 3 week period. As with the hurling finals it would culminate in Croke Park on August 4, to be followed by 2 quarter-finals in the Bank of Ireland Championship.

It all began on July 7 following the completion of the early rounds of the respective provincial Championships, and there was a few interesting pairings in the first round.

Carlow made the trip to Dungarvan with a very depleted team and were walloped by John Kiely's Waterford, who for the first time in their history lashed in 8 goals and tacked on 10 points for good measure, while in reply the team with the distinctive colour jerseys could only register 7 points.

Páidí Ó'Sé took his Clare team to play Ardfinnan in Tipperary and in a tightly contested game emerged winners by 1-13 to 0-12. This game also marked the end of Declan Browne's inter-county career. Generally recognised as one of the game's outstanding footballers, Browne, at 29 years of age, felt it was time to go, and he left a rich legacy behind. The Moyle Rovers' man won 2 All-Star awards, a unique achievement for a Tipperary footballer and also had the honour, richly deserved, of captaining his county to Tommy Murphy Cup glory in Croke Park in 2005.

Antrim had a comfortable win over London by 4-11 to 1-10, while Mick O'Dwyer's first association with the competition was a winning one as his Wicklow side defeated Leinster rivals Offaly by 5 points, 1-16 to 1-11. After this

Mick O'Dwyer celebrates with temporary Wicklow manager Arthur French after Wicklow won the Tommy Murphy Cup Final [Football]. Wicklow v Antrim. Croke Park. 4 August 2007.

loss John Crofton stepped aside as manager of Kildare.

A week later on July 14, the curtain came down on Páidí Ó'Sé's tenure in Clare as his side suffered a shock 1-11 to 0-10 defeat to Antrim in the semi-final.

Wicklow's summer was extended further when they reached the final with a good win over Waterford, 2-15 to 0-14, and once again the genial Micko was back in a final. It may not have been the

one he wanted, but for Wicklow any appearance in a final was welcome.

Croke Park has often been the graveyard of Wicklow dreams but on this particular occasion, the Garden County men left the stadium with the sweet smell of victory in their nostrils and in dramatic circumstances at that. Antrim made the brighter start but could only muster 1 point and that after 27 seconds, as the Wicklow defence, in particular corner-backs Ciaran Hyland and Alan Byrne, excelled at repelling waves of Antrim attacks. Wicklow, taking their cue from the excellence of their defence, improved and struck for a crucial goal on 15 minutes. Tommy Gill and Don Jackman did the spadework and Derek Daly rifled home the first goal.

Midfielders James Stafford and Thomas Walsh were magnificent and it came as no surprise that they conjured up a second goal. Tony Hannon waltzed through the porous Antrim defence, delivered a pinpoint pass to Leighton Glynn who made no mistake and with 25 minutes gone Wicklow had a 6-point lead, 2-3 to 0-3.

Antrim introduced Michael Magill and his influence helped swing the game his side's way. Points from Conor McGourty and Michael McCann saw the gap reduced to 2-5 to 0-8 at half-time.

In the second-half Wicklow stretched their lead to 4 points, but Antrim never gave up and battled away throughout a gripping 35 minutes that produced some fine passages of play.

With the sands of time running out Antrim's persistence was rewarded when they won a penalty for a foul on Kevin Brady. McGourty held his nerve to narrow the gap to the bare minimum. Two minutes into injury-time, they forced the game into extra-time when McGann landed the levelling point, 2-12 to 1-15. Much to the delight of the saffron supporters their dreams of glory was very much alive. Not so happy were the Cork and Sligo teams who now had to wait almost 30 minutes for their game to begin.

As often happens in extra-time, tiredness sets in and scores are scarce, so it came as no surprise that at the end of the first period it was still level 1-16 to 2-13. Would there be a winner at all or in keeping with Wicklow's season would it require a replay? Remember they were involved in 2 replays in the Leinster Championship.

Three minutes into the second period Antrim got their noses in front with a point and for all their efforts it looked like heartbreak again for Wicklow. In the energy-sapping heat the game had slipped into the second of the 2 minutes of added time at the end of extra-time, and there was to be one final twist. Wicklow came in search of the levelling point. Leighton Gill pumped the ball high in the direction of the Antrim goal. Stafford fielded it and fed Captain Tommy Gill, who seconds before had missed a simple free that would have tied the game. This time he made no mistake and with the Antrim defence awol, he blasted the ball past Sean McGreevey for the winning goal, 3-13 to 1-17 – from villain to hero in seconds! The joys of sport!

It was the final act of a dramatic decider and cruel on a gallant Antrim team who had one hand on the Cup but somehow let it slip agonisingly from their grasp.

Gill climbed the steps to end the long wait for Wicklow as Micko celebrated with his backroom team, in particular Arthur French who assumed the role of manager after the genial Waterville ace took ill during the season, which limited his role for a while.

In reference to his health problems Micko said, 'it was a wonderful way to win, but it's not good for the heart I can tell you.'

He has won the highest honours in the game with the most decorated football county of the lot – his native Kerry, but he derived tremendous satisfaction from this win, and why not? It was a great day for Wicklow football and they rightly celebrated in style.

Tommy Murphy Cup Final result Wicklow 3-13 Antrim 1-17 (aet).

Tommy Murphy Cup Final (AET)	
Wicklow	3-13
Antrim	1-17

Christy Ring Cup

Confined to teams in Division 2, only 8 counties took part this year and there was annoyance that a Special Congress last year decided that for the winners there would be no promotion to the top tier of hurling in 2008.

Two groups of 4, with the top 2 in each qualifying for the semi-finals. Westmeath winners in 2005 were defending an unbeaten run in the competition while London, 2006's champions, were hoping to replicate that success.

There were some exciting games in the group stages. Westmeath had a narrow win over resurgent Down, 2-13 to 1-15. It was a defeat that proved costly for the Ulster side. Neighbours Meath and Westmeath also played out a thrilling draw. It finished Meath 2-16 Westmeath 1-19. The fact that both had already guaranteed semi-final spots did not lessen the intensity of an exciting contest.

It was much clearer in the second group and even a loss to Carlow did not prevent Kildare from joining their Leinster neighbours in the semi-final. Both games were down for decision on July 21 in O'Connor Park, Tullamore, and Kildare caused a major upset when they had a narrow but deserved win over a fancied Meath side. They did not help their cause with some wayward shooting but a goal by Brendan Byrne gave them an interval lead of 1-9 to 1-7.

It was a keenly contested second-half and on occasions Meath threatened to make it a second successive semi-final defeat for Kildare but in an exciting finish the Lily Whites held on to win 1-14 to 1-13 to reach their first major hurling final. Billy White made a major contribution with a personal tally of 6 points, carrying on his good form of last year in which he also racked up some impressive totals.

Westmeath looked in control of their semi-final with Carlow, when 2 goals by John Shaw and another by full-forward Daniel Carty helped them to a commanding 11-point interval advantage. Carlow, though, staged a tremendous comeback and with 20 minutes gone in the second-half they had drawn level, thanks to goals from Robert Foley and Craig Doyle. They looked in a winning position, having briefly taken the lead. However, Westmeath did not panic. Instead, they regrouped and their greater experience at this level of competition surfaced. Corner-forward Derek McNicholas struck home a goal; midfielder Pat Clarke tacked on a point as the challenge of 14-man Carlow faded.

Westmeath held on 4-11 to 2-15 to reach their second final in 3 years and it would be an all-Leinster decider against Kildare.

The final was fixed for Sunday August 5 on the same bill as the semi-final clash of Wexford and Kilkenny and the Cork v Waterford replay. However the throw-in time of 12.15pm upset Westmeath boss Seamus Qualter who described it as a 'kick in the teeth, it's the same old story. They'll look after the big boys and have no regard for the smaller counties despite all the work we are doing for hurling.'

It may have been an early start but it did not affect the men from the Lake County who won a disappointing contest in which Kildare, for all their effort and it was significant, never looked like winning. Westmeath led 0-4 to 0-1 early on and the writing was on the wall for Kildare following the game's first goal which came courtesy of John Shaw in the 15th minute. The sides swapped points, and then the result was written in tablets of stone when in the 23rd minute a dreadful mix-up between Kildare goalkeeper and defender Ronan Tynan allowed Andrew Mitchell in for goal number 2. That left it 2-7 to 0-3 for Westmeath at half-time and even the gathering supporters for the 2 big games

Westmeath captain Darren McCormack, with GAA President Nickey Brennan in the background, lifts the Christy Ring Cup at Croke Park. Westmeath v Kildare. Christy Ring Cup Final [Hurling]. 5 August 2007

were finding it hard to maintain interest in a drab encounter.

It got worse for Kildare on the resumption as Westmeath extended their lead to 2-11 to 0-4 and up in the Hogan Stand the 'maroon and white' ribbons were already on the Cup. Kildare did get a run of a few points from Billy White, Paddy O'Brien and Mattie Dowd but they merely took the bare look off the scoreboard that read 2-15 to 0-13 with Barry Kennedy's late point for Westmeath, thus giving wing-back Darren McCormack the honour of lifting the Christy Ring Cup and becoming the second Westmeath man to accomplish that feat.

Christy Ring Cup Final	
Westmeath	2-15
Kildare	0-13

Qualter acknowledged afterwards that the goals decided the game, 'they put a bit of daylight between us and once we did not concede a goal we were always comfortable.'

A couple of days after this win it was announced that Westmeath will compete in next year's Leinster hurling Championship. They can also defend their Christy Ring Cup, but are still disappointed at being excluded from the Liam McCarthy Cup. Their hopes for 2008 were dealt a blow, though, by mid August when manager Seamus Qualter resigned his position and it shocked the hurling fraternity in the county. Qualter was at the helm for 4 years and it was a successful period for the county, winning the Christy Ring Cup twice and a number of creditable displays in the Leinster Championship, including a shock win over Dublin, and in the qualifiers against Kilkenny and Waterford.

The Galway native served as a player, selector and finally as a manager and he leaves hurling in Westmeath in a far healthier state than when he took over in difficult circumstances from Tom Ryan in 2005.

The Cup competitions for 2007 were complete and it was now celebration time for the hurlers of Westmeath and Roscommon and the footballers of Wicklow, to shorten the winter in these counties.

Aidan Fogarty, Kilkenny, is quickest to catch a breaking ball, chased by Seamus Hickey, No 4, and Stephen Lucey, Limerick. Kilkenny v Limerick. All-Ireland Hurling Final, Croke Park. 2 September 2007

23

Kilkenny
v
Limerick

HURLING FINAL

*Could the impossible happen? Could this
David v Goliath battle provide the shock
of the season as eager hopefuls Limerick
made their way to GAA HQ to take on
the team that utterly dominates hurling
in today's game?*

23 Kilkenny v Limerick

Hurling Final

Can 'Cats' take Title?

Hurling's biggest day dawned on the first Sunday in September, the Guinness All-Ireland Final, with Kilkenny bidding to retain the title and Limerick hoping to bridge a long gap, 1973, since their last success. It was also the first meeting of the counties in a final since 1974, which Kilkenny won having lost 12 months previously to the Shannonsiders. Incidentally the respective managers, Brian Cody and Richie Bennis, played in that final.

It was a damp and dull morning in Dublin as the respective supporters descended on the capital. Many from Limerick were up since Saturday, but in keeping with tradition the majority of Kilkenny supporters arrived on the morning of the game. Tickets that were so scarce all week now seemed to be in plentiful supply and the demands of most were met. The attendance was almost capacity at 82,127. There was a hint of rain in the air as inside the stadium the pre-match routine of so many was underway – stewards, first-aid officials and gardaí – before it was gates open and let the action get underway.

Cork and Tipperary met in the ESB All-Ireland Minor Hurling Final and it was victory for the young men in blue and gold trained by Tommy Dunne and Declan Ryan. Sean Carey and Robert White traded first-half goals as Tipperary led 1-9 to 1-6 at half-time.

Michael Heffernan got a second goal for Tipperary on the resumption, giving them a commanding lead. Late on Carey and Luke Farrell for Cork had further goals but by then the Irish Press Cup was heading to the Premier County for the 18th time, on a 3-14 to 2-11 scoreline.

It also meant Tipperary joined Cork and Kilkenny at the top of the roll of honour and they also won back-to-back titles for the first time since 1953 in this first ever meeting between the counties in a minor All-Ireland final.

The hour of reckoning was drawing ever nearer as the build-up continued with the introduction of the Kilkenny jubilee team of 1982/83 to the crowd by RTÉ's Marty Morrissey. Familiar names back in a stadium that is much changed from the time when this team won successive titles – Fennelly, Henderson, Fitzpatrick, Ruth, Cummins – household names in Kilkenny. A special day also for GAA President Nickey Brennan a member of the 1982 team who was

Eoin Larkin, Kilkenny, tries to retain the ball, chased by Peter Lawlor, Limerick.
Kilkenny v Limerick. All-Ireland Hurling Final, Croke Park. 2 September 2007

accorded a rousing reception from supporters of both teams.

The Liam McCarthy Cup is placed on a podium on the edge of the pitch and the teams will pass it as they race onto the green sward that is Croke Park. No problems with the pitch this year which is a tribute to the hard working and efficient ground staff.

At 3.05pm champions Kilkenny arrive on the field to a huge roar, but at 3.07pm when the men of Limerick enter the arena, the decibel levels almost lift the roof off the stadium. It seems as if everyone from the Treaty City and County is in the ground, but only 15 at any one time can play. Uachtarán na hÉireann, Mary McAleese, and her husband Martin arrive and are introduced to the teams. The parade follows. *Amhrán na bhFiann* is sung by Paul Byrom as the clock moves ever nearer to throw-in time. Taoiseach Bertie Ahern was in his seat for the minor

237

game.

A special day also for referee Diarmuid Kirwan from Cork officiating at his first final, emulating his father Gerry who refereed the 1988 decider between Galway and Tipperary. Interestingly Limerick goalkeeper Brian Murray's father Terence was also a former inter-county referee and took charge of the finals of 1987 and 1993.

Pre-match predictions were that Kilkenny would carry too much firepower and experience for Limerick, but manager Richie Bennis said, 'we are not coming up just for the final, we are here to win.' Kilkenny boss Brian Cody was cautious but confident that 'if we play well we will be in a good position to win.'

Bennis had announced an unchanged team from that which beat Waterford in the semi-final. Kilkenny goalkeeper PJ Ryan was passed fit after an anxious few weeks with a hand injury, as Willie O'Dwyer got the nod ahead of Richie Power in attack.

At 3.30pm the game got underway and a hesitant start for Limerick as the tension of the occasion got to them. Only 2 players Ollie Moran and Mark Foley have played in an All-Ireland final. Even the reliable Andrew O'Shaughnessy missed an easy free; it did little to calm the nerves.

No such problems for Kilkenny. Captain Henry Shefflin, operating at full-forward, as he fired over a free. In the next attack Eoin Larkin scored from play. Both sides missed a couple of chances and Limerick were under increasing pressure as Tommy Walsh and Michael Kavanagh were on top in defence. Then in the space of 60 seconds this game was turned on its head and Limerick were dealt a double blow.

With 9 minutes gone Walsh's sideline cut was grabbed by Eddie Brennan who ghosted past Seamus Hickey and struck a powerful shot to the corner of the net passed a helpless Murray. It immediately got worse for Limerick. Kilkenny won the puck-out and James 'Cha' Fitzpatrick hoisted the *sliotar* in the direction of Shefflin, who grabbed it and despite the close attention of Stephen Lucey, the man they call 'King Henry' batted the ball to the net. Larkin added a point. With just 10 minutes gone the score read Kilkenny 2-3 Limerick 0-0 – shades of Kerry and Mayo in last year's football final.

Throughout the Championship Limerick have displayed remarkable resilience. If ever it was needed, now was the time and to their credit they were not found wanting. In the next 8 minutes they outscored Kilkenny by 5 points to 1, with centre-forward Ollie Moran leading the charge as he landed 2 brilliant scores. Kilkenny were dealt a blow when full-back Noel Hickey went off with a hamstring injury that had made him doubtful in the build-up to the game. A re-shuffle as John Tennyson came in at centre-back with Brian Hogan going to full-back and normal service was quickly resumed. Larkin, Brennan and Shefflin scored points and Kilkenny were still 8 ahead. In the closing 10 minutes of the first-half, the sides share 6 points, 5 from play including one from Kilkenny wing-back Tommy Walsh. As the teams disappear under the tunnel for half-time the champions are in control 2-10 to 0-8.

The half-time entertainment was provided by Frankie Gavin and Hibernian Rhapsody. There is little doubt that the supporters in 'black and amber' enjoyed it more then their worried counterparts in 'green and white'. It was generally accepted that the champions were just 35 minutes away from their 30th title. Limerick for all their bravery were finding it difficult to break down a resolute Kilkenny side who were playing with their usual power and intensity.

A slight chance, though, with the news from the dressing rooms that

Darragh McGarry, son of James and late Vanessa, assists Kilkenny captain, Henry Shefflin in lifting the Liam McCarthy Cup. Kilkenny v Limerick. All-Ireland Hurling Final, Croke Park. 2 September 2007

Shefflin was out of the second-half with a suspected cruciate knee ligament injury, Michael Fennelly would take his place. Limerick started well and O'Shaughnessy and Niall Moran landed points, but worryingly their inside line of

O'Shaughnessy, Brian Begley and Donie Ryan were making little impact. In fact all three failed to score from play.

Richie Power was introduced after 26 minutes for the ineffective O'Dwyer and he assumed the free-taking duties in Shefflin's absence. He duly converted the next 3 and it was now 2-13 to 0-10. A gap of 9 points – a comfortable lead for Kilkenny and even the massive Limerick support was losing heart.

Suddenly they were thrown a lifeline when their best player, Ollie Moran, lashed in a fine goal, 2-13 to 1-10. The next score was vital. Crucially it went to Kilkenny as Walsh fired over his second point of the game. O'Shaughnessy landed another free to keep his side within touching distance but was it enough? Apparently not, as Fitzpatrick and Fogarty landed points for Kilkenny, who still held an 8-point lead.

A pivotal moment in the 55th minute when Limerick won a free. Up stepped O'Shaughnessy and his powerful shot was deflected around the post by JJ Delaney. The resultant '65' was missed and it looked as if Limerick's last chance was gone. To their credit they got the next 3 points as Bennis re-jigged his team with a couple of substitutions and they had now reduced the deficit to 5 points, 2-16 to 1-14.

Would there be a grandstand finish to a final that ever since the 2 goal salvo in the 9th minute was heading in only one direction? That course was not altered. Kilkenny battened down the hatches, confined Limerick to just 1 more point, while Power and Brennan with 2, closed the game out. As referee Kirwan sounded the final whistle of the 2007 Guinness Hurling Championship, Kilkenny were celebrating again, winners by 7 points, 2-19 to 1-15.

| Kilkenny | 2-19 |
| Limerick | 1-15 |

Cody punched the air and embraced his injured captain Shefflin as the players from both sides acknowledged the result. The Kilkenny supporters brushed the stewards aside to race on and greet their heroes. Shefflin hobbled up the steps to be met by another proud Kilkenny man, Nickey Brennan. As the presentation got underway they were joined by two special people, James McGarry and his son Darragh, still grieving at the loss of Vanessa in a tragic road accident a short few weeks earlier.

Nickey performed his duty and handed the Liam McCarthy Cup to Henry who immediately turned to Darragh and in a hugely significant

**Kilkenny manager, Brian Cody celebrates with Henry Shefflin after the game.
Kilkenny v Limerick. All-Ireland Hurling Final, Croke Park. 2 September 2007**

gesture the young lad with tears streaming down his face raised the precious cup high into the September sky.

In his wonderfully eloquent speech Shefflin paid tribute to all involved with this special team, had words of praise for Limerick and his own manager Brian Cody, before striking a chord with the thousands still in the stadium. This win he said, 'is dedicated to Vanessa McGarry who was very much a part of the Kilkenny set-up. She is not here to-day but she is with us in spirit. James may not have an all-star at home but to us he is a special star and we are very proud of the part he has played with this team.'

Head bowed, James acknowledged Henry's word with a nod. Nickey Brennan gave him a tap on the back, while the Kilkenny supporters chanted his name 'McGarry, McGarry' as a slight smile slipped across the face of a proud Darragh.

It was a poignant moment on what was an emotional occasion.

In the bowels of the stadium as the *Rose of Mooncoin* was being sung with gusto from the winners' dressing-room, Brian Cody spoke to the assembled media. 'It means everything to us, it's a terrific feeling, great craic really what else would you be doing, the team, the supporters are fantastic, there is an honesty and genuineness in our team and that's what drives us on.' Before finishing he had a go at Ger Loughnane for his remarks about this team, 'he praised us often enough, and now suddenly we are a dirty team. That is terribly wrong, we are respected by our opponents far and wide and we accept defeat in the same way we celebrate victory.' And then he was off, no doubt to join in the singing, a happy man.

As for Limerick, Richie Bennis was as honest as he has been all year in his assessment – 'the early goals killed us. We were playing catch up after that, but at least we gave it our best shot. We will drown our sorrows, regroup and hopefully come back stronger next year.

We will benefit from the experience gained today, and I am very proud of my players – they never gave up.'

Twenty-four hours later the respective teams began the journey home. Over 15,000 greeted gallant Limerick in O'Connell Street and vowed they would be back.

Champions Kilkenny were welcomed home by over 20,000 in Market Street, their fifth victory parade of Cody's reign. They were now level with Cork on 30 titles and already thoughts of players and supporters alike were turning to 2008 and the 3-in-a-row.

That's the beauty of sport – the next challenge awaits.

The 2007 All-Ireland Hurling Champions – Kilkenny . . . sounds familiar!

Note: The final marked the end of Guinness' sponsorship of the hurling championship, which in 2008 will have a new format. The group stages are no longer, Galway and Antrim will meet in a first-round tie, the Leinster and Munster champions will go directly to the All-Ireland semi-finals, which means 2 instead of 4 quarter-finals in 2008.

Colm Cooper, Kerry, tries to shake off
the tackle of Graham Canty, Cork.
Kerry v Cork. All-Ireland Football
Final, Croke Park, 16 September 2007

24

Kerry
v
Cork

*Two neighbours – one cup. It was an
all-Munster affair in Croke Park
for the 2007 Bank of Ireland football
final. Cork began their quest to take
Sam out of Kerry hands.
Kerry, however, had other ideas.*

24 Kerry v Cork

Historic Football Final

Historic Pairing

It was billed as the game that would define history, Munster's keenest footballing rivals, Cork and Kerry, meeting in the 2007 Bank of Ireland All-Ireland Football final, with more than just bragging rights at stake.

For Kerry, the reigning champions and with 34 All-Ireland titles, 'losing was not an option' according to one player, while for Cork a win would put them in credit for a long time to come.

The build-up was intense. It may not have captured the imagination of the public nationwide, but along the Cork/Kerry border they were enjoying the occasion.

Baile Mhuirne in Cork, Rathmore in Kerry are hotbeds of football and in Ballydesmond, another village straddling the border, the excitement was mounting, as the GAA club here draws its players from both sides of the famed 'county bounds'.

Kerry were favourites, appearing in their fourth successive final and bidding to become the first team since Cork in 1989/90 to put titles back to back. It was no real surprise when manager Pat O'Shea named an unchanged team from the semi-final win over Dublin.

Cork were dealt a blow 8 days before the game when experienced defender Anthony Lynch suffered a hand injury in training, which almost certainly ruled him out of the final.

Billy Morgan delayed his team announcement for 48 hours, but it made no difference. Lynch was out, but on the plus side James Masters, who missed the semi-final win over Meath, was back.

Dublin on All-Ireland day is special and this was no exception as the supporters from Munster made their way to the capital. More accustomed to gathering in Killarney under the Magillicuddy Reeks or by the Banks of the Lee in Cork, fans in O'Connell Street provided a sea of colour and at first glance, 'green and gold' was dominant.

As always on football final day, the quest for tickets was relentless. While most were accommodated, it is a tribute to both counties that despite earlier predictions, the attendance was 82,126. A repeat of the pairing in the Munster final it may have been, but this was different.

Cork and Kerry enjoy a healthy rivalry but there was a nervous tension around the place, particularly from the

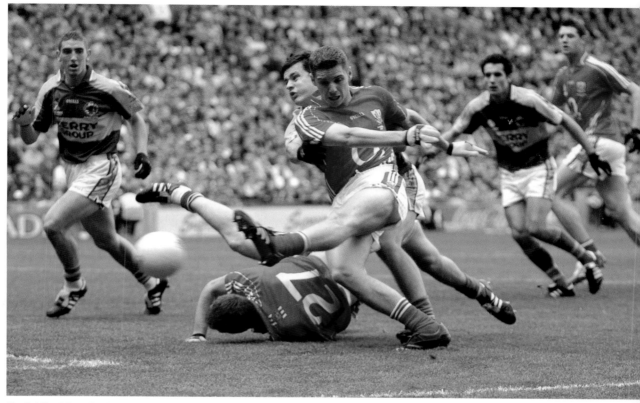

**Daniel Goulding, Cork, scores his goal against Kerry despite the tackle of Pádraig Reidy.
Kerry v Cork. All-Ireland Football Final, Croke Park, 16 September 2007**

Kerry supporters as the pressure to avoid defeat was huge. For Cork it was pressure of a different kind – to end a run of poor results against their neighbours in Croke Park.

Opinion was divided on the likely outcome although the 'experts' felt Kerry's big match experience would swing the game the way of the Kingdom.

Weather conditions were favourable despite a grey leaden-filled sky spilling early morning rain. By throw-in time a light freshening breeze and sunshine

had descended on HQ.

The traditional pre-match pageantry gave way to the ESB Minor Final and the young players from Galway and Derry served up a cracking contest.

Gavin McGeehan's goal gave Derry an early advantage that they held until the 57th minute, when Galway corner-forward Damien Reddington scored a smashing goal and the Connacht champions were in front for the first time. Derry fought desperately to save the game but in a welter of excitement

Galway hung on to win by one point, 1-10 to 1-9.

It was a proud Paul Conroy who accepted the Tom Markham Cup from Patron of the GAA, Archbishop Dr Dermot Clifford. Conroy was the sixth Galway captain to lift the famous cup, and it was the county's first win in the minor Championship since 1986.

A special moment then arrived for the Jubilee team and in an ironic twist it was the Offaly footballers of 1982 who were being introduced to the crowd. Back then a late Seamus Darby goal denied Kerry a historic fifth successive title. All credit to the huge Kerry support in the stadium, the Offaly footballers were very warmly received.

The names and the memories came flooding back as the several brothers on the team were given a huge welcome – the Lowrys, Fitzgeralds, Connors along with Martin Furlong, Liam Currams and a host of household names. However there was, Darby apart, a special welcome for that prince of footballers Matt Connor now confined to a wheelchair following a car accident some years ago.

Throw-in time was now little over 30 minutes away as the Cork team made their way onto the field, led by captain Derek Kavanagh. In an unusual move, instead of bursting past the line of stewards and the Sam Maguire Cup, which had been placed on a pedestal in front of the Hogan Stand, they calmly walked to the bench in the middle of the field for the army of photographers lined up on the opposite side of the field. A statement of intent, that they were ready for the task ahead.

Minutes later Declan O'Sullivan and his colleagues raced out from the tunnel to a tumultuous roar, confirming both the arrival of the champions and that the Kerry supporters had travelled in numbers.

To the strains of '*The Star of the County Down*', Uachtarán na h-Éireann Mary McAleese was then introduced to the teams and match officials. The pre-match parade followed, as just before 3.30pm Cork-based but Dublin-born Elaine Canning backed by the Artane School of Music sang *Amhráin na bFhiann.*

Minutes later with the watching crowd holding its breath in anticipation referee Dave Coldrick got the 100th Championship clash between the counties underway.

There was a tense and nervous opening to the game and the tactical switches were quickly noted. Defensively Kerry detailed Aidan O'Mahoney to mark Kevin McMahon, while Tomás

Kerry players [left to right] Mike Frank Russell, Colm Cooper and Kieran Donaghy celebrate after the match. Kerry v Cork. All-Ireland Football Final, Croke Park, 16 September 2007

Ó'Sé was given the task of curbing Pearse O'Neill – both Cork players were very effective in the semi-final win over Meath.

Midfield quickly resembled 'Times Square' at rush hour such was its congested area, with Kerry determined to deny Nicholas Murphy the dominance he enjoyed in previous games. As a result over the 70 minutes Dara Ó'Sé was to

249

emerge as the pivotal figure, and in the process win his fifth medal.

Cork drew first blood with a James Masters free, but by the 12th minute it was all square at 0-3 each. Donnacha O'Connor had converted 2 more Cork frees, while O'Mahoney from play and Colm Cooper and Bryan Sheehan had Kerry points from frees.

Mistakes were plentiful on both sides. Kerry hit a couple of bad wides while Cork coughed up possession regularly, suggesting big match nerves had got to the players, but Kerry's forceful and aggressive play was also a factor.

Then came the game's first defining moment, and while we were not to know it at the time, it had a huge bearing on the outcome. Another spilled ball in the middle of the park was grabbed by Seamus Scanlon, who launched a high ball in the direction of the Cork goal. Cooper and Kieran O'Connor were under it when Cork goalkeeper Alan Quirke entered the equation and just as he did the 'Gooch' got a fist to the arriving O'Neill's leather and in an instant it was nestling in the net. Kerry 1-3 Cork 0-3, 17 minutes gone.

Kerry were now a different team as if the goal had lifted a huge expectant weight from their shoulders. Two minutes later they nearly got another goal. Cooper's pace took him past Kieran O'Connor but his powerful drive went over instead of under the bar – a diving Cork defender may have just done enough.

Masters had another free, cancelled out by a Paul Galvin point from play and Cork were now in danger of being swamped. They had yet to score from play and badly needed something to ignite their challenge. Cork also had a let-off when Kieran Donaghy had justifiable claims for a penalty turned down by the referee. It was a decision that infuriated several Kerry players.

Cork then conjured up their first score from play, well taken by full-forward Michael Cussen. Then when Masters, who was clearly showing the signs of his lay-off, added another point from a free only 2 points, 1-5 to 0-6, divided the teams after 31 minutes.

Crucially the last score of the first-half went to Kerry as Tomás Ó'Sé drilled over his by now obligatory point in a Championship game and as the sides headed for the dressing room Kerry were in front, 1-6 to 0-6.

Was the final about to go the way of previous deciders in which Kerry had filleted the opposition or was there a kick left in Cork, who had been expected to bring a manic desire to the table but were now eyeballing a heavy defeat in the face unless they improved?

As the crowd enjoyed the wonderful half-time entertainment provided by Liam O'Connor, one team stood on the edge of greatness and in the next 35 minutes they would achieve it.

Billy Morgan introduced Daniel Goulding for the ineffective Masters, but before many had resumed their seats for the second-half, this game had lost its pulse.

The Cork defence so solid all season handed the game to Kerry in bizarre fashion. Donaghy ripped the ball from the arms of Ger Spillane and found himself staring at an empty net, goalkeeper Quirke having already moved away expecting a pass. 'Star' recovered his composure to stroke home the game's second goal.

Cork were shattered and the life drained from their challenge while Kerry began to play with the swagger of champions elect. In the next 4 minutes, Sheehan, Seamus Scanlon, O'Sullivan and Cooper all had points and with the score at 2-10 to 0-6 pockets of empty seats appeared in the stadium.

In an effort to lift their sagging spirits Cork brought on Anthony Lynch, but by now the only issue that needed deciding was the margin of Kerry's victory.

Goal number 3 duly arrived in the 48th minute and again the Cork defence was culpable, as Donaghy had the simple task of hitting the ball into an empty net,

Kerry's Paul Galvin lifts the Sam Maguire Cup. Kerry v Cork. All-Ireland Football Final, Croke Park, 16 September 2007

3-10 to 0-7.

This was a massacre disguised as a beating as yet another one-sided All-Ireland final played out its last breath. Goulding did get a Cork goal and a point, O'Connor chipped in with a couple of points, but as Kerry boss Pat O'Shea emptied the bench, the 'Gooch' stamped his class on the final.

With the contest long dead on its feet he embellished a wonderful display as he teased and tormented the Cork defence and signed off with 2 classy points, bringing his tally to 1-5 in a 'man of the match' performance.

In an ironic twist the stadium announcer called 'gardaí and stewards to end of match positions' – the end had come a lot earlier in a grossly one-sided decider.

Referee Coldrick finally took Cork out of their agony by bringing the 2007 All-Ireland final to an end. Kerry were worthy and deserving champions on a 3-13 to 1-9 scoreline.

Kerry	3-13
Cork	1-9

On the sideline Billy Morgan congratulated Pat O'Shea. The huge Kerry support ignored calls to stay off the pitch and raced onto the field to embrace their heroes and celebrate in style.

It was a special day for Kerry captain Declan O'Sullivan as he climbed the steps of the Hogan Stand to accept the Sam Maguire Cup, thus joining one of Gaelic football's most exclusive clubs.

Only 6 players have collected the 'Sam' twice, Joe Barrett (Kerry), Jimmy Murray (Roscommon), John Joe Reilly (Cavan), Sean Flanagan (Mayo), Enda Colleran (Galway), Tony Hanahoe (Dublin). O'Sullivan, from the Dromid Pearses Club in South Kerry, became the seventh.

For one other man in the stadium it was a poignant occasion as Liam Mulvihill was attending his last final in an official capacity. The Ard-Stiúrthóir will retire in a few months time, and in a lovely gesture President Nickey Brennan asked Liam to present the Cup to O'Sullivan.

The Ard-Stiúrthóir duly obliged and O'Sullivan lifted the famous cannister into the bright September sky to the raucous acknowledgement of the thousands of 'green and gold' clad supporters who were gathered on the green sward beneath them.

By winning their third title in 4 years Kerry assumed the mantle of a great team. In fact only a defeat to Tyrone in

2005 has stopped them from completing a 4-in-a-row. There are those who questioned the merits of this particular side. Not any more. They deserve their place among the best teams the GAA has seen.

A special day also for likeable manager Pat O'Shea, who in his first year at the helm guided his county to glory, just a short few months after suffering a heartbreaking defeat in the club final with his beloved Dr Crokes.

Sam Maguire was a proud Corkman, but the cup he presented to the GAA for the Senior Football Championship is once again about to spend another few months in familiar surroundings and few will argue it's in its rightful place at the end of an eventful Championship.

Thirty-three counties started out in May, some with little hope of winning, others with a bit more, but as summer gives way to autumn, the men in 'green and gold' ensured it will be short winter in *An Ríocht*.

Note: To compound matters for Cork boss Billy Morgan, he was handed a 24-week suspension after the final for remarks passed to a linesman, which rules him out of inter-county football until March 2008.

Ciara McDermott, Mayo, tries to get a pass away, closely marked by Briege Corkery, Cork. Mayo v Cork. All-Ireland Ladies' Football Final, Croke Park. 23 September 2007.

Ladies' Days

CAMOGIE AND LADIES' FOOTBALL FINALS

The Senior Camogie Championship saw a new force emerge – Wexford put their best team forward in an effort to break Cork's stranglehold on the O'Duffy Cup. Meanwhile, the Ladies' Football Championship saw the two top teams in the country go head to head again – Cork v Mayo.

25 Ladies' Days

Camogie and Ladies' Football Finals

The growth of camogie and ladies' football in recent years has greatly increased the awareness of these sports among the general public. In the process an appreciation of the efforts the players in both codes make has also grown. Camogie is into its second century while ladies' football has been described as the fastest-growing sport in the country, although the drop in attendance at recent All-Ireland finals must be a worry to the officers of Cumann Peil Gael na mBan.

The profile given to both games in print and other media outlets has also improved. TG4 now sponsor and give extensive coverage to the Ladies' Football Championship. TG4 also covers the league, which is sponsored by Suzuki. In this regard camogie is a bit behind in that it is reliant on RTÉ who cover the Senior Championship, including a Sunday Game programme on the night of the All-Ireland final. However, the Camogie Association should seek more coverage of their games, as it remains a very attractive game with a high-skill level evident in all teams. The arrival of Setanta Sport has also benefited camogie as they cover the club finals along with extensive highlights of the Féile Na Gael in both codes.

Naturally most attention is focussed on the Senior Championship and this year Cork were in pursuit of the much coveted 3-in-a-row in both codes. To attain that milestone would be a unique achievement, especially as several dual players were involved.

Gala Senior Camogie Championship

The format for this year was unchanged from the previous season with all 6 counties playing in a round robin series of games with the top 4 qualifying for the semi-finals, the pairings for which would be decided on an open draw basis. Cork were favourites and, having retained the league, were in a good position going into their opening game.

However, the league did offer some hope that a new force was about to emerge in the game, which was welcome as Cork and Tipperary's dominance had become stale and a change would benefit all concerned. Wexford were offering a realistic challenge to the big '2' while Dublin were hinting at a revival on the back of successive wins at junior level.

Mary Lacey, Wexford captain, lifts the O'Duffy Cup while Liz Howard, President of the Camogie Association, looks on. All-Ireland Senior Camogie Final, Cork v Wexford. Croke Park. 9 September 2007.

Galway continued to struggle as did Kilkenny who would have to wait some time before their promising under-age players would blossom at senior level.

A week after a heartbreaking defeat in the league final [a late goal gave Cork victory], Wexford travelled to Leeside determined to make amends, and they did so in emphatic fashion. On a gloriously sunny afternoon they blitzed the champions 4-12 to 0-14 to signal their arrival as genuine contenders. In Cork's defence it was their sixth game in a short space of time, as they were involved in a draw and replay which went to extra-time against Tipperary in the Munster Championship, but coach Fiona O'Driscoll was offering no excuses – the better team won.

On the same day Tipperary had an easy win over Galway, as Dublin caused a major surprise by hitting 6 goals past a hapless Kilkenny in a 6-7 to 1-7 win. As the series continued it was obvious that Kilkenny and Dublin, despite their early promise, were beginning to lose pace with the group leaders. Cork recovered from their initial loss to win their

257

remaining games and easily secured their place in the semi-final.

Wexford lost only one game – that was to Tipperary. Galway, with wins over Kilkenny and Dublin, made it to the last four which was completed by Tipperary who could afford to lose to Kilkenny in the final group game. That win gave the once mighty ladies from the Marble County their only success in a miserable campaign.

The semi-final draw brought a sigh of relief as it guaranteed a different pairing in the final which would breathe new life into the Association's big day. Only one of the big two would make it to Croke Park on September 16. Cork would play old rivals Tipperary with Wexford facing Galway. Both games were fixed for Nowlan Park on Saturday August 11.

In the opening game, Wexford had a comfortable 2-11 to 0-9 win over Galway with goals from Kate Kelly [she finished with 1-11] and Michelle Hearn. Their early season promise was maintained as they had reached the final for the first time since 1994, while their last win was in 1975.

Much was expected of the second semi-final between the two sides that between them had won the previous 9 titles. But it was never a contest as the champions eased into the final, with a 2-18 to 0-14 win, the goals coming from

Angela Walsh and Una O'Donoghue.

The stage was set then for the decider, a fifth between the counties, and it stands at 2 wins each, Cork's victories coming in 1971 and 1992, while Wexford emerged victorious in 1968 and 1975.

For the second year in a row the Senior Camogie and Under-21 hurling final would form an attractive programme in Croke Park, while also on the bill was the Junior Camogie decider. This featured Clare and Derry and what a riveting contest they served up with the lead changing hands several times over the hour and beyond as Cork referee Cathal Egan played 6 minutes of added time.

It was in this period that the game was eventually won and lost. It looked odds-on that the New Ireland Cup was bound for the Banner County, but in the dying embers of a cracking game the girls from Derry snatched victory when Aisling Diamond grabbed the winner. Derry won by the narrowest of margins 3-12 to 2-14, agony for a gallant Clare team, but it was a proud captain Claire Doherty who received the cup from Camogie Association President Liz Howard, in the presence of the North's Deputy First Minister Martin McGuinness, himself a proud Derryman.

It's a pity that the under-21 final which followed did not produce such excitement. In fact as a contest it was dead in the water after 10 minutes as Galway ripped the Dublin defence apart with quality goals. In the end they won in a canter by 5-11 to 0-12. Now it was over to the ladies of Cork and Wexford to determine the destination of the new O'Duffy Cup for 2007. Cork, as champions and on the cusp of a historic three-in-a-row, were favourites, but Wexford under the guidance of Stella Sinnott were not just in HQ to make up the numbers, and they posted their intent early on.

Yet is was Cork who got the opening score from Jennifer O'Leary in the first minute. They also hit 2 bad wides and were then dealt a blow in the third minute. Poor defending allowed Una Lacey grab a goal and when Kate Kelly added a point, Wexford after a hesitant start suddenly settled and grew in confidence. Emer Dillon got a Cork point, but the champions were not to score again for 23 minutes. It would prove a costly period. In the 15th minute Lacey once again breached the Cork defence to net her second goal and Wexford were 2-1 to 0-2 in front. Scores were scarce for the remainder of the half, both sides registering just 1 point each, Kelly for Wexford and Orla Cotter for Cork. It left the Leinster girls still ahead

2-2 to 0-3 at half-time.

Wexford's defence was outstanding in that 30 minutes, never allowing the much-vaunted Cork attack the space they thrive on, as evidenced by their tally of seven first-half wides. Could the champions respond to save their crown or would Wexford keep their composure in the face of the expected onslaught?

As the Cork backroom team plotted their comeback in the bowels of the stadium, out on the field the successful Cork team of 1982 and 1983 were taking their bow as the Jubilee champions. A special day for a wonderful team as among them Sandy Fitzgibbon, Mary O'Leary, Val Fitzpatrick, Pat Moloney and Cathy Landers enjoyed the limelight one more time.

Gemma O'Connor, the Cork captain, got the first point of the second-half, but it was quickly cancelled out by a similar score from Ursula Jacob. Cork then struck for a goal – a brilliant strike by Emer Dillon, who was a constant threat to Wexford's ambitions all afternoon. The goal signalled a good spell for Cork who scored 3 of the next 4 points. The gap was down to a single point 2-4 to 1-6 and central to Cork's fightback was captain O'Connor who was now dominating in midfield.

Crucially they could not get the

levelling point and cushioned by their 2 first half goals, Wexford belied their big match experience to ride out the storm. In the space of 4 minutes they hit 3 points, Kelly, Jacob and substitute Katriona Parrick scoring. With 57 of the 60 minutes played, the cup was heading to the Model County. But champions die hard and back came Cork. O'Connor and Briege Corkery had points – just 2 between the sides again entering injury-time. One last chance as Orla Cotter headed for goal and her powerful shot had winner written all over it. However, Wexford custodian Mags D'Arcy was equal to the challenge, batted the *sliotar* clear, and the incoming O'Connor drove it harmlessly wide.

It signalled the end of Cork's reign. As referee John Morrissey from Tipperary brought a pulsating final to a conclusion the Wexford supporters in an attendance of 33,317 were in raptors. Despite the best efforts of stewards and officials, they made their way onto the field to greet the new heroines of camogie and who could blame them. It had been a long wait.

In the period since their last win they had endured some dark days but now they were worthy champions on a 2-7 to 1-8 scoreline and the party was about to begin. And so it did, as soon as captain Mary Leacy took possession of the O'Duffy Cup. The cheer that greeted her as she raised it high into the Dublin sky could be heard back on Vinegar Hill.

Wexford	2-7
Cork	1-8

'A dream comes true', said Stella Sinnott, but the dream was now a reality and when they returned to their native county the following day and night, they were rightly feted. Enniscorthy, Gorey and Wexford town had not witnessed scenes like it since the hurlers came home triumphant in 1996. Now the proud people of Wexford had new and worthy champions, the Senior Camogie team of 2007.

For Cork the dream was over, now could the dual players salvage their season?

TG4 Ladies' Football Championship

In comparison to the Senior Camogie Championship, the equivalent in ladies' football, features 4 provincial campaigns that also include a 'back door' system and in 2007 there was an added ingredient. Once the provincial Championships were concluded the 16 top teams in the country were then divided into 4 groups to play off in a champions league style format, after which the top 2 in each section would qualify for the quarter-finals.

The idea behind this was to provide more games and with it more exposure for the sport. While in theory it sounds good, the simple fact is that some of the games were meaningless. As with the hurling Championship the quarter-finalists quickly became known and in most of the groups the final series of matches was of little benefit to the participants.

There was of course a number of interesting developments throughout the provincial Championships, the most notable being that once again, despite losing their league title and with it an unbeaten 32-match run, Cork were back on form and in hot pursuit of the 3-in-a-row.

Mayo were making all the right noises in the West, especially with the brilliant Cora Staunton back in the fold. The Army Officer demonstrated her prowess by scoring 2-13 of her side's total of 3-16 in the Connacht final win over Galway.

Even at this early stage of the Championship, the prospect of Cork and Mayo going head-to-head for the title appealed to most fans, but would they get their wish?

The group stages did offer the prospect of some intriguing games when the draws were made for this phase of the Championship. Cork, Galway, Roscommon and Monaghan were in Group 1. Group 2 contained Mayo, Dublin, Kerry and Waterford. Leinster champions Laois were in Group 3 along with Tyrone, Sligo and Donegal. In Group 4, 2006's runners-up, Armagh, were joined by Kildare, Meath and Down.

Apart from a place in the last eight of the Championship, the prize for winning your group was a top seed, thus avoiding the other group winners.

Cork got their campaign off to the best possible start with a hard-earned win over a fancied Galway side, 2-13 to 1-11. Monaghan and Roscommon offered only token resistance and the champions easily secured top spot in the group.

The surprise here came from Monaghan edging out Galway for the runners-up spot and sending the Tribeswomen packing a lot earlier than many anticipated – one of the favourites falling at the first fence so to speak.

Mayo also encountered few problems in their group. Like Cork, they emerged as the top seed, which ensured they would not meet at the quarter-final stage. Along with Cork and Mayo, most of the big guns, Galway apart, did make the quarter-finals with Dublin, Armagh, Tyrone, Monaghan, Laois and Kildare

261

completing the line-up.

There was another shock at this stage when in the all-Ulster clash, Tyrone scored 4 goals in a 4-7 to 0-10 win over Armagh. Mayo were given a stiff test before seeing off resilient Monaghan by 5 points 1-12 to 1-7. Cork hammered Dublin, 3-17 to 1-4, while in the all-Leinster clash former champions Laois saw off Kildare by 2-10 to 0-7.

The semi-final pairings resulted in the Championship favourites, Cork and Mayo, avoiding each other. Cork would face Laois with improving Tyrone standing between Mayo and a place in the final.

Kingspan Breffni Park was the venue for the Mayo v Tyrone clash and what a cracker they produced, including a controversial incident that helped shape the contest. Five minutes before half-time referee Tony Clarke awarded Mayo a penalty that was dubious to say the least. Cora Staunton's effort was saved by goalkeeper Elaine Mallaghan, but the rebound fell to Staunton who made no mistake at the second time of asking. Mallaghan then reacted to apparently being goaded by the Mayo star and was immediately sin-binned by Clarke and the Ulster girls were without their number 1 goalkeeper for a crucial 10 minutes.

It was level 1-5 each at half-time but Mayo were that bit better in the second-half. Staunton finished the match with a total of 1-8 as the Connacht champions made it to the final on a 2-13 to 2-8 scoreline, leaving Tyrone shattered at the manner of their defeat.

There was no such drama in the second semi-final. Even with home advantage in O'Moore Park, Portlaoise, Laois were powerless to deny Cork a place in the final. It ceased to be a contest from very early and goals by Valerie Mulcahy (2), Deirdre O'Reilly and Laura McMahon eased the champions to an emphatic 4-14 to 0-6 win. The dream final was on – Cork v Mayo – yet another Sunday in September to look forward to.

Sadly, a few days after their defeat to Cork in the semi-final, Laois suffered another blow with the untimely death at 35 years of age of former player Lulu Carroll. Lulu was an outstanding player with her club Timahoe and won an All-Ireland senior medal with Laois in 2001. She was also an All-Star award winner in 1996. Despite her ongoing battle with cancer she acted as selector with the team in the loss to Cork. Tributes poured in for the young lady who was a wonderful ambassador for the game and a huge loss to all who knew her, especially her family.

Cora Staunton, Mayo, evades the tackle of Bríd Stack, Cork. Mayo v Cork. All-Ireland Ladies' Football Final, Croke Park. 23 September 2007.

Final's Day

It was to be the last big day in Croke Park for 2007 and an occasion graced by President Mary McAleese and Taoiseach Bertie Ahern. Six counties representing all four provinces would do battle for the final 3 All-Ireland titles of yet another super season on the GAA fields.

Teams from Kilkenny are quite used to appearing in Croke Park in the ninth month of the year, but a football team from the Marble County in an All-Ireland Final is a rarity.

It made for an unusual pairing in the junior decider with Kilkenny facing the exiles from London. Unusual it may have been but both were there on merit and proceeded to entertain the early arrivals in a lively contest. Kilkenny got a great start with goals from Sara McCarthy and Lynda Phelan, but a goal scored by Shauna Keogh boosted London at a time when Kilkenny were reduced to 14 players following the sin-binning of Marie Dargan. Kilkenny went a long period without a score and a second London goal by Sharon Lynch brought the sides level at 2-5 each. It ensured a frenetic finish before Kilkenny edged home when an effort by Orla McCormack somehow found the net in a crowded goalmouth.

London fought hard to gain parity but Kilkenny hung on to win by 3-5 to 2-5, so in a tradition normally reserved for the likes of hurlers Henry Shefflin and Jackie Tyrell, Kilkenny captain Catriona Grace climbed the steps of the Hogan Stand. She was joined by Emer Roantree whose brother tragically died a week before the game and the win was dedicated to the Roantree family, as yet another All-Ireland Cup was heading to the Marble County.

Just 2 weeks after winning senior camogie medals, five Wexford girls were back in HQ, bidding to make it a double as Leitrim provided the opposition in the Intermediate Final, which like the junior decider produced an exciting contest. Wexford opened up an early 0-5 to 0-1 lead, but 34-year-old veteran Ann Marie Cox led the fightback and getting good support from Eileen O'Donoghue and Sarah McLoughlin, Leitrim drew level. The Connacht girls were now the dominant team and they were in front 0-8 to 0-6 at the break. Wexford battled back and a goal from camogie star Kate Kelly restored their lead, but it was to be short-lived as Leitrim were determined to land the title, and they took inspiration from Cox, whose free-taking was impeccable. The veteran attacker drilled over 4 frees in a row and with 7 minutes remaining it was 0-15 to 1-8 for Leitrim.

Wexford were now struggling and while they did get the next 2 points, Leitrim closed the game out with the last 2 scores of the game, one from play by Cox, bringing her tally to 0-8 and the title was bound for the West. Leitrim were winners by 0-17 to 1-10.

It was only fitting then that in the inaugural year of the Intermediate Championship that a Leitrim captain Sinead Brennan should take possession of the Mary Quinn Cup. The cup presented by the Quinn family commemorates a woman who rendered the game in the county tremendous service, and with a team that had Mary's daughter, midfielder Maeve, play a pivotal role in the historic win on a special day for the ladies from Leitrim.

Main Event

With the curtain-raisers and the pre-match preliminaries so much part of All-Ireland final day out of the way, the heavyweights of Ladies' Gaelic Football took centre stage.

Cork on the cusp of history against a Mayo side keen to feast at the top table – something they had not done since their last success in 2003. The champions were favourites but were dealt a severe blow in the build-up to the final when experienced dual star Mary O'Connor was ruled out with a serious knee injury. It was also to be Mary's last inter-county football game with Cork as she is concentrating on camogie in 2008.

Mayo, though, were confident and with ace forward Cora Staunton in splendid form they felt they had the firepower to outgun Cork and derail their 3-in-a-row ambitions.

Eamonn Ryan, the Cork coach, is a wily campaigner and he set his stall out early and a superb display of defending particularly in the opening 10 minutes laid the foundations that helped stifle Mayo's best-laid plans. At the other end the Cork attack sparkled, none more so than young Amanda Murphy, in for the injured O'Connor. She had the satisfaction of getting the game's first point. It signalled an excellent period for Cork and in quick succession they added 4 more points from Deirdre O'Reilly, Juliet Murphy, Geraldine O'Flynn and Nollaig Cleary. With 15 minutes played, Cork were 0-5 to 0-0 in front and already Mayo had a mountain to climb.

It was clear that the Cork game plan was working. Juliet Murphy was covering acres of ground in midfield, while at the back, the perceived threat from Staunton never materialised, principally because of the excellence of the Cork defence. Mayo had deployed Marcella Heffernan as an extra midfielder in an effort to create space inside for Staunton, but the plan never really worked. Brid Stack at centre-back was superb, while full-back Angela Walsh was just as effective with good support from Rena Buckley and goalkeeper Elaine Harte.

Mayo finally got on the scoreboard with a point from Catherine McGing, quickly followed by another from Staunton. Amanda Murphy and Diane O'Hora traded points and at 0-6 to 0-3 for Cork, there was a hint of a Mayo revival approaching the half-time break.

Then came a pivotal moment. Cork's Norita Kelly tumbled in the small square and referee Eugene O'Hare awarded a penalty. It seemed a harsh call and the Mayo defenders were very annoyed at the decision. Kelly received extensive treatment for an injury to her ankle. She was eventually forced off. Despite the delay, Cork's Valerie Mulcahy kept her composure and superbly drilled the penalty to the net, thus enhancing her reputation as an outstanding penalty taker. It was her second in All-Ireland finals.

It gave Cork an interval lead of 1-6 to 0-3, but more importantly it had restored their confidence following a period of Mayo pressure that almost produced a goal but for an excellent block by Cork defender Linda Barrett on full-forward Aoife Heffernan.

On the resumption, there was a mirror image of the previous week's football final when a goal effectively decided the contest, but unlike seven days earlier, this time it was Cork who got the goal. It was created by a clever reverse pass from Laura McMahon [whose brother Kevin had played in that football final with Cork] to Valerie Mulcahy who scored with another clinical finish. It was now 2-6 to 0-3 for Cork and the champions were in an almost unassailable position.

The goal more or less ended Mayo's challenge. Cork remained in control in defence and maintained a consistently high standard throughout the second-half. Further points from Murphy and O'Flynn extended their lead and while Mayo did create a couple of chances, they were denied – first by the vigilance of Cork goalkeeper Harte and then when a Staunton effort came back off the upright. Even the most ardent of Mayo supporters must have sensed it was not going to be their day.

Cork have moved 2-11 to 0-6 in front and used their full complement of substitutes when Mayo's persistence was finally rewarded. The Connacht champions won a close-in free which Staunton hit powerfully to the net and then with the game a mere 13 seconds away from the final whistle, they got a second goal from Fiona McHale.

However, it was a case of too little too late, except that it showed what they might have been capable of had they been allowed express themselves.

Cork's outstanding play over the 60 minutes ensured that long before the final had run its course the 'red and white' ribbons would adorn the Brendan Martin Cup for another year.

| Cork | 2-11 |
| Mayo | 2-6 |

A special day too for team captain Juliet Murphy as she accepted the cup from Ladies' Football President Geraldine Giles. In a nice touch she asked the injured Mary O'Connor to share the unique moment and she becomes the first ever Cork captain to lead a team to 3 All-Ireland wins in a row.

Afterwards Mayo boss Frank Browne, while acknowledging the better team won, was at a loss to explain how poorly his own side performed. 'We worked hard in the last few months and we did

Cork captain, Juliet Murphy, left, and Mary O'Connor hold aloft the Brendan Martin cup after winning three-in-a-row. Mayo v Cork. All-Ireland Ladies' Football Final, Croke Park. 23 September 2007.

not become a bad team overnight. We will go away lick our wounds and hopefully come back stronger next year.'

For Cork captain Juliet Murphy it was a significant win apart from achieving the 3-in-a-row; 'it was a good thing that we were playing Mayo in the final. They set the standards a short few years ago and the question was could we beat them in an All-Ireland final? We were very determined to do that and we are delighted now that we have done it.'

So the curtain comes down on yet another exciting chapter in Ladies' Football as the winners and losers made their way home to enjoy the celebrations or contemplate what might have been. The girls from County Cork are already planning for 2008, and dare I mention it – the 4-in-a-row?

Darren Magee and Declan O'Mahony, Dublin, win possession despite the efforts of Pádraig Clancy, Laois. Dublin v Laois. O'Byrne Cup Final. O'Connor Park, Tullamore, Co Offaly. 28 January 2007

26

Best of the Rest

Whilst the country's attention is fixed on the All-Ireland finals in Croke Park, plenty of other contests and sporting rivalries are played out the length and breadth of the island throughout the year. Here's a round-up of them.

26 Best of the Rest

Winners As Well

Beyond the glare of publicity generated by big match days in Croke Park, Thurles, Cork or Clones, the GAA and its games reach into the very fabric of Irish society and while it is easy to be part of such big days, there are many more as well.

It is now of course a 12-month season with very little respite as clubs, counties and colleges go about their business with a professional approach that would put other sports to shame.

The inter-county year begins in January with the four Provincial Councils running their respective cup competitions. The participation of the Third Level colleges in these competitions works well as they, like the counties, are preparing for the season ahead.

In Leinster, Dublin won the O'Byrne Cup in football, Kilkenny retained the Walsh Cup in hurling, while the McKenna Cup final in Ulster attracted a huge crowd as Tyrone retained the trophy, a similar tale in Munster as Cork kept possession of the McGrath Cup.

Babs Keating guided Tipperary to the *Waterford Crystal Cup* and in the Connacht football FBD League the winners were Sligo IT, who caused a huge surprise by beating Galway in the final and so secured a trip to New York for their efforts.

In Third Level competitions the much sought-after Fitzgibbon (hurling) and Sigerson (football) Cups are contested as keenly as ever. Davy Fitzgerald put his troubles in Clare behind him to guide Limerick Institute of Technology to victory in the Fitzgibbon, while on home soil in Belfast, Queens won the Sigerson. The Ashbourne Cup in camogie was won by UCD.

Plenty of drama and excitement as well at college level with All-Ireland titles at stake in both codes. Omagh CBS won their first senior 'A' football title and St Mary's from Edenderry won the 'B' Championship.

In hurling, glory for De Le Salle from Waterford in the 'A'. In 'B' FCJ Bunclody garner the honours.

The Vocational Schools body continue to promote their games in an exemplary fashion. In hurling St Brigids, Loughrea emerged as champions, with Virginia College from Cavan taking the football title for the second year in a row.

At Inter-County level, the 2006 winners both retained their titles, Tyrone

Noel Earls, Kilmoredaly tries to win the ball as he is tackled by Brian Foley, Robert Emmetts, London. Kilmoredaly, Galway v Robert Emmet's, London. All-Ireland Intermediate Hurling Final. Croke Park. 11 March 2007.

defeating Meath in football, while in hurling Cork made it 3-in-a-row with a win over Galway.

The decision taken some years ago to extend the club championships for Intermediate and Junior to All-Ireland level was an excellent one – further enhanced by playing these finals in Croke Park.

The deciders in 2007 were also played in HQ, but this time under the newly installed floodlights, making it an even more memorable occasion for the participants. They may have been played before small crowds, but the enthusiasm generated matched that of All-Ireland day – after all, the club, be they big or small, are the very rock on which the Association is built.

Greencastle from Tyrone won the Junior football crown with a 0-13 to 0-12 win over Kerry champions Duagh, while there was joy for the Kingdom in the Intermediate final as Ardfert, who were

Junior champions in 2006, made it back-to-back titles by defeating Eoghan Ruadh from Derry in a low scoring decider, 1-4 to 0-5.

Danesfort from Kilkenny [where else?] won the Junior hurling title with a 2-16 to 2-8 win over Clooney Gaels from Galway.

However, the real story came in the Intermediate final as Robert Emmetts from London took the honours amidst scenes of unprecedented joy. They beat Killimordaly from Galway convincingly by 1-14 to 0-8. It was the first time ever that a club title was won by a team from outside the 32 counties and reflects greatly on the hard work been done by 'exiles' on behalf of the GAA in cities abroad.

Emmett's, based in North London but drawing their players from various parts of that huge city, received a tumultuous reception on their return home. It was a proud night then in Croke Park, for the men with a passion for hurling in the city of London.

The highly prestigious Kilmacud-Crokes seven-a-side hurling and football competitions are keenly contested at various venues around Stillorgan on the Saturday of the All-Ireland hurling and football finals and generate great excitement. Sarsfields from Cork took

the 2007 hurling title, while in football after a feast of action the honours went to Longstonew. Both competitions are now in their 35th year and it is a tribute to that fantastic club that they grow in stature every year.

Eoin Kennedy from Dublin won the Martin Donnelly sponsored All-Ireland 60 x 30 singles handball title. Brendan Cummins, another goalkeeper who had a mixed year, won his third Puc Fada title in four years over the Cooley Mountains with a total of 49 pucks. John Brennan from Carlow won the MBNA Kick Fada competition and the legendary Mick O'Dwyer was inducted into the Hall of Fame.

Sadly the association lost several outstanding members during 2007, including two former Presidents. In February Tipperary's Seamus O'Riain who served from 1967 to 1970 passed away. The Moneygall native was one of the founders of Féile Na Gael and was instrumental in establishing the first links with Australian Rules Football Association.

Con Murphy had the distinction during his term of office, 1976-1978, of presenting the McCarthy Cup to 3 winning Cork hurling captains. Con won 4 All-Ireland senior hurling medals and while still an active Inter-County hurler refereed the All-Ireland Finals of 1948 and 1950. Con also devoted a lot of his time working to secure the return of the Crossmaglen Grounds to the club from the British Army. It was only fitting then that shortly after his death that became a reality. The club was well represented at his funeral.

Canon Bertie Troy, the man who coached Cork to the 3-in-a-row hurling titles of 1976-78, passed away, as did Eamonn Coleman, the man who guided Derry to their only All-Ireland senior football title in 1993. Bertie Coleman whose foresight help set up the All-Ireland Club Championship also slipped away after a long illness.

Outstanding Dublin dual star Mick Holden, one of the great GAA characters in the capital, died suddenly in September. Mick was a member of the Dubs' team that won the 1983 All-Ireland title in a controversial final against Galway, in which Dublin finished the match with 12 players.

Back at Inter-County level, All-Ireland honours came to the Cork junior football team who defeated Wexford 1-14 to 3-2 in the final, while there was compensation for Wexford in Intermediate hurling as they beat Waterford 1-11 to 1-9 in an exciting final.

Having lost the Cadbury's Under-21 football final to Mayo in 2006, Cork bounced back to claim the 2007 title. They completed a 4-in-a-row in Munster, had a thrilling 1-point win over Armagh in the All-Ireland semi-final before beating Laois in a cracking final.

Laois looked likely winners but a late goal by Colm O'Neill and an injury-time point from Daniel Goulding's free gave the Rebels their tenth title on a 2-10 to 0-15 scoreline.

In Under-21 hurling four first-half goals ensured Galway were never in trouble against Dublin and easily won the county's ninth title on a 5-11 to 0-12 scoreline.

The Féile Na Gael hurling competition was hosted by Kilkenny and the Christy Ring Trophy for Division 1 went to Castleknock of Dublin. The football equivalent was jointly hosted by Sligo, Leitrim and Roscommon and O'Donovan Rossa from Derry took the Division 1 title.

Cork retained the Division 1A Senior National League title in Camogie, while Limerick won Division 1B, and in Ladies' Football the league title went west to Mayo.

Brian Whelehan, an iconic hurling figure throughout a wonderful career, retired, as did Kieran McGeeney, the man who captained Armagh to

All-Ireland glory and also led Ireland in the Compromise Rules series. However, the Armagh man was quickly back into the game as the newly appointed Kildare manager – his first venture into the coaching arena at inter-county level.

The much troubled Compromise Rules series set for October 2007 was cancelled after violence marred the second test in Croke Park in 2006, with the aggressive approach adopted by the Australians posing a danger to the Irish players.

It was also announced that the GAA's Ard Stúirthóir, Liam Mulvihill is to retire, but will stay in office until his successor is appointed which is expected to be early 2008.

Surprisingly, Tommy Breheny resigned as Sligo football boss while former star Joe Dooley took over as Offaly hurling manager.

A good year for Dublin hurling and signs that the game in the capital is continuing to make strides – the seniors retained their Division 1 status while Leinster Championships won in both Minor and Under-21 grades. Finally after a long and protracted debate, rugby and soccer came to Croke Park. With Lansdowne Road being redeveloped both codes will use the GAA's 'jewel' until the work on the new stadium is complete.

That is just a brief glance at some of the other many and varied games and stories that made up the GAA year of 2007.

It's just a snapshot of what really goes on from Mizen Head to Malin Head in an organisation that is at the heart of every town and village in the country, just as the founders hoped it would be all those years ago.